PSYCHOMETRIC SCALING:
A TOOLKIT FOR IMAGING SYSTEMS DEVELOPMENT

Peter G. Engeldrum

Winchester, Massachusetts, USA

Psychometric Scaling: A Toolkit for Imaging Systems Development

By Peter G. Engeldrum

Published by:
Imcotek Press
P.O. Box 17
Winchester, MA 01890-0017
USA

First Printing 2000

Publishers Cataloging-in-Publication Data

Engeldrum, Peter G.

Psychometric scaling : a toolkit for imaging systems development / Peter G. Engeldrum. – 1st ed.

p. cm.

Includes bibliographical references and index.

ISBN 0-9678706-0-7

1. Imaging systems–Image quality–Psychological aspects. 2. Imaging systems–Image quality–Psychological testing. 3. Psychometrics

I. Title

TK8315.E54 2000 621.36'7'019

QBI00-285

To Carol, Edna and George.
Without them this would have been impossible.

Table of Contents

Disclaimer

This book is designed to give information regarding the subject matter covered. It is sold with the understanding that the publisher and author are not engaged in rendering legal, accounting, engineering, or other professional services. If legal or other expert assistance is required, seek the assistance of industry-specific professionals.

It is not the purpose of this book to reprint all the information available to the author or publisher, but to complement, amplify, and supplement other texts. You are urged to read the available material, learn as much as possible about psychometric scaling, and tailor the information to your needs. For more information, consult the references in the back of this book.

Every effort has been made to make this book as complete and accurate as possible. However, **there may be mistakes**, both typographical and in content. Therefore this text should be used only as a general guide and not as the ultimate source of psychometric scaling information. Of course, this book contains information on psychometric scaling that was available as of the date of printing.

The purpose of this book is to inform the reader. The author and the publisher will have neither liability nor responsibility to any person or entity for any loss or damage caused or alleged to be caused, directly or indirectly by using or applying any of the contents of this book or accompanying software.

If you do not wish to be bound by the above, you may return this book to the publisher for a full refund.

Preface

My interest in psychometric scaling was sparked during my undergraduate days at the Rochester Institute of Technology. I was always fascinated with the idea of getting people to judge all sorts of imaging attributes. Since there were no courses on the topic at RIT at the time, it remained an idle curiosity until my first job.

One of my first jobs was to make simulations of aerial images having various attributes for a psychometric scaling study. Over the next few years, I was only casually involved in psychometric scaling, however. In attempting to learn more about this topic, I was continually frustrated that there was no text written for scientists and engineers that described this interesting and essential tool.

By the early 1970s, when I went to work for the Xerox Corporation, one of the major technical and market issues for the company was "copy quality." Clearly identifying "copy quality" requires a human judgment, so a wide-ranging effort was expended by a group of scientists and engineers to come to grips with the "copy quality problem." This effort included spending a lot of time sorting out scaling methodology issues. At that time, Stevens' (1975) *Psychophysics: Introduction to its Perceptual, Neural, and Social Prospects* was published. Stevens' book summarized ratio scaling, but it did not go into methods in any detail. The difficulty of learning scaling, from an engineering perspective, remained. There were some introductory texts, mostly for psychology majors, but the only books written that included detailed methodologies were Guilford's (1954) and Torgerson's (1958) texts. The comprehensive work, *The Measurement and Prediction of Judgment and Choice* by Darrell Bock and Lyle Jones (1968), seemed to be largely unknown in the early 1970s.

"Copy quality" is still a complex topic that is difficult to convey succinctly. Out of my efforts to explain to management what the broad "copy quality" issues were, I began constructing a framework for understanding image quality–a tool now called the Image Quality Circle. The group of scientists and engineers I interacted with had various orientations to the copy quality problem, depending on their particular backgrounds. I associated with image and color scientists and engineers that thought image measurements and models were the answer, and psychologists who thought scaling was the "true calling."

After a decade with the Xerox Corporation, an opportunity arose to form Imcotek, a consulting company that provides expertise in image and color science to organizations in the imaging industry. What soon became apparent was that "copy quality" got transformed into the more general "image quality." The need for psychometric scaling was still very much alive.

The last quarter of this century has been a period of dramatic change in the imaging industry. Product development teams have been challenged by rapid emergence and acceptance of new core imaging technologies. Mastering basic science and technology are understandable objectives for R & D teams, and, for many, the focus on core technology leaves little time to extend their understanding of analytic techniques. In most companies I have worked, management at least implicitly encourages their technical staff to "use the library" to learn a new field, and not to reinvent the wheel. The literature covering imaging applications of psychometric scaling has been sparse, so even "library-inclined" staffers have had little with which to work.

Psychometric scaling has not died, thanks to several chapters by Jim Bartleson (Bartleson, 1984) in Volume 5 of the *Optical Radiation Measurement* series, and the psychophysics texts by John Baird and Elliot Noma (1978) and by George Gescheider (1985, 1997). These texts were very useful, but Bartleson's work had the added bonus of focusing on imaging and color. However, given the shrinking product development cycles there is precious little time available to the engineer to put the methods outlined in these texts to work.

Both personal computer software and hardware have become powerful enough to take on the troublesome matrix arithmetic that is an essential part of applying psychometric scaling techniques. With powerful mathematical tools such as Mathematica®, MatLab®, and MathCad® available to all, it seemed to me that the time was ripe to put together a book that emphasized the tools of psychometric scaling, as opposed to the theory. This turned out to be a bigger chore than I had envisioned, partly because I wanted to provide the most mathematically exact methods available. What I soon discovered was these exacting methods were buried in literature 50 years old! The "old timers" knew their math but did not have handy computer resources to set up the more exact methods. Inverting a matrix greater than three by three by hand is a real chore, so practical approximations were sought. These approximations have survived over the years, and the more exacting techniques long forgotten.

In *unidimensional scaling* (the topic of this book), the items of interest lie along a line or a dimension in the "psychological space." In the areas where unidimensional scaling was used, it had been recognized that many attributes were multidimensional. With the rise of digital computers in the late 1950s, the complex calculations for deriving scales of many dimensions were possible, and thus a new approach to scaling was born: multidimensional scaling (MDS). At that point, developments in unidimensional scaling largely stopped.

Over the years working with scientists and engineers, I have learned that scaling is largely of peripheral interest to them, in spite of immense practical benefits scaling can offer their development programs. Although product development people may not have a strong interest in psychometric theory, they *are* interested in clear application boundaries. When they encounter a gray area in the application of some method, a common reaction is to pick and choose the tools they need to "get quick results." I have written this book in a way that is intended to deliver such "quick results." To meet the needs of practitioners who have to move quickly, this book is decidedly light on theory, and has almost entirely avoided psychophysical laws and models such as Stevens' Power Law, Weber's Law and Fechner's Law, and all their variants.

The emphasis on method over theory is both philosophical and practical. On the philosophical side, I do not see that rehashing these laws will contribute to the wider use of the Image Quality Circle. On the practical side, and in the context of the Image Quality Circle, understanding scaling is the major task, not understanding psychophysical laws. In any specific circumstance, the scale is the sought-for end.

Acknowledgments

Many people helped in making *Psychometric Scaling: A toolkit for Imaging Systems Development* a reality. This book owes a lot to the reviewers who graciously gave their time to comment and make helpful suggestions. Thanks to Dr. John Baird (Dartmouth College) for his major contributions to the final structure, and for keeping me honest; Dr. Julian Bullet (Polaroid Corporation), and Dr. Mark Fairchild (Rochester Institute of Technology) for sharing their scaling experiences; and to Perry Lieber (Hewlett-Packard), who had to learn psychometric scaling the hard way, for his "user" insights. Roger Dooley (Adri Research), my first "teacher" on psychometric scaling and now a consultant, was responsible for helping me understand the topic and keeping me on the straight and narrow during the years we both worked at the Xerox Corporation. Marie Ariel and the reference staff at the Winchester Public Library helped ease the considerable effort in acquiring original source material.

The fact that this book is in readable form is entirely due to my editor and friend Michael Zeis of Blackstone Research Associates. The cover design is by Cynthia Eggers, of the Moonlit Creative Group, who challenged me to describe psychometric scaling in simple terms.

The Image Quality Circle evolved over decades and has benefitted from many discussions with many colleagues. During my time at the Xerox Corporation and for all these years, Dr. Rodney Shaw (Hewlett-Packard) has been a source of keen insights on the topic of image quality.

To all of you, a big thanks.

I would appreciate hearing from readers and users of the methods contained in this book. Any suggestions and errata would be welcome. I can be reached by E-mail at pge@imcotek.com or by regular mail at Imcotek, POB 17, Winchester, MA 01890.

Peter G. Engeldrum
Winchester, MA
January 2000

Chapter 1

Image Quality and Psychometric Scaling

A product development person responsible for image quality has to work in an area where myths and mysteries endure. One of the major myths is the idea that humans cannot perform as meters. Skepticism abounds in the hard-science community on this topic. Thus, observations and judgments by humans are largely avoided in favor of measuring images with instruments–territory that is much more familiar to scientists and engineers. Taking the safe approach is indeed unfortunate, because measuring images with instruments completely ignores the ultimate end user of the image, the human customer. Worse yet, measuring images can lead to incorrect trade-off decisions in product development, since one may be attempting to optimize a quantity not well correlated to human judgment. There are many historical examples of this, but the most recent one is the so-called ink jet printer "dpi war," where the addressability of imaging elements is the sole arbiter of image quality.

How does one use humans as reliable meters? *Psychometric Scaling: A Toolkit for Imaging Systems Development* introduces the basics of psychometric scaling, and provides many useful scaling ideas and techniques that have practical applications in the study of image quality. The goal is to eliminate some of the impediments to a full and useful application of psychometric scaling to the solution of the image quality evaluation problem.

For the purpose of this book, an *image* is defined as a distribution of a colorant arranged to convey information to the observer. The term colorant could include ink, wax, toner, phosphors or light sources, for example. *Image quality* is the integrated set of perceptions of the overall degree of the excellence of the image.

A term that encompasses the measurement of image quality is *image evaluation*. Two distinct divisions of image evaluation were recognized quite early. The first type, *objective image evaluation,* involves physically measuring image quality components with instruments. *Subjective image evaluation*, the second type, is not viewed as having quite the same scientific status since it involves obtaining human judgments of the various aspects of image quality.

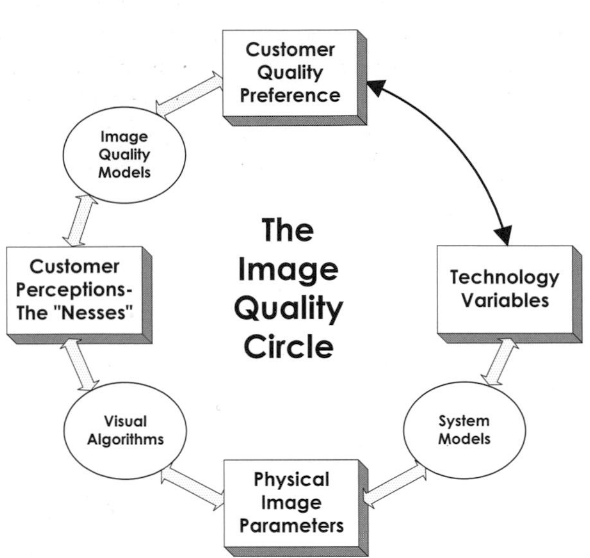

Figure 1.1 - The complete Image Quality Circle showing all the connecting links.

The *Image Quality Circle*, shown in Figure 1.1, is a framework, model, or process which helps to understand and manage image quality. Chapter 2 gives a complete description of the Image Quality Circle.

Human judgments provide a measure for two of the four components (boxes in Figure 1.1) of the Image Quality Circle: Customer Perceptions–the "Nesses," and Customer Quality Preference. Image Quality Models and Visual Algorithms, two links in the Image Quality Circle (ellipses in Figure 1.1), also require these human judgments. Obtaining these human judgments is the topic of *psychometric scaling*.

For quality estimates, we need the customer's judgment of the quality of the image. For visual algorithm development, we need a human judgment of the "nesses." Lightness, colorfulness, and sharpness are examples of Customer Perceptions. Human measurement, or psychometric scaling, is crucial to the successful implementation of the Image Quality Circle.

1.1 Psychometric Scaling

Psychometric scaling, literally "mind measuring" (Nunally and Bernstein, 1994), has not been given the appropriate level of attention by product development personnel, probably because the tools and theory of human measurements have been the domain of particular scientific disciplines not often encountered by physical scientists and engineers. Psychologists, psychophysicists, social scientists, and some market researchers use psychometric scaling, but not much of this rich resource has found its way into the physical sciences or engineering. One of the barriers to free information flow is discipline-specific technical jargon which is not easily translated from one discipline to another. However, there are some widely used industrial applications of psychometric scaling, particularly in food product development where it is called "sensory evaluation" (Bock and Jones, 1968; Meilgaard, *et. al.*, 1991; Chambers, *et. al.*, 1996).

1.2 The Scope of This Book

Psychometric Scaling: A Toolkit for Imaging Systems Development provides practical guidance and useful tools for working scientists and engineers who need a robust and organized framework for incorporating judgments from human observers into their imaging systems development effort. Although this book was not written for psychophysicists, psychologists, or social scientists, the methods and the computational tools provided should be useful to them.

In my experience, psychometric scaling is largely unknown to product engineers and scientists. When they are aware of the topic, they are somewhat skeptical of it. It doesn't appear to be "hard science." Indeed, scaling studies are often referred to as "beauty contests."

The tools described here are oriented toward business and consumer imaging, as opposed to the use of imagery for diagnostic purposes such as medical imaging or military reconnaissance. These applications have their own set of tools.

There are a small number of statistical hypothesis tests presented in this book. The guiding principle for inclusion was uniqueness. If the test was more or less unique to psychometric scaling, it was included. Otherwise it was left out. Since this book focuses on interval scaling, most standard parametric hypothesis tests applicable to psychometric scale values can be found in statistical text books.

No attempt has been made to provide a comprehensive treatise on scaling, psychophysics, or psychometric theory. For those readers interested in more theoretical aspects of psychometric scaling and psychophysics, the texts by Geschieder (1997), Baird (1997), Bartleson and Grum (1984), Baird and Noma (1978), and Torgerson (1958), will provide a more complete picture.

1.3 The Contents of This Book

Chapter 2 sets the context for this book. It describes the Image Quality Circle and puts image quality in a broader historical context. Chapter 3 provides an overview of the scaling process and offers practical suggestions on conducting the scaling study.

Psychometric Scaling: A Toolkit for Imaging Systems Development is organized roughly along the lines of Stevens' (1946) definitions of psychometric scale types. "Chapter 4: Measurement Scales" defines nominal, ordinal, interval and ratio scales. Procedures for determining thresholds and just-noticeable-differences of the "nesses" are described in Chapter 5. "Chapter 6: Ordinal Scaling" describes methods for developing ordinal scales. Interval scaling, the main focus of this text, begins with "Chapter 7: Direct Interval Scaling" and continues with "Chapter 8: Indirect Interval Scaling–Case V and Paired Comparison." "Chapter 9: Indirect Interval Scaling–Generalization of Thurstone Case V" provides techniques that expand Thurstone's Law of Comparative Judgment beyond the traditional Case V. "Chapter 10: Indirect Interval Scales-Category Scaling Methods" completes the coverage of the interval scaling methods. Chapter 11 explores Stevens' final category, ratio scaling methods. Selecting the best method for scaling studies can be found in the last chapter, "Chapter 12: Selecting the Best Method."

1.4 MathCad® Sheets

Since this book is written primarily for physical scientists and engineers, I have taken advantage of the greater mathematical and computer skill set often found within this group. With today's powerful personal computers and sophisticated data analysis/mathematical software, we can use calculation techniques and offer mathematical detail that go beyond the approximations often presented in traditional psychophysics texts, and implement some original and more exacting data reduction techniques.

Having sufficient computer power enables us to illustrate points with compact matrix representation whenever we need to. Attempts have been made to make the matrix-vector mathematical presentation consistent. Sometimes, though, matrix-vector presentation causes something fundamentally simple to appear cumbersome. In these situations, the simpler summation notation is used.

The reader will notice a distinct absence of examples in the text. In order to save considerable space, the many worked examples are provided externally. All of the methods described in this book have a corresponding MathCad® solution worksheet that illustrates the method. These can be found on the CD-ROM attached to the back cover of the book. The purpose of these worksheets is to enable readers to calculate scale values using their own data. The worksheets are generally structured so that the first step is to read a basic data matrix into the sheet. Data collection and data matrix construction are performed externally to the MathCad® solution work sheets.

To use these work sheets you need at least MathCad® version 7.0 on a Windows® PC or a Macintosh®. Those without MathCad® can download an evaluation version from www.mathsoft.com that will run the sheets but not save the computed results.

A final word on the math in this book. A detailed understanding of the equations in this text is not an essential prerequisite for using the methods. The MathCad® solution sheets are intended to help solve practical scaling problems. All that is required for using these tools is preparing a data matrix for proper input to the solution sheet, and analyzing the results.

Chapter 2

The Image Quality Circle

This chapter introduces the broader subject of image quality to establish a reference for psychometric scaling. It highlights how psychometric scaling fits within the overall theme of image quality. This larger framework of image quality is called the Image Quality Circle (Engeldrum, 1995).

2.1 Imaging Technology Perspective

The topic of image quality did not develop overnight. The notion of image quality has its genesis in the field of optics. Optics, as a science and technology, dates back to about 1200 B.C. with the invention of curved mirrors (Hecht and Zajac, 1974). The invention of the optical microscope by Janssen and the telescope by Lippershey in the first decade of the seventeenth century surely established the concept of a visual image. But the images in those days were transient and unrecorded.

Permanent recording of images had to wait for the development of photography in the first half of the nineteenth century. Attempts at making permanent images started with Joseph Nicéphore Niepce in 1822, using a photopolymerization process. The first commercially successful imaging process was developed by Louis Jacques Mandé Daguerre in 1837. Photography, the two-step negative-positive process we know today, is credited to William Henry Fox Talbot, who developed it during the period 1835 to 1845 (Coe, 1976).

Photography integrates two image-forming processes comprising the first imaging system. The first imaging process is performed by the lens, creating an image of a real-world object on the light-sensitive film. The second process is performed by the photographic film, recording the quantity of light falling on a particular location. Once these two steps are completed, a latent image is on the film, and film development and print-making produce finished images.

The twentieth century brought the development of television and digital imaging. The development of the iconoscope tube for image capture by Vladimir Zworykin in 1923 and the demonstration of a complete television system by Philo Farnsworth in 1935 ushered in the age of electronic imaging. Like the images in Galileo's telescope centuries earlier, live television images are also transient. Photographic film was used to record images in the early days of television, before magnetic tape recording. In its day, the system for recording a television broadcast was the most complicated imaging system devised, comprising optics, photography and electronics.

Launching of the Sputnik satellite by the Soviet Union on October 4, 1957 lit the fuse on the race into space. Imaging probes have always been a principal component of space exploration. The first probes imaged the moon; later they were sent to outer planets of the solar system. These probes ushered in the age of digital imaging with both terrestrial and space applications.

Today digital imaging has progressed from expensive one-of-a-kind space applications to achieving widespread commercial importance, starting initially in diagnostic medical imaging and the prepress area of commercial printing. Digital imaging has been developing in the consumer and office sectors only since the advent of the personal computer. And this is only the beginning.

Looking at the history of imaging technology, we see that image quality has not been at the top of the list of design criteria during the initial phases of technology development. The imaging system first had to "work" and record an image. Process sensitivity to light was, and still is, a high priority. Only after achieving successful image recording does image quality become a high priority.

The first image quality topic to be addressed was the rendering of tones that comprise the image, then the spatial structure or the image details. Finally, as an imaging technology develops, attention is focused on the color quality of the image.

2.2 Image Quality Today

Image quality is not to be ignored. Market studies consistently show that image quality is one of the top customer considerations in purchasing a product, along with such purchase factors as cost. Achieving good image quality still requires substantial effort, even with so-called "mature" technologies. It is not a solved problem. There are several reasons why, after so many years, image quality remains such an elusive target.

The first reason is that the emphasis for the study of image quality, past and present, has been on *objective image evaluation*, which involves physical measurement of images. This was a difficult task and required substantial investment in instruments called microdensitometers. A major goal of objective image evaluation is to make the connection between image quality and technology variables, but this has not been universally achieved. Present emphasis is on gathering extensive image measurements, and empirically exploring relationships among the measurements to elucidate predictors of image quality. Collecting vast amounts of image data is feasible today because the costs of instruments, equivalent to the microdensitometers of old, are orders of magnitude less, and the measurement speed is far greater. These efforts have not yielded robust relationships between the physical image parameters and image quality because they generally fail to account for the characteristics of a human observer. Simply making more and more image measurements has not brought us closer to elucidating the underlying relationships.

Secondly, image quality has not gotten the attention of academics. The study of image quality today is a multidimensional, multidisciplinary topic, driven by equipment and supplies manufacturers' product development efforts. As a scientific pursuit, image quality has few academic adherents. But this is slowly changing with the traditional role of industrial research and development migrating into the universities.

Even though the study of image quality is driven by manufacturers, an Image Science or Image Quality function rarely appears on a corporate organization chart, even when the corporation is principally in the imaging business. Making image quality happen is typically left to product development engineers, perhaps in concert with the marketing function. With no top-level concern or assigned responsibility, it is no wonder image quality sometimes falls between the organizational cracks. What's worse is that, since we are all human observers, the easiest path is to bypass expensive and complicated image quality programs completely: we establish image quality by decree, with a statement such as "I can tell if the image quality is good enough by looking at it."

Still another reason image quality is elusive is that a set of myths and mysteries surrounds collecting image quality and other attribute judgments from human customers. This process of collecting and analyzing judgments is termed *subjective image evaluation* in the photographic industry, and has been treated as a poor second cousin to objective image evaluation.

The prevailing myth is that "humans can't be meters, so why should we even ask them." This view is unjustified. A major objective of this book is to show how we *can* make humans be reliable meters. In a very real sense, the customer is the ultimate "meter" when making the final buying decision. (Of course, the buying decision is complicated by many non-image-related factors.)

A corollary to the myth about the inability of humans to perform as meters is the mystery of psychometric scaling itself. Since the origins of psychometrics are not in the physical sciences, they are categorized by some as "soft science," with the implication being that psychometrics are not "good enough" to be called real science. In fact, there is nothing "soft" about the science of psychometric scaling. Indeed, some of the greatest contributors to psychometric scaling started their careers as physical scientists.

Finally, the lack of a unifying view of image quality has kept people from taking an organized and comprehensive approach to the discipline. Image quality was, and still is, a difficult topic to understand. For more than half a century a plethora of terms described various *components* of image quality, but there was no way to get a view of the "big picture."

This lack of a unified view of image quality has lead to confusion and chaos, which has prompted an array of questions. Where does image quality fit relative to the perceptual attributes that people see? What are image quality models? Does objective image quality translate to image quality *per se*? Where does subjective and objective image evaluation fit into all of this? And the questions continue.

In an attempt to bring some order to the existing chaos, the Image Quality Circle (first described as the Four Way Approach) was developed (Engeldrum, 1989). The basic structure established in 1988 and 1989 remains in place, and continues to be enhanced (Engeldrum, 1995).

2.3 The Image Quality Circle

The *Image Quality Circle* is a robust framework which organizes the multiplicity of ideas that constitute image quality. It also serves as a process model that can simplify and focus product development activities. In the decade since its inception, the Image Quality Circle has been applied in industry by several leading manufacturers of imaging products. It helps manufacturers implement workable image quality projects, and integrate image quality into their product development cycle.

Before describing the details of the Image Quality Circle, a few definitions are essential to establish a frame of reference for the terms *image* and *quality*. Not all of the definitions presented here are recognized by international standards bodies.

In this book, we use the term *image* to mean a colorant arranged in a manner to convey "information." Colorant is used in its most general sense. It can be ink, plastic (toner), wax, dye, silver, phosphors, and so on. The function of the image is to visually communicate information, which can be in the form of text, graphs, graphics, images, or even fine art. The idea of an image is very broad, and need not be a "hard copy" on a physical substrate. It can be a "soft copy" image on some form of electronic display, or any other appropriate medium.

Quality is the integrated set of perceptions of the overall degree of excellence of the image. The set of perceptions can be defined or undefined. For example, in medical imaging, quality relates to the diagnostic capability of the image, and there are specific protocols which have been defined for making this evaluation. In most other areas of imaging, image quality has no set of protocols, and is typically a "beauty contest." Here, the ultimate measurement of adequate image quality is the purchase of the imaging device or system.

The *Image Quality Circle* is a process that connects the Customer Quality Preference, shown in the top box in Figure 2.1, to the Technology Variables of the specific imaging system or technology, shown in the right-hand box. In practice, the Image Quality Circle provides a structure for putting image quality into products.

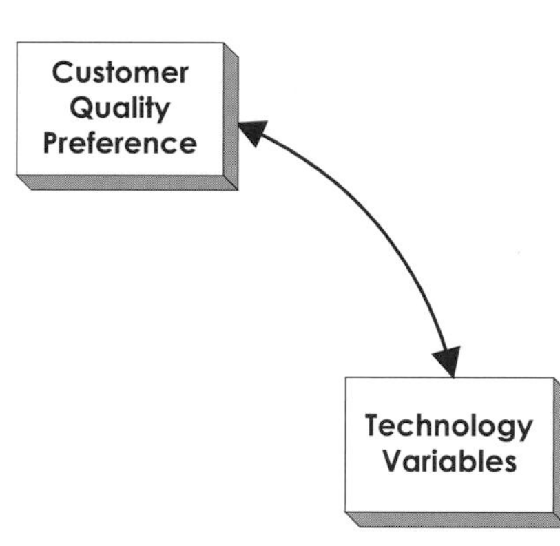

Figure 2.1 - Customer Quality Preference (judgment) from samples having variations in Technology Variables.

2.3.1 Customer Quality Preference–The Image Quality Value

The Image Quality process begins with determining *Customer Quality Preference.* The Image Quality Circle element labeled Customer Quality Preference (Figure 2.1) represents the judgment a customer renders for a sample image. In a typical judgment situation, a set of image samples is given to human observers, usually customers or customer surrogates, and the observers make a judgment about image quality for each sample presented.

This value represents the customer's opinion of image quality, and in the Image Quality Circle framework is context-independent. The underlying assumption is that the customers know image quality when they see it and, under experimental conditions, they can express a judgment about it.

During the measurement of Customer Quality Preference, it is preferable to avoid tying explicit or implicit image applications to the image quality judgment, for a very good reason. A frame of reference or context constrains the image quality scale values to being valid only for that context. For example, suppose the market application of a product is for casual snapshots of the family. The usual approach is to ask customers for a response in context of the application; e.g., "Please express an image quality rating for these samples to be used as family snapshots." This context results in values on a scale of image quality for "use as family snapshots." A scale constrained in such a way would not be valid for office documents or any other application.

Viewing image quality in an abstract or context-independent way is a departure from conventional wisdom. The main argument for this treatment is based upon the repeated empirical observation that experts and non-experts judge image quality similarly when the task is application-independent. Performing the judgments in an application-independent environment lowers the confusion in understanding, interpreting, and using Image Quality Preference values. Put another way, this approach results in an image quality scale that is more "absolute."

There is general agreement that image quality requirements are contingent on the application or use of the image. However, if image quality scales are *not* designed to be context-independent, then a set of potentially confusing application-dependent scales will evolve. In such an environment, Customer Quality Preferences can never be stated emphatically, and decisions resulting from the use of the

Image Quality Circle will always have application caveats associated with them.

Product applications are considered an overlay to the Customer Quality Preference values to avoid the proliferation of different image quality scales that are application specific. To generate the overlay, the customer is asked application-specific questions *after* a scaling study or presentation of the image quality scale via physical examples.

The applicable tool set to determine the Customer Quality Preference or the image quality value is psychometric scaling. Getting customers to be "quality meters" requires an understanding of the tools, and is one of the motivations for this book.

2.3.2 Technology Variables–The Things We Control

These are the items that are used to describe an imaging product, such as dots or pixels per inch, dot or pixel size, paper thickness, or waterfastness of the image materials. The list of Technology Variables is almost endless.

Imaging system technologists are in control of the Technology Variable list. Their primary function is to choose the best set or sets of Technology Variables or parameters from the list that yields the required image quality. This is easier said than done.

The process implied by Figure 2.1 is never-ending. Change Technology Variables. Make samples. Have customers give image quality judgments. Manipulate Technology Variables. Make new samples. Get more customer judgments. There must be a better way!

2.3.2.1 The Simple Process

Especially in a field with some degree of complexity, newness or unfamiliarity, we tend to latch onto those aspects that are concrete. Technology Variables are very concrete. So are Physical Image Parameters (to be introduced below). We measure them because they are measurable. We change technology variables because we *can*.

What happens if we combine objective tools that are more familiar and easier to implement with subjective image evaluation? If one accepts that humans participating in scaling studies *become* measuring tools, a much more thorough understanding about how to use technology to satisfy customer needs will develop, if for no other reason than the discipline of having to think of our products in human terms. Consider how important hearing human-term appraisals (both pro and con) of one's product concepts can be. But the principal benefit of integrating subjective and objective tools into a product development process is not from hearing observer commentary about our product plans. Rather, one develops command over image quality underpinnings and develops the ability to *predict* image quality.

Among the advantages of using the "make changes-make samples-collect judgments" work flow is that the process is intuitive and simple. It can be quickly implemented, and customer feedback is direct.

On the other hand, there are several disadvantages. It is an expensive process that, in principle, never stops. Conducting studies of this kind often requires the services of a market research firm to organize the study, recruit (sometimes for a fee) study participants, and write or present the results. It is rare today that product design cycle times permit even one of these types of studies. In short, the simple process is expensive in both time and resources, and never-ending.

The "make changes-make samples-collect judgments" process is only useful for the technology variables that are changed to produce the samples. Of course, technology variables have their highest uncertainty during the early stages of imaging product development. At best, studies conducted during this phase of the development process are snapshots of limited longevity. Tomorrow's new technology advance will almost certainly raise questions on the usefulness and validity of today's study.

The results apply only to the imaging technology tested. The customer quality judgment is explicitly tied to the samples that were judged by the customer. Many technology variables contribute to image quality in complex and poorly understood ways. Only at some very global level is it reasonable to develop generalizations about technology variables. As we develop the Image Quality Circle, it will become clear that customers do not judge image quality on technology variables at all.

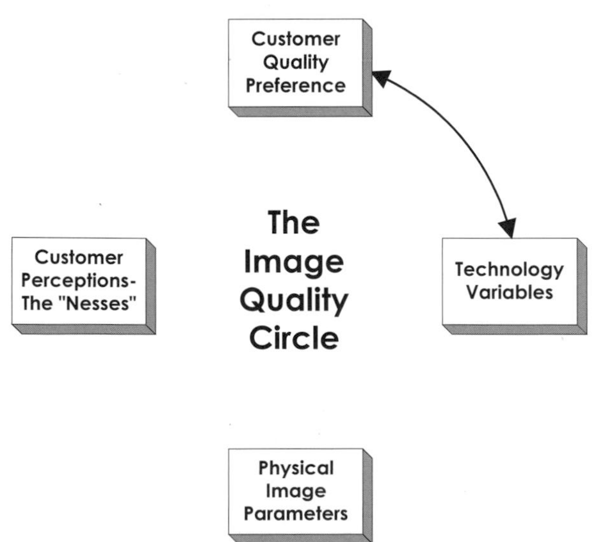

Figure 2.2 The Image Quality Circle with added elements, Customer Perceptions-"Nesses" and the Physical Image Parameters.

Although the simple process is quick and it gives fast results, it does not contribute in an organized way to understanding the overall image quality issues of the product or technology over the long run. To be sure, conducting repeated customer studies on image quality will increase overall knowledge about both technology variables and customer preferences. But it is highly unlikely that these studies by themselves help one understand the components of image quality or help one proceed on a path to the robust image quality prediction.

To address the longer term, both in terms of understanding and prediction, and to provide a comprehensive framework for image quality, two additional elements need to be added to the Image Quality Circle. These additional elements are Customer Perceptions and Physical Image Parameters (Figure 2.2).

2.3.3 Customer Perceptions–The "Nesses" –The Things We See

Customer Perceptions are the perceptual attributes, mostly visual, that form the basis of the quality preference or judgment by the customer. A *percept* is a sensation or impression received by the mind through our senses. An *attribute* is a characteristic of the image. So a *perceptual attribute*, or "ness," is a characteristic of an image that we sense (see). Most visual perceptual attributes end with the suffix "ness," so this is the telltale clue. Some examples from imaging are sharpness, graininess, colorfulness, lightness, and brightness. In this book "ness" is used as a short-hand notation to mean some perceptual attribute, to emphasize the connection to human perception, and to distinguish a Customer Perception from a Physical Image Parameter.

Understanding Customer Perceptions is a key to understanding the Image Quality Circle. Customers or observers do not make image quality judgments on Technology Variables, *per se*, as many technologists believe. Instead, they make a quality judgment, or express a preference for a particular image, on the basis of what they see, the "nesses."

Although we use the shorthand term "ness" to characterize the Customer Perceptions, not all Customer Perceptions end in "ness." There are some perceptions in imaging that are more complex, such as "tone reproduction." In color imaging, we have the percepts of "hue" and "chroma." For clarity in identifying Customer Perceptions, the suffix "ness" will sometimes be attached to such traditional terms. In all likelihood, nowhere but in this book will the reader encounter "hueness," which we use to describe the perceptual attribute of color, denoted by words such as blue, green, red, and yellow.

No single "ness" completely encompasses the idea of image quality, since we define image quality as the *integrated* perception of image excellence. However, it may happen that a given set of images may have only one "ness" that varies, so when customers are asked to judge the quality of such a set, they will typically respond on the basis of that "ness" varying in the image set. (Factors affecting observer judgments are covered in Chapter 3.) In this special case, the resulting scale will not be one of image quality, but a scale of the single "ness" that varies. One must not be drawn to the erroneous conclusion that a specific "ness" constitutes image quality. A large number of "nesses" are possible in any image set. Fortunately, only a small number of them vary in typical images, and it is this small set of Customer Perceptions that drives the judgment of image quality (Stultz and Zweig, 1962; Sawyer, 1980; Bartleson, 1982; Engeldrum, 1995).

Again we see that establishing a "ruler" for the "nesses" requires human judgments and thus the application of psychometric scaling.

2.3.4 Physical Image Parameters–The Things We Measure (Image Physics)

Physical Image Parameters are quantitative, usually obtained by physically measuring the image with instruments. Physical image parameters have historically been called *objective* measures of image quality. Typical of such measures, or parameters, are optical density or spectral reflectance factor. More complex, both in terms of description and measurement, are functions of spatial frequency such as modulation transfer, Wiener spectra, or amplitude spectra. The field of image science has a strong focus on physical image parameters (see Dainty and Shaw, 1974).

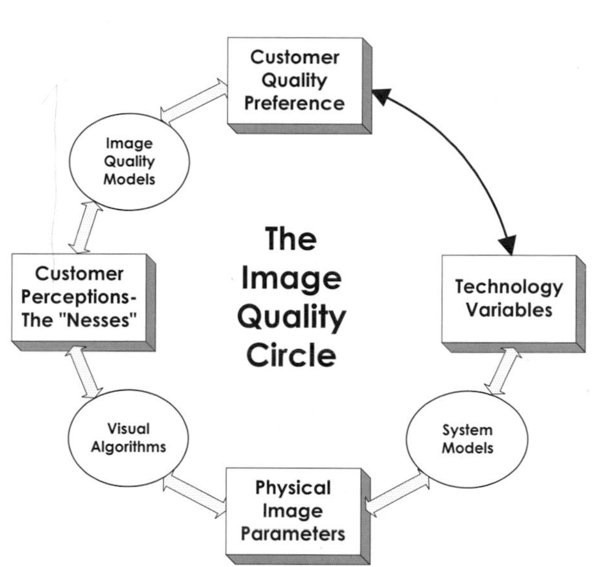

Figure 2.3 - The complete Image Quality Circle showing all the Connecting Links.

In Figure 2.3 we note that Physical Image Parameters are diametrically opposite Customer Quality Preferences. The very configuration of the Image Quality Circe on the page implies that Physical Image Parameters are not "close" measures of image quality. In fact, they are not: when compared to Customer Quality Preferences, customers don't see Physical Image Parameters, they see "nesses."

2.3.5 Image Quality Circle Connecting Links

To complete the Image Quality Circle we need the connecting links which allow us to move back and forth around the Circle. Moving around the circle is exactly analogous to performing a system design or trade-off analysis. Generally one question is something like, "What set of Technology Variables do we need to yield X image quality in our product?" To answer this question one would proceed counterclockwise around the Image Quality Circle starting with the Customer Quality Preference. On the other hand, what if the question was something like, "How does increasing the Z Technology Variable by 100% affect our image quality?" The approach now is to start at the Technology Variables element and go clockwise around the Image Quality Circle. Using the Image Quality Circle in these two directions is illustrated by the wide two-headed arrows in Figure 2.3.

The three connecting links are illustrated in Figure 2.3 as ellipses. We shall start the link descriptions, commencing at the System Models and going clockwise around the circle.

2.3.6 System Models

System Models, sometimes referred to as image models, are formulas, physical models, algorithms, or computer code that predict the Physical Image Parameters from the Technology Variables. The double arrow indicates that these models can be used in both directions. Conceptually, the inputs and outputs can be both the Technology Variables and the Physical Image Parameters, depending on which way one is traveling around the circle.

Placing the System Models in this part of the image quality process is a break with past conceptualizations. Previous arrangements have used system or image models directly to predict "nesses" or image quality, a difficult and all-encompassing requirement. The underlying motive for this new construct is to minimize the requirements of such models. Requiring the System Model to predict only Physical Image Parameters instead of image quality or "nesses" simplifies the System Models, increases their modularity and portability, and increases the success rate.

Most practical System Models are developed with specific inputs and outputs, but the System Model's concept is not constrained by such practicalities. System Models that take Technology Variables as inputs and generate Physical Image Parameters as outputs are called forward models. Forward models are often easier to build and therefore more popular. Since the Image Quality Circle concept has no defined inputs and outputs–one can go either direction around the circle–forward models need to be invertible. Another logical possibility is to construct "reverse" models that have Physical Image Parameters as the inputs and Technology Variables as the outputs. Such models are not easy to construct simply because it is a one-to-many problem; one Physical Image Parameter can result from many Technology Variables.

No constraints are put on System Models other than that they provide the linkage of the Physical Image Parameters to the Technology Variables. In some cases a System Model is simply a measurement. Pragmatic engineers and scientists often use models that relate just a few critical technical variables to a few critical physical image parameters. The relationships can be purely empirical, like a multivariate equation developed via regression analysis, or one based on fundamental detailed physics.

In the early stages of an imaging technology development, there are no models at all. Rather, they tend to evolve over time, which makes building System Models a long-term process. The simple long-term objective of the System Model connecting link can be summarized as the capability to predict the measured spectral radiance factor (color) of an arbitrary image point.

2.3.7 Visual Algorithms

Visual Algorithms connect Physical Image Parameters to Customer Perceptions (see Figure 2.3). The function of a Visual Algorithm is to predict a value on a "ness" scale from a suitable set of Physical Image Parameters. Like System Models, these algorithms can be formulas, models, or computer code, recipes that are used to compute a value of a "ness" (e.g. sharpness) from something like the measurement of the gradient of a printed edge. The "units" of these scales are "ness units," and are therefore different one from another. Although we use the term visual algorithm, it should not be seen in only a visual context. It is quite possible that important "nesses" are not visual at all. The substrate of an image is an important quality factor, but it is often described by tactile "nesses," not visual "nesses."

Visually-based algorithms have an extensive history in photographic image quality, and in recent years have been extended to electronic imaging.

Robust Visual Algorithms must include at least two fundamental properties of the human visual system: the nonlinear response to light (luminance) and bandpass-like spatial frequency properties.

See Wandell (1995) for a modern view of visual science that relates directly to visual algorithms.

There are a few internationally standardized visual algorithms. In the field of color science, the definition of CIE lightness is a visual algorithm in the context of the Image Quality Circle. The CIE definition of lightness is given by: $L^* = 116(Y/Y_n)^{1/3} - 116$, where Y is the CIE luminance or Y Tristimulus value and Y_n is the Y value of the reference white. In this example, the visual algorithm connects Physical Image Parameters to Customer Perceptions in two steps. First comes the calculation of Y from the spectral properties of the image, which would include the light source of the viewing illuminant for reflectance or transmittance images (Physical Image Parameters). Then, lightness (L*) is calculated from Y and Y_n, using the CIE defining equation.

In the CIE L*a*b* system of color coordinates there are other visual algorithms for "chromaness" (chroma, C*) and "hueness angle" (hue angle, h_{ab}). The physical image parameter is the same: the spectral reflectance, transmittance or radiance property of the colored object.

Color "nesses" are practical examples of the many-to-one mapping characteristic of the clockwise rotation around the Image Quality Circle. In this case the "many" are the spectral properties at thirty or more wavelengths (reflectance factor, for example), and the "one" (three really) are the lightness, hue and chroma "nesses." The complete CIE colorimetric system has its roots in psychophysical scaling. See Fairchild (1997) for a recent view of color and color appearance.

Some "nesses" have to do with the spatial structure of images; e.g. the variation in nominally uniform areas called "uniformityness." A well-known subset of "uniformityness" is graininess. Developing a successful visual algorithm for graininess would require the incorporation of the spatial frequency properties of the human visual system (Engeldrum and McNeill, 1985; Dooley and Shaw, 1979).

Visual Algorithms are not unique to the Image Quality Circle concept. Examples of visual algorithms can be found in the areas of computational vision, visual processing, and human visual models. See Watson (1993) and Landy and Movshon (1994) for recent surveys on computational vision and visual information processing.

2.3.8 Image Quality Models

Image Quality Models link Customer Perceptions, the "nesses," with Customer Quality Preferences. The Image Quality Model inputs are values of "nesses" and the output is the image quality value. This is the ultimate destination in the many-to-one mapping process of the Image Quality Circle: a one-number summary description of image quality. By adopting a long-term strategy of building robust Image Quality Models with a suitable set of "nesses" that link to the customer, expensive image-quality scaling efforts can be minimized.

Building Image Quality Models is an empirical endeavor that combines scales, or rulers, of both image quality and the "nesses." They are statistically derived, but the mathematical formalism underlying successful Image Quality Models attempts to capture characteristics of human judgments, so they are not merely blind exercises in regression analysis (Engeldrum, 1995).

What is particularly valuable and efficient about Image Quality Models, in the Image Quality Circle framework, is that most of the model construction relies on psychometric scaling studies. Thus, investments in hardware infrastructure are minimal, compared to the considerable resources required for the measurement of Physical Image Parameters and Technology Variables.

The details of image quality modeling are complex and beyond the scope of this book. But for some starting points, see Sawyer (1980), Bartleson (1982, 1984), de Ridder (1992) and Engeldrum (1995, 1999). For a more general view on how humans perform when asked to make integrated judgments like image quality judgments, see Massaro and Friedman (1990) and Baird (1997).

2.3.9 Image Quality Circle Short Cuts

Two short cuts can be created by following a diameter instead of the circumference of the Image Quality Circle. One short cut connects Customer Quality Preference to Physical Image Parameters, while the other connects the Technology Variables to the Customer Perceptions. Neither of these two diameter paths are generally recommended.

The image science and image processing/compression literature describes many attempts to develop values of image quality by taking these short cuts. The popularity of the short cuts rests on the widely held idea that a generic mean-squared-difference measure is adequate for image quality. Some short cuts that have "worked" are often found to be feeble when either the Physical Image Parameters or Technology Variables associated with the imaging technology change. Often, these approaches are doomed to failure because fundamental attributes and properties of the human visual system have not been taken into account, either via Visual Algorithms, or via the "nesses" that are the components of image quality.

However, there are some exceptions to this rule. One such exception is in the quality assurance function in a manufacturing environment. If all the components and the connecting links of the Image Quality Circle are known, then the Physical Image Parameters that yield a particular value of image quality are also known. This offers the opportunity to perform the quality assurance function at the Physical Image Parameter level, say, instead of the Customer Perception level. Thus the evaluation of image quality components, the Physical Image Parameters, can be highly automated. Other possibilities, no doubt, exist.

2.4 Psychometric Scaling and the Image Quality Circle

Roughly one-half of the Image Quality Circle, from Visual Algorithms to the Image Quality Preference, requires human judgments. Without some means for obtaining measurements from actual customers or customer surrogates, we cannot determine in a numerical fashion Image Quality Preference, nor the Customer Perceptual Attributes, or develop Image Quality Models or Visual Algorithms. In short, we have an incomplete Image Quality Circle unless human observers are involved.

Psychometric scaling is an absolutely essential tool for implementing the Image Quality Circle. The remainder of the chapters in this book present methods for determining the numerical value of the "ness," or the image quality, for a set of image samples.

Chapter 3

The Process of Scaling and Some Practical Hints

Simply stated, the goal of scaling in the context of the Image Quality Circle is assigning numbers to image quality and the "nesses," or attributes. A *scaling study* is the process of establishing these numbers or scale values. On the surface, it appears quite simple to ask observers to express a judgment or an opinion about some images, but it is more subtle than that. The purpose of this chapter is to give an overview of the process of designing and conducting scaling studies, and to provide practical guidance or hints.

The hints and suggestions presented here are oriented toward a product development environment where the overriding factor is to deliver "quick, useful results." Some of these hints may not be applicable for academic research. However, the hints provided in this chapter should have appeal to anyone interested in scaling or the use of scale values as response variables in statistical experimental design, since all scaling endeavors, be they published works or private studies done to support internal product development efforts, are probably undertaken to develop accurate and precise image quality or "ness" scales.

For some "nesses," such as brightness, there is a well-understood physical correlate (luminance); but for others, such as graininess or glossiness, the physical correlates (Physical Image Parameters) are not so obvious. In particular, it is necessary to combine several physical variables in order to obtain a correlate of these "nesses." In order to do this, one needs a Visual Algorithm or a model of some kind to link the multidimensional physical stimulus to the subjective perception. In some cases such algorithms have been worked out, but in other cases they have not. One of the great advantages of methods discussed in this book is that we are able to devise perceptual scale values without requiring that we have a well-understood Visual Algorithm to define the combination of Physical Image Parameters that form the basis for the "nesses." Only in the case of plotting a psychophysical function between a physical variable and a perceptual variable is it necessary to have a rigorous definition of the stimulus. This is also why this book concentrates on the indirect methods of scaling pioneered by L. L. Thurstone. His original motivation for developing these methods was to provide quantification of such variables as "excellence of handwriting" and "preference for wrist watches." These are subjective variables that do not have a readily defined physical stimulus correlate.

It is a practical impossibility to cover all possible factors affecting the results of a scaling task and provide specific recommendations for each of them. Attempting to do so would take a book in its own right. The objective here is to limit the hints to some key areas relevant to imaging. Readers interested in the topic of biases in judgments should see Poulton (1989).

3.1 The Process

At one level the scaling study appears deceptively simple. Anything so simple would not appear to need extensive planning. However, diving headlong into a scaling activity without a plan is almost guaranteed to yield poor results, results that may be useless or totally inaccurate. In a schedule-driven product development environment, this headlong dive is more the rule than the exception, though. The message is simple: before you begin, you need a scaling study plan. The following sections describe some of the many factors that need careful consideration in developing a scaling study plan.

The process of developing the scale values for a "ness" or image quality consists of seven basic steps:

1) Select the samples (stimuli).
2) Prepare the samples for observer judgment.
3) Select observers.
4) Determine observer judgment task or question.
5) Present samples to observers for their judgment or preference.
6) Collect and record observer responses.
7) Analyze observer response data to generate the scale values.

These steps interact, often in unforeseen and unpredictable ways. Serious consideration and planning of the scaling study is needed for successful results. The remainder of the chapter discusses issues and provides some useful suggestions for completing the first six of the seven steps outlined above. Succeeding chapters cover the analysis methods for actual scale generation.

3.2 Sample (Stimuli) Selection

Selection of image samples, or stimuli, is governed by the objective of the scaling study and many other practical factors. Sample selection is, in practice, one of the most difficult parts of the scaling study, and is not often given the serious attention it requires. Failure to collect or generate a suitable sample set has derailed numerous scaling studies because many of the selection factors are elusive or undefined. By focusing on a few critical factors, the process of sample selection can be substantially simplified.

Table 3.1 Sample Categories

Sample Category	Properties/Characterisitcs (After Bartleson, 1986)
Random and Independent	1) Every image has an equal chance of being selected (random). 2) Selection of one image does not influence the selection of another (independent).
Stratified	The above, plus: 1) Population is classified according to some relevant distinction. 2) Number of items in each class reflects the population of interest.
Contrast	A stratified sample with additional items in classes of particular interest. Does not reflect the population.
Purposeful	One, but not both, of the following conditions: 1) Represents the population 2) Varies independently in some attribute.
Incidental	1) A random independent sample of subgroups of particular interest, or, 2) A special existing collection that is unique and cannot be added to ("sacred samples").

Four key factors that need to be addressed during the sample selection or sample generation phase of the scaling study planning are:

1) What *categories* should the samples represent?
2) What *range and distribution of "nesses"* should the sample set contain?
3) What *image size* should be used?
4) What *image content* or image elements should the samples contain?

Although all of these factors are key, there is no universal optimum set of these four elements suitable for all scaling studies. The choice of elements will depend on many practical considerations and the necessary trade-offs.

3.2.1 Categories

Bartleson (1984) proposed five categories to describe samples of imagery, and listed their basic properties. These categories, shown in Table 3-1, can be used as a guide in sample image selection.

The real value of Bartleson's categorization is that it represents an organized way to make a rational sample selection; and, conversely, identify what properties the sample does not possess. Following the categories in Table 3-1, some practical suggestions are offered for selecting an appropriate set of image samples for a scaling study.

Random and Independent–Random and independent sampling of images, although statistically interesting, is difficult in practice to implement. A major issue is the difficulty of defining a population that can be randomly and independently sampled. There is no single reservoir of "the population" of images, although, as digital imagery continues to develop, there are an increasing number of firms on the

Internet offering image files in an increasingly large number of image classes. Handy as they may be, files of existing imagery may have only limited usefulness when image and color characteristics must be quantified.

Stratified–Stratified sampling or imagery is becoming more practical due to the wide availability and accessibility of image databases. Imagery can be defined in classes such as text, graphics and photographs. The class "photographs" can be further stratified into various subclasses such as landscapes, portraits, and groups of people. Stratified sampling is a very practical approach with wide availability of digital image files.

Contrast–Contrast sampling is common in a product development environment. Usually there is an interest in knowing the quality requirements or performance of a particular imaging device with respect to some class of imagery. The classes are shaped by the market for the product. For example, if the imaging device is a color computer printer for the office desk, then the image quality performance requirements for text and color graphics would need to be known. If, on the other hand, the imaging device was a consumer product to print "pictures," then performance over a wide class of photographs would be of interest. Selecting imagery classes relevant to the product application is also efficient because it ignores irrelevant classes.

Purposeful–A purposeful sampling can be extremely useful during product design. During the product development process, questions arise that require engineering trade-offs. Often the prototype product produces some unexpected "ness," and raises the question, "What level of the (unwanted) 'ness' is acceptable?" A set of sample images that exhibit various levels of the "ness" in question would comprise the sample set to be used in a scaling study.

Incidental–Incidental sampling is, arguably, the most widely used sample category in imaging product development. Typically, a set of images is selected as the "reference" set, supposedly representing product performance requirements. These images then become the "gold standards" or "sacred samples." These incidental samples are often selected by the product development team to represent a readily understood image quality contract between the relevant product development organizations–marketing and engineering, for example.

3.2.2 Range and Distribution of "Nesses"

The samples define the context of the scaled "ness" or image quality. There are two aspects to this depending on whether a "ness" or image quality is being scaled. When scaling a "ness," if the "ness" of interest does not vary in the sample set, any resulting scale cannot be a measure of the "ness" in question. The context was incorrect and it will be a scale of some, perhaps unknown, "ness." In scaling image quality, the context is the specific set of "nesses" and their range in the sample set. It is common in image quality scaling studies that the quality judgment varies due to the variation of only one "ness." The resulting scale from this sample set will not be one of image quality, although it may be labeled as such, but a scale of the single "ness" that varies in the sample set. Much care is needed in identifying the "nesses" in a sample set in order to avoid these pitfalls.

Bartleson and Woodbury (1962) illustrated the change in image quality judgments that can occur when photographic transparencies vary in color balance ("color balanceness"). They conducted three scaling experiments. The first experiment had samples that ranged in color balance from "cool" (blueish) to "normal;" the second varied from "normal" to "warm" (yellowish); and the third was the combination of the "warm" and "cool" sets. Each set had a uniform distribution with respect to "color balanceness." Bartleson and Woodbury showed that observers' quality judgments change according to the set (context) they are judging. The sample images were photographic transparencies viewed in a darkened room, and chromatic adaptation of the human visual system was the main reason for the sample-set dependence of the quality judgments.

Two solutions to counter chromatic adaptation were suggested. The first was to interleave "high-quality representative photographs" with the samples when viewing. The second solution was to view a 0.2 neutral density filter for 15 seconds between sample presentations (Bartleson and Woodbury, 1962). In an image quality experiment, interleaving an area of constant luminance for 20 seconds–equivalent to viewing a neutral density filter to control adaptation–has also been suggested (Westerlink and Roufs, 1989).

With some scaling methods, the distribution of the "ness" in the sample set can also have a significant influence on the scale values. In category scaling, observers have a tendency to use all categories equally often (Gescheider, 1997). For example, if a large fraction of the samples have high values of a "ness" and only a few have low values, observers tend to make fine discrimination at the high end and lump the low-valued "nesses" together in the bottom categories. This judgment behavior results in scale distortion. The best solution is to have equal numbers of samples that uniformly span the range of "ness" of interest.

Generating samples using computer image simulation or rendering techniques can help achieve the required "ness" range and distribution. This powerful method can be used for sample generation without having to actually construct the imaging device or system. Image simulation is not a trivial undertaking, however. A substantial and thorough knowledge of the imaging technology is required to correctly simulate the desired "ness." Since no imaging device is perfect, these images will ultimately be limited in the "ness" and image quality by the imaging characteristics of the simulation output device.

To reiterate a point made earlier, securing a set of samples that have the desired "ness" or "nesses" with the desired range and distribution is often a very difficult problem to overcome. It is more than worthwhile to expend the effort to select or generate a sample set that meets the scaling study requirements.

3.2.3 Image Size and Spatial Sampling

Image size and object sizes in the image are well-known factors in "ness" and image quality judgments (Corey, *et. al.*, 1983; Westerlink and Roufs, 1989). These studies used photographic prints and transparencies, both color and monochrome, which varied in sharpness. The results indicate that the larger the image size, the higher the quality or sharpness rating, all other things being equal.

In general, expect image size to be a factor influencing observer judgments, one way or another. The simplest strategy is to keep the size of the images in a scaling study constant, thus eliminating or minimizing image size as a judgment factor. Keeping sample image size constant does not eliminate any context-of-scene dependence factor, though.

Image size also enters in an indirect way. The scale values of samples from an imaging system should not be limited by the inherent quality of the *input* image or object. Evaluating the quality of computer printers, for example, should not depend on the spatial sampling frequency (pixels per distance) of the image file being printed. It is not uncommon for sample images used for output device testing to have a sampling frequency, pixels per distance, lower than the addressability (resolution or dots/inch) of the output device. This tactic of using low-resolution images ties the "ness" or quality judgments directly to the sampling frequency of the input, rather than the inherent imaging characteristics of the output device. A good rule of thumb is to have the sampling frequency of the test samples be at least equal to the addressability of the output device. This rule also implies a limit to the size of an image from any given file.

Fortunately there are practical upper limits to the sampling rule. Otherwise, file sizes can become excessive for high-addressability output devices. A useful upper bound for spatial sampling frequency is about 10 samples or pixels per mm for images viewed at "normal" distances of about 14 inches. If the viewing distance changes, the upper bound on the maximum sampling interval scale changes in an inverse manner. Closer viewing distance would require a proportional increase in the sampling frequency, while an increase in viewing distance can use a lower sampling frequency. The key is to keep the angular sampling frequency (pixels/degree or pixels/radian) constant.

3.2.4 Image Content

There are a host of contexts, overt or implied, within which a sample is viewed and judged. A helpful rule to remember is, "Preferences do not occur in a vacuum, they are always formed relative to a context" (Mellers and Cook, 1996).

The spatial configurations of the elements and the object content in sample images are well known "context" factors. The breadth of spatial configurations can vary from large areas of color (or dark areas), to areas that change rapidly from point to point (so-called "busy" images). This dependence of judgments on spatial configuration, or context, is called *scene dependence*. The term *spatial configuration* is preferred to scene dependence because it more accurately relates to the judgment factor.

Complicating spatial configuration issues are the inherent interactions of Technology Variables and the "nesses" in real-world images. Some spatial configurations can amplify poor attributes or defects of the imaging system, while other configurations minimize them. Graininess is a good example of this effect. If an imaging system produces noticeable levels of graininess, typically most visible in large midtone areas, then any image sample with a large midtone area will be judged to have high graininess.

To generate useful scales, a balance must be achieved between the spatial elements and objects in sample images. This is the driving reason for using more than one image in scaling studies. The assumption is that assorted spatial configurations will average out spatial-configuration effects. Assuring that the "correct" spatial configurations have been selected prior to the scaling study is not usually possible. However, assessing the dependence of scale values on the spatial configuration of sample images can be accomplished after the scale values are determined. One approach is to use an appropriate statistical experimental design incorporating analysis of variance (ANOVA), where the spatial configuration can be tested to see if it is a factor in determining the scale values.

Most people have fairly consistent preferences for a few "critical" colors, such as flesh tones, green grass and blue sky. It is well known that the preference for *reproduced* versions of these colors is quite different from the preference for the actual colors themselves (Bartleson and Bray, 1962). These colors provide a context for observer judgments of image samples, and the judgments may be substantially altered by their inclusion.

Image classes are also known to exert an influence on judgments. For example, the sharpness of portraits of people and landscapes are judged differently (Freiser and Biederman, 1963). In fact Freiser and Biederman found that if portrait sharpness is too high, observers find the image "disagreeable." Portrait photographers have known for a long time that images taken with a "soft focus" (low sharpness) are preferred.

Emotional involvement, or potential involvement, of the observer in the sample image or scene content is another context factor. It is no secret that sex sells, and for this reason advertising agencies use alluring women and men in product advertisements. The same idea applies in the scaling of sample images. The choice of sample, or scene, can affect the scale values in both positive and negative ways, through emotional involvement of the observers. Emotional involvement also applies to "my images" versus someone else's images. A bond or attachment to the persons or objects in the images causes altered judgments.

Electronic image displays are often used to simulate images on substrates such as paper and clear polymer. But the use of such self-luminous displays does not provide the same mode of appearance as reflection images. Stokes, *et. al.* (1992) suggested an interesting device to provide better correlation to reflection, or hard-copy, images. They suggest a pair of hands on a gray background holding a white card. The sample image is placed in the white card, thus providing a constant context for the observers' judgments.

Although the emphasis has been on pictorial imagery, the same general rules hold for text and graphic images. For example, samples of text composed of unfamiliar typefaces (fonts) may create a foreign context for the observer, and not give a useful scale. Similar arguments hold for graphic image classes.

There are no hard-and-fast rules that govern the content or spatial arrangement of image samples. One useful strategy is to include samples from various image subclasses such as portraits, landscapes, people groups, and so on. This tactic will tend to average out potential observer biases. An additional option is to maintain different scales for different image classes; e.g., a pictorial image quality scale, a text quality scale, and so forth. However, this is not recommended because of the potential for confusion among the scale users. A better approach is to treat the image subclasses as an overlay to the "absolute" image quality scale.

When scaling image quality, it is important to include image classes that are familiar to, or requirements of, the target market of the product. Do not limit the selection of image types to those readily available within the organization. Consider taking advantage of the vast array of images available on the Internet, but beware that they may not have important image and color-characteristic descriptive information.

3.3 Sample Preparation

Once the samples have been selected, it is then appropriate to consider how these samples should be prepared for presentation to observers. Careful preparation will not only preserve the samples, but will reduce unwanted, and often unknown, influences on observer judgments.

3.3.1 Sample Handling and Maintenance

When the scaling study requires a large number of observers, such practical issues as routine sample handling and keeping the samples clean become important.

One useful technique for keeping the sample images clean is to mount the samples on a rigid base such as cardboard. Care needs to be taken to ensure that the color of the base or backing does not alter the appearance of the samples in undesirable ways. For example, a nonwhite base or sample backing will change the color appearance of the sample if the sample substrate is not completely opaque. A simple method for dealing with low substrate opacity is to back the sample with a highly opaque white material such as a highly reflecting white cardboard.

Images generated by some imaging technologies are prone to damage due to mechanical abrasions of the imaging material. A cover of heavy paper or plastic material, hinged on one edge of the sample, is one means of providing protection. If the cover is transparent, it can also minimize or hide surface textures from the observer, which may be useful in some situations.

3.3.2 Sample Border or Mask

In addition to mounting on cardboard, placing a frame, border or mask around the samples has some advantages. The frame, border or mask is usually a neutral gray cardboard, which serves two purposes. The first is to mask off, by covering any white border surrounding the sample. Masking the border may not be appropriate if the whiteness of the image substrate is of interest. However, if the sample set is produced on a variety of substrates, using a mask around the edge of the sample will eliminate substrate whiteness as an observer cue, thus eliminating the chance that an unwanted "ness" might influence observer judgments.

Some imaging technologies have built-in cues, such as substrate thickness, tactile feel, image gloss, and image surface texture, that let observers deduce substantial information about the sample. A simple mask or border, in conjunction with a backing material if the image substrate has low opacity, can minimize the cues and allow the observer to focus on the "ness" rather than the imaging technology. It is not a rigid requirement that samples be mounted and have neutral gray masks, but it should be considered as a useful tool to isolate the "nesses" you want the observers to focus on.

Another important use of the gray mask is to provide a constant visual reference or adaptation point. When scaling color "nesses," a constant visual reference is important because it stabilizes the chromatic adaptation point of the observer, and forces the white point reference to be in the image sample.

When viewing projected transparent images (overhead transparencies in a typical office environment, for example), the surround, which is usually white, significantly influences the perception of lightness in color and monochrome images (Bartleson and Breneman, 1967). This "surround effect" causes an increase in the "image contrastness" when the surround is light, and a decrease in "contrastness" when the surround is dark. Usually photographic slides and motion pictures are viewed in a dark room, or equivalently a dark surround, so an expected range of surrounds from light to completely dark occurs in many practical viewing situations. The border or mask surrounding an image is a primary tool in controlling the image appearance and should receive careful consideration.

The previous discussion focused on hard copy imaging technologies, but the same ideas apply to electronic image displays. The tan-colored bezels surrounding the actual displays have almost the same hue and lightness. However, their influence on observer judgments can be affected by the illuminance on the display, which is not usually a factor with images on opaque substrates.

3.3.3 Sample Labeling

Hiding the sample identification helps reduce the chances that helpful observers will "solve" the visible code and respond to the sample identification and not the "ness" of interest. Placing identifying numbers or letters on the samples in areas that are visible to the observers is generally not a good practice. In addition, one should avoid sequentially labeling samples in the order of some technology variable. The preferred labeling practice is to put the identification on the back of the sample. If it is essential that some alphanumeric identification be visible to the observer, use a non-obvious code of some sort, such as a four-digit sequence of random numbers.

Bar coding of samples can speed data recording and reduce errors. Bar code generation software and code-reading hardware for PCs is inexpensive and easy to use. Labels can be inexpensively produced on conventional office printers, and have the added advantage that they are not readily decoded by observers, so they can be safely placed in the viewable image area if necessary. Software is readily available to scan the bar code and have the data directly placed in a spreadsheet.

3.3.4 Numbers of Samples

In scaling studies, the number of samples depends on the scaling method, covered in later chapters, and the time and resources available. Using many samples in an attempt to cover all the sample-selection considerations discussed so far is often impractical. Depending on the needs of the study, the number of samples can be anywhere from about three to about thirty.

Scaling method and sample quantity interact considerably. Some scaling methods are most efficient with small numbers, say less than ten, while other methods may only yield satisfactory results with larger numbers. Another consideration is physical sample size. Manipulating poster-size images is physically difficult, so the number of samples must be necessarily small if the prints are large.

The length of time it takes an observer to complete a scaling task is a key consideration. Time is largely driven by the quantity of samples.

Too many samples can force the observer to lose interest and hurry through the judgment task, to the detriment of scale quality. Scaling conducted hastily usually results in scale values with high variance and bias. If the scaling activity takes an inordinate amount of time and resources, or gives poor results, it may lose support and wind up on the organizational pile of "ineffective tools that we tried but did not work." Discriminating judgment needs to be applied in deciding the sample number.

An alternative strategy is to conduct two scaling studies, each with a smaller quantity of samples. Methods to merge scales generated from two different scaling studies are presented in later chapters.

3.4 Observers–"Type" and Number

A commonly held belief among newcomers to psychometric scaling is that experts see things differently, or give different scale values, than unsophisticated observers. This may or may not be true, and it depends on the scaling task. Observers who participate in scaling studies are usually eager to help, and will often use various methods to provide the "correct" answers. These factors are real and must be addressed to assure high-quality scale values.

A general discussion of observer selection is outlined in Chapter 8 of Meilgaard, *et. al.* (1991). ASTM Standard E 1499-97 (1997), which is primarily oriented to color appearance judgments, gives detailed guidelines for the selection, evaluation and training of observers.

3.4.1 Expert Versus Average Observers

Observers who have experience in judging or evaluating images usually fall into the expert observer category. In their vocation, they may learn to make very fine distinctions of the "nesses" they experience. To a much greater degree, experts can distinguish among categories of a specific "ness": their "ness"-scale resolving power is often much greater than average or untrained observers. This may become troublesome with some scaling methods, particularly category scaling, where the trained or experienced observers distinguish among categories that average observers do not. Conversely, there are applications in product quality assurance that require fine quantization or categorization of "ness" values and the detection of small differences. Trained or expert observers are needed in this type of scaling task.

For specific "nesses" that are relatively unique to a particular imaging system (a defect for example), experienced observers may give scale values that are markedly different from average observers. When this occurs, it may be due to *stimulus errors,* which simply means that observers are making a judgment on a Technology Variable and not a "ness." Product development personnel are often very familiar with the Technology Variables of the imaging system, so recruiting them as observers is not generally recommended. Product development personnel tend to be more sensitive to "bad" "nesses" than average observers. After all, their job is to make the bad "nesses" disappear. If the potential observer is knowledgeable about failure modes or technology variables of the particular imaging system, and the scaling study is trying to simulate typical customer response, then such observers should not be considered for the scaling study.

If the objective is to generate a "ness" scale for average or typical customers, the safest course is to use typical customers as observers. On the other hand, if the scaling task is to scale a fundamental "ness" not specifically associated with a particular imaging device–colorfulness, for example–most human observers will respond similarly.

Observer training and task familiarity both play a role in understanding the task and the speed of executing the scaling task. Experts generally give scale values similar to average observers when scaling fundamental or basic "nesses," but they often do it faster.

The most common situation is where expert and average observers often give distinctly *different* responses when answering a preference question. If the scaling task requires a response to any of the following questions:

"Which sample do you prefer?"
"Which one do you like?"
"Which one is best for the xxx application?"

then it is a preference task. Confusion about whether the judgment task is a basic "ness" or a preference is probably the origin of the myth about expert vs. average observer difference. Statistical testing is warranted if there are concerns that observer group expertise may distort scale values.

3.4.2 Number of Observers

"How many observers do I use?" is a common question when planning scaling studies. The answer to this question can become complicated, but there are some practical guidelines.

The fundamental advantage of having a large number of observers is the increased precision of the estimated scale value. Using more observers decreases the error in the scale value, depending on the details of the statistics of the scale estimate. However, the general rule is that scale precision increases as the square root of the number of observers, a familiar statistical result. Because of the square root factor, doubling the number of observers does not double the precision of the scale value. It only decreases the error by a factor of 1.4, the square root of two.

The number of observers to use in scaling studies is typically governed by availability. Scaling studies in the imaging arena are conducted with as few as four observers, and with as many as fifty. A recommended range is from ten to thirty for typical scaling applications. This is not intended to be a rigid rule, only a guideline subject to scale precision requirements and the experience and knowledge of the study administrator. Better estimates of observer numbers can be obtained by establishing a desired scale precision, and using the statistical relationships between numbers of observers and scale standard deviation. Most methods described in this book provide formulas for estimating scale-value standard deviation.

Increasing observer numbers only affects the scale-value precision, or variability about its average value. There is no practical way to know the absolute accuracy of a scale value, so the choice of observer number, *per se*, does not affect scale accuracy.

3.5 Observer Task Instructions–It's All in the Question

Next to the sample image set, observer instructions are the most significant item that controls the context of the observers' judgments in a scaling study. Sadly, it is far too common to see the observers' task instructions get only passing consideration.

To achieve useful and meaningful results, observers need to be told what they are to do.

1) What, exactly, is the attribute they are to judge, and what is their judgment task?
2) Is there an explicit or implicit context to the scaling task?
3) What criteria or definition should they use in their judgment?

No samples are perfect, particularly in the early stages of product development. Should the observers be instructed to ignore certain aspects or defects of the samples?

These considerations are key to any successful scaling study, so we devote this section to providing guidance. Instead of including prototype instructions here, each chapter describing the data analysis methods includes some suggestions from which to model observer instructions.

3.5.1 What is the Attribute and Judgment Task?

A common scaling scenario is to use the paired comparison data collection method instructing the observer to answer the question, "Which do you prefer?" by selecting one of the pair. In reporting the results, the scale is termed an "image quality" or some other "ness" scale. This is grossly incorrect because the instructions to the observer are, "Which do you prefer?" No question was asked about image quality or a "ness" preference, so the final scale is nothing more than a basic scale of preference. No reason can be given for the preference of one sample over another from this type of experiment. The preference rating may be for overall image quality reasons, or more likely because of the dominance of one or two "nesses" in the sample set.

The general rule is specifically to ask the observer to make a judgment on the appropriate "ness" or image quality. For an image quality scale, the appropriate instruction to the observer should be something like, "Select one of the two samples that has the highest image quality."

The judgment task instructions should be clear and should avoid complex or fuzzy ideas, technical jargon, and the use of Technology Variable labels. Matching the instructions to the ability of the observer group is also essential. If there are any time constraints or other limitations, then these should be clearly stated.

Use of scripts, explained later in this chapter, helps by formalizing the task for the observers. A recommended procedure is to present a set of written task instructions to the observer to read. The study moderator then asks if the observer understands the instructions. The scaling administrator needs to be alert at this point, because over-helpful observers can use this opportunity to obtain some clues about what answers you want from them. Good practice would have the scaling administrator provide concise answers, without elaboration. This is like walking a tightrope–you want to make sure the observer understands, and yet you do not want to provide background material or explanations that may bias the observer's judgments.

3.5.2 What is the Context?

Observer instructions and scripts frequently set the context of the judgment in a scaling task. It comes about when the scaling is set in the background of an application for the image. For example, the context of the judgment can be set by suggesting that image quality is, "The quality of images you would give to friends and family." We now perform an experiment where the observers judge image quality using paired comparisons. In a paired comparison judgment, observers then may be asked, "Select the sample that has the highest image quality." The resulting image quality scale would have a context of "images that would be given to friends and family." To say that this scale is applicable to the quality of office documents is to seriously mislabel the resultant scale.

Integrative attributes such as image quality are much more context- or application-dependent than "nesses" such as image sharpness and graininess. Image quality, within the framework of the Image Quality Circle, is an abstract or absolute concept, and is not tied to an application.

Even when the question and context are carefully described to the observer, there is no guarantee that the desired results will be achieved. For example, suppose the observer follows instructions and scales a set of samples according to image quality. Yet if the sample set varies only in the "ness" dimension of, say, "textureness," the resulting scale has to be called an image quality scale; image quality is in fact the question posed to the observer. However, the scale is really a scale of "textureness" by virtue of texture being the only "ness" dimension that varies in the sample set! This is, sadly, an all too common problem.

In some scaling paradigms, such as the graphical rating scale, the orientation or context of the scale is not obvious and has to be explicitly stated. Is it a "goodness" scale where the attribute increases in "goodness" from left to right? An example of a "goodness" scale might be a sharpness scale, since an increase in this attribute is generally considered "good." Going from left to right on the ruler, as the sharpness increases, the "goodness" increases in the same direction. A "badness" scale is related to a "ness" such as graininess that is "bad" or unwanted. The scale increases in "badness" left to right.

Although grasping the notion of goodness and badness scales is easy, there are some attributes that may switch depending on the amount. Too much of a good thing, such as colorfulness in images, becomes a bad thing (de Ridder, 1996). Scaling study planners should be alert to such possibilities when selecting anchors or references, because the scale may extend substantially beyond the high or low references.

The context of the scaling experiment can also be established by an introductory script that describes the purpose of the scaling. If establishing a context for the judgment is important, then explaining to the observer the purpose for the scaling may be useful. There are mixed views about this. I am from the minimalist school that believes in giving the observer only the minimum of information that is needed to do the task. Extra information may distract the observer from the task at hand. In addition, a long verbal explanation may allow the observer to pick up extra clues in order to be helpful. Finally, an excessive question and answer session consumes precious time for the observer and the administrator. Let the observer spend time giving you answers, not vice versa.

3.5.3 Criteria and Definitions

Depending on the scaling objective, the "ness" may or may not be explicitly defined. There are several ways to define a "ness":

- One can use words and define the "ness" in observer instructions.
- One can use visual references, which are often used as anchors.
- One can let the "ness" be defined by the observer using some internal criteria.

When an observer uses his or her own internal definition, it is of no use unless the observer somehow conveys its meaning to the study administrator.

If an explicit "ness" definition is used, it should be unambiguous and easily accessible to the observers during the scaling study. A card with the written definition can provide a handy reference. Visual references are often used as anchors in graphical rating scale experiments, but they can be used with most any other scaling method. These references are often employed where a word description would be difficult, or where they supplement a written definition.

Instructing the observers to be either highly critical or tolerant in their scaling judgments can result in significantly different scale values for a set of samples. For example, instructing observers to be "critical" in their judgment of the image quality of projected photographic transparencies produced the lowest quality scale values when compared with instructions of "liberal," "objective," or "tolerant" (Bartleson and Woodbury, 1965). There seem to be few practical situations where instructing the observer how to apply personal judgment criteria is appropriate, so it is best to avoid doing so.

3.5.4 Looking Through the Haze–Imperfect Samples

Few samples used in real-world scaling studies are perfect or defect-free, particularly in the early stages of product development. To compensate, we can ask observers to ignore scratches or dirt, or not consider image composition in their judgments. Although instructing observers to ignore certain aspects or defects of the samples is not uncommon, there is no guarantee the observers will do so.

If the attribute of interest does not interfere with, or is different from, the sample defects, then expecting that observers will respond to the "ness" of interest is reasonable. However, if the sample set has streaks and you are asking the observers to judge "bandingness," it is doubtful that, without training, observers can reliably ignore the streaks and judge only "bandingness."

Clearly the best strategy is to use samples that do not exhibit any unwanted "ness," but this is not wholly realistic. With imperfect samples, asking the observer to ignore such unwanted "nesses" via the instructions would be prudent.

3.5.5 Prototype Instructions

Observer instructions are so important to a scaling study's success that prototype instructions appear with each scaling method. These examples are provided with some reluctance, since no observer instruction set is ever perfect. Less experienced scaling enthusiasts are advised to use the instructions as they are. Attempts at word-smithing these prototypes may make the instructions more cumbersome and confusing. After gaining experience with scaling, the instructions can be refined for particular scaling needs.

3.6 Presenting and Viewing Samples

Viewing conditions and the mode of sample presentation are key factors in scale accuracy, precision, and scaling study efficiency.

3.6.1 Presentation Mode

The presentation of sample stimuli to observers occurs in two basic ways–all at once or one at a time. Obviously some scaling methods and situations require one or the other. For example, the paired comparison method requires that the samples be presented in pairs, while judging images displayed in electronic form may require that a single sample be presented at a time. There are various views regarding each presentation method, so judgment on the part of the scaling planner is required.

If there are no visible references or anchors, then single-stimuli presentation is prone to a host of influences, including observer criterion drift. In addition, study planners must account for sequential effects.

Two methods are available for reducing observer criterion drift. The first is to have the observer do a prescaling on a subset of sample stimuli covering the full "ness" range of the main sample set. This familiarizes the observer with the range of "ness" within the set.

A second technique, which aims to achieve the same result with less effort, is to present samples to the observer that represent the maximum and minimum of the "ness" to be scaled. Stabilizing and "calibrating" the observer's criterion is the primary goal of prescaling. Since the observers' responses are not yet stabilized, this "training data" is usually discarded when computing the final scale values.

The sequence of sample presentation can often affect observers' judgments. The simplest solution is to randomize the sequence using a computer's random number generator, or a table of random numbers. This option may not be available for all scaling methods.

Multiple-stimuli presentation, giving observers the complete set of samples at once, offers a simple and efficient way to stabilize observer criteria. Observers can get calibrated by viewing the complete sample set. No prescaling is needed, which saves time and can reduce the number of samples required.

A strong motivation for using multiple-stimuli presentation is that it simulates the typical observing condition. In a retail sales situation, the customer may view several print samples before choosing a computer printer. For sample sets greater than about twenty, the all-at-once presentation mode can become unwieldy, but it depends on the particular details of the scaling method. In order to assure effectiveness of using the all-at-once presentation method, part of the observers' instructions should explicitly request the observer to review the sample set before commencing the scaling.

3.6.2 Viewing Distance

Generally speaking, "nesses" associated with spatial image structure such as sharpness, graininess and raggedness will have scale values that vary with the distance over which the observer views the samples. Changing the viewing distance alters the perceptibility, detectability, or characteristic, and so the scale value of a spatial "ness." Raggedness and graininess are more visible when the viewing distance is small. Sharpness values, on the other hand, decrease as the sample distance decreases. This result suggests that the viewing distance may need to be controlled during the observers' judgments, but it depends on the scaling objectives and the level of scale precision required.

Letting the viewing distance "float" will tend to increase the spread of the judged scale values over a group of observers. Some experimenters fix the distance with a mechanical restraint such as a chin rest, bite bar, or physical barrier.

3.6.3 Sample Illumination

Light incident on a surface and spectral "quality" are the two principal illumination variables to control. The absolute light level incident on the samples, the illuminance, is measured in lumens/m^2 or lux. For emissive displays, such as CRTs and LCDs, the appropriate term for the amount of light coming from the object or surface is the luminance, in candelas/m^2. The absolute light level on the sample, illuminance (or luminance in the case of CRTs and LCDs), affects the perception of colorfulness, "tone reproductionness," graininess and other "nesses." Increasing the illuminance on a sample increases the colorfulness (the Hunt effect), makes graininess more visible, particularly in the dark areas of the image, and generally increases the sensitivity of the human visual system to spatial details. These effects are substantial when one shifts from indoor to outdoor illumination, but they do not vary much under typical indoor lighting. If the image application will be outdoors in noonday sun, a billboard for example, then performing the scaling under the same condition would be appropriate.

The second consideration is the source spectral power distribution, often stated as the Correlated Color Temperature (CCT), although these two terms are not exact equivalents. All color-related "nesses" are affected by the spectral power distribution of the illuminating source simply because the color appearance changes according to the spectral quality of the source. (See Fairchild, 1997, for a complete discussion of color appearance issues.) Scaling a set of color samples under a light source that is different from the application's expected light source will not provide a good prediction of the scale values under the actual viewing source.

Many common light sources have been standardized by the CIE, an international standards body for light, illumination and color. There is a series of CIE Daylight sources–the D Series–that represent various phases of practical daylight. These sources have nomenclature such as D5000 (D50 for short) or D6500. The D stands for daylight, and the four-digit number represents the CCT in Kelvins. Eleven common flourescent sources have also been standardized as the CIE

F Series. F2 is the designation for the popular cool white lamp that has a CCT of approximately 4200K.

The lamp's spectral power distribution can also have a substantial effect on the fluorescence of some sample substrates. Many paper makers incorporate "brighteners" or fluorescent dyes into their papers to improve the paper's "brightness." These dyes are stimulated by short wavelength ultraviolet radiation, UV, that converts the mostly invisible UV to visible blue light. This increased blue light compensates for the yellowish hue of the paper and makes it appear whiter and brighter. When viewing brightened paper samples under light sources deficient in UV, the paper and any colorant on the paper will be quite different in appearance. Sometimes colorants have fluorescent properties, and the color appearance is dependent on sources' UV content. Tungsten lamps generally have low UV output, while fluorescent lamps, popular in offices, offer far more output in the short wavelengths.

The key thing to remember is that, since color appearance varies depending on light source and absolute light level, the scale values also vary. The relevant standard for viewing prints, transparencies and substrates for graphic technology and photography is ISO-3664, *Viewing conditions–Prints, transparencies, and substrates for graphic technology and photography*. This standard specifies a D50 source and two levels of illumination for viewing prints: 2000 lux and 500 lux.

Another factor that is often ignored is the geometry of the sample illumination. For samples with intermediate levels of gloss, illumination geometry is critical in controlling the surface appearance. The recommended viewing practice is to illuminate the sample at 45 degrees from the normal to the surface, and view the sample normal to the surface. This geometry is easily accomplished using a viewing booth, which is therefore recommended for scaling studies. When the illumination geometry cannot be controlled, the configuration and size of the illuminating light source should be reported.

3.6.4 Environmental Factors

The scaling study environment, if not carefully examined or controlled, can have adverse effects on the scale values. The most significant factors to consider in planning the scaling environment are psychological and physical comfort, noise, and surround.

Ensuring the physical comfort of an observer may seem obvious, but it is easily overlooked. Such simple things as providing a comfortable chair and having sufficient space to spread samples out while doing the scaling task can become major problems if not attended to.

Check to see if the support items such as image references, mouse buttons or other signaling or data-recording devices are conveniently positioned. Control other obvious items such as room temperature and humidity.

Psychological comfort of the observer is also important. Instructions or scripts can establish a mindset within the observer. For example, observers should not be made to feel that someone is watching, or that they are taking a test. Words in the instructions addressing these concerns can increase the psychological comfort level. Explicitly informing the observers that they are not taking a test and that you want their opinions, is often helpful. Clearly, scaling is a task that can be a challenge, and may generate some psychological stress. The study planner and administrator should be conscious of environmental issues in order to reduce the influence of stress on the scale values.

Noise can affect our ability to perform tasks. Scaling usually occurs in rooms that are nominally quiet, but may have noises that could distract some observers. Two ubiquitous noise sources are the 60-Hz hum of fluorescent light fixtures, and the periodic noise of HVAC systems. In selecting an area for scaling, a review of these and other noise sources is in order.

A factor that can affect color appearance is the color of the scaling study room. If a viewing booth is not used, the color of the walls will combine with the illuminating light source to give an unknown and arbitrary illumination on the samples. In addition, highly colored walls can alter the observer's state of adaptation, possibly changing the color appearance of the samples. Highly colored surfaces such as tables, desks and walls are to be avoided in favor of gray or pastel colors. For critical scaling applications, ASTM E 1808, *Standard Guide for Designing and Conducting Visual Experiments* (1996) recommends that the area immediately surrounding the samples should have a color similar to the samples. The remaining area, the ambient field, should be neutral with a Munsell Chroma less than 0.2, pastel, and a Munsell Value between N6 and N7, corresponding to a visual reflectance of between 0.29 and 0.49. For viewing and scaling images, the standard practice (ISO 3664, ANSI/NAPM/PH2.30) is a neutral gray background having a reflectance factor of less than 0.20. Note that the ISO and ASTM are not entirely consistent in their recommendations.

3.6.5 Observer Motivation

A factor that is sometimes overlooked is observer motivation. Scaling studies conducted in concert with market research studies commonly offer observers a small amount of money, about $50. Offering rewards has not been a common practice when observers are drawn from within an organization, but it is on the increase. These "internal" observers are usually given a tangible premium to compensate them for their voluntary efforts. Sometimes a larger reward, such as tickets to a concert or sporting event, or a dinner, is given for continued scaling service. There is no fixed rule, particularly within organizations. In most organizations, observers will volunteer without any expectation of a reward if they feel that they are contributing to the organization's success in some way.

3.7 Conducting the Scaling Study

A large number of possible methods for conducting the scaling study are available. There is no universal agreement on a standard method. Scripts and pilot studies are two recomended tools that can help eliminate costly errors and improve scaling studies over the long run.

3.7.1 Scripts

Scripts are the written sequence of procedures, questions, or instructions to be followed by the scaling administrator. The foremost purpose of the script is to present a consistent narrative to all the observers. Most observers look, ask, and listen for cues about what the scaling administrator really wants. They search for cues because they are usually interested in the scaling process, and they want to be helpful and do a good job. Scripts are usually read aloud by the scaling administrator, word for word, as a means of enforcing the consistency of presentation. Using a consistent procedure (the script) also reduces the effects of unintended moderator bias as a factor in observer judgment.

Included in scripts are instructions to observers on how to perform the task, what criteria to use in the judgment, and pointers to external and internal references (anchors) that need to be considered. It is essential that the script should not imply or refer to criteria, definitions, or other items that can affect observer judgments.

There are several significant benefits to using a script. First is the ability to test and modify it in order to fine-tune the experimental procedure. The script should be considered a variable during study design, and a given during the study itself. Secondly, the well-tested script can be used multiple times, and simultaneously in multiple locations, and thus ensure that later scalings will be conducted in the same manner as earlier ones. Finally, it formally documents the complete methodology of the scaling study. Using a script is no guarantee that results will be identical, since the observers will no doubt be different, and other factors may change over time. Nevertheless, using a script will reduce the influence of factors that can affect scale consistency.

Commonly included as part of the script for the scaling administrator is a list of the environment requirements, such as a specification of the lighting, a list of equipment, any associated software, and calibration methods. All of these factors can affect the perception and judgment of "nesses" or image quality. The rigorous specification of these environmental requirements will assure identical conditions for any subsequent scalings.

All of this may seem like a lot of effort just to generate a "ness" scale. However, anyone experienced in doing physical measurements usually has a measurement procedure. In this respect, scaling or the measurement of human response is no different.

3.7.2 Pilot Studies

Pilot studies are small-size trials to test and debug the scaling study script and response-collection process. One should not expect a script to be correct without a trial. Pilot studies offer the opportunity to fine-tune the script and ultimately to save substantial effort. They are essential in my view.

It is sometimes argued that pilot studies are not needed for the "casual" study. I wonder what a "casual" scaling study is. In almost all cases, the motivation for the scaling is to answer some product-related question. The answer usually has a non-trivial economic impact, so the "casual" scaling study is an example of false economy.

Pilot studies are designed to give study planners quick feedback regarding the script. A pilot study is conducted using a small number of samples and observers, along with the draft script. The objective at this point is to test and debug the script, not collect precise data.

Script testing and debugging require feedback from the observers at the completion of the scaling. This is the time to ask observers questions about the scaling task they just performed. Some of the relevant questions are:

- "Are the instructions clear on what to judge?" A lot of questions on the part of the observer prior to and during the scaling give clues about areas of the script that need improvement.
- "Is the visual judgment task easy or difficult? What parts?" These are critical questions, because you may unknowingly be asking observers to do an impossible task. Most observers will do *something*, even if the task is difficult or impossible.
- "Is the data recording method intrusive?" A popular method today is for the experimenter to enter the observer's response data directly into a spread sheet. This, or any other data recording method, should be transparent to the observer and not interrupt the flow of the study.
- "Were samples presented in a way that was easy to work with?"
- "Were you physically comfortable during the experiment?"
- "What suggestions do you have that might improve the scaling task?" This is probably the most important question that can be asked of the observer. Encourage the observer to give feedback on any and all topics, but be aware that the observer will likely have a number of questions about the scaling process, the samples, and the imaging technologies involved.

Observer responses to these questions should be used to amend the script, particularly the observers' instructions. At this point the scaling study plan is in good shape, and there can be high confidence for success.

3.8. Analyzing Observer Response Data

The computed "ness" or image quality scale values are a combination of two scaling study parts–the sample presentation/data collection method, and the data analysis method. Both together define the scale properties to be discussed in the next chapter. Referring to "the scaling method" as if it is a data collection method, without reference to the data analysis, is quite common. This is at best confusing, and often misleading, simply because it is incomplete. I encourage the readers of this book to describe both parts; for example, a paired comparison data collection method combined with Thurstone's Law of Comparative Judgment. These *two pieces* in combination define the generation of scale values.

The next chapters in this book define what is meant by scale types, and the mathematical properties they convey. After this groundwork, the remaining chapters discuss all the data analysis options for scale generation.

Chapter 4

Measurement Scales

Measurement of human response is not a new field. The well-established fields of psychometrics, psychophysics, and sensory evaluation are rich resources of measurement methods and data analysis.

The words psychometrics, psychophysics, and scaling are often used interchangeably, which leads to confusion. Additionally, appreciation of basic scale types is not very common in the physical sciences, and it is a source of much bewilderment and, quite literally, miscalculation. To clarify these topics, the following sections provide definitions, scale type descriptions, and a set of important cautions about possible misunderstandings when generating scales and analyzing results.

4.1 Vocabulary of Scaling

Psychometrics (mind measuring) encompasses measuring human response to the "nesses" or image quality. The field of *psychophysics* covers the human response to a stimulus specified by physical parameters (Physical Image Parameters). The shorthand term *scaling*, as used in the imaging field, means the generation of a scale or ruler of the observer's response to a "ness " under study. The output or result of a scaling study is a scale of, say, sharpness, or image quality. In particular, *psychometric scaling* is the generation of rulers, or scales, of the "nesses" and image quality by human measurement.

Different disciplines have different words for the same ideas. Underlying a scale is a continuum, often called the *psychological continuum*, or sometimes a *psychological dimension*. When this continuum can be directly related to some sensory organ or system, e.g., touch, it is called the *sensory continuum*. Sometimes a "ness" cannot be related to a sense organ, *per se*. Image quality is one such example. Another example can be found in the food technology realm, where the term *hedonic* scale or continuum is used when describing the continuum of likes and dislikes of food products. In this text, we use psychological dimension or psychological continuum, since our subject matter–image quality–does not relate directly to a sense organ, and as a result has no underlying sensory continuum.

The term *observer* in this text is used to describe the humans that view, touch, or feel images. They are variously called subjects, respondents, judges, or, customers, but in this text these terms are all equivalent.

The images or *samples* we ask the observers to respond to are, strictly speaking, called *stimuli*, simply because they stimulate human sensory systems. In scaling images, the sensory system of interest is the human visual system, but sometimes the tactile sensory system is also involved. Samples and stimuli will be used more or less interchangeably unless distinguishing between them is appropriate. Stimuli are also called stimulus objects, psychological objects, or just objects (Bock and Jones, 1968).

Strictly speaking, when we ask the observers to respond to image stimuli we are asking for a *judgment,* which is distinguished from a *choice* (Bock and Jones, 1968). The judgment implies that the observer is acting "objectively," whereas the choice implies some form of personal preference in the response. We mostly speak of an observer making a judgement, as opposed to a choice, but on occasion observer choices are requested.

The term *scale value* is used consistently throughout this book as the numerical value obtained from a scaling study. Usage of the term "scale value" is associated mostly with imaging. L. L. Thurstone, after starting his career as an engineer and later becoming a great psychometrician of the twentieth century, used the term *affective value*. This term is commonly used in the food technology field (Bock and Jones, 1968; Meilgaard, *et. al.*, 1991).

A *scaling study*, sometimes called a *scaling experiment*, is a term used here to mean the activities or processes that comprise all the elements needed to generate a scale. Chapter 3 describes a scaling study in detail. Preference is given to the term "scaling study" because it is in line with other forms of studies; e.g., market research studies. The word *experiment* in the term *scaling experiment* carries the unfortunate connotation of being a risky venture that may not provide useful results.

4.2 Stevens' Scale Classifications

All scales are not equal, either in their classification or the mathematical operations that can be performed on them. In 1946, Stanley Smith Stevens, a world-renowned psychophysicist and later the director of the Psychophysics Laboratory at Harvard University, put forth a scale definition and classification system that has provided the reference ever since (Stevens, S. S., 1946).

So far, the term *measurement* has been used rather loosely. To shore up the idea operationally, we use Stevens' definition (Stevens, S. S., 1946):

"Measurement is the process of assigning numbers to objects or events by rules."

The key words in Stevens' definition are process and rules. Both define the scale properties.

Table 4.1 Stevens' Classification of Scale Types

Scale Type	Operations	Permissible Transformations
Nominal	determination of equality	y = f(x), any one-to-one transformation
Ordinal	determination of greater or less than	y = g(x), any monotonic transformation
Interval	determination of equality of intervals or differences (distance)	y = ax+b, any linear transformation
Ratio	determination of the equality of ratios	y = ax, any constant scale factor

Stevens described four scale types: nominal, ordinal, interval, and ratio, as shown in Table 4.1. He ascribed the scale types with "basic empirical operations," "mathematical group structure," and "permissible statistics."

Recently, Velleman and Wilkinson (1993) have challenged Stevens' classification of "permissible statistics" concerning the scale types as too restrictive. Since this book does not contain a rigorous analysis of scale statistics, we do not need to involve the reader in the debate, and have included only "permissible transformations" in Table 4.1. As published by Stevens, Table 4.1 had a fourth column, called "permissible statistics" which is not included here.

The mathematical "power" of the scale types in Table 4.1 increases as one moves through the scale types from the nominal scale to the ratio scale. Every scale type below a particular type has the properties of that scale type plus all the types above. For example, an interval scale has the property of an ordinal scale and a nominal scale. In practice, this means that we can "demote" a scale to one of lesser power, by using a different data reduction or data analysis method. From the point of view of scale generation, demotion is not very common, but there are some situations where it is convenient for performing statistical tests.

4.2.1 Nominal

A *nominal scale* has names or labels assigned to objects or events. An easy way to remember is that "nominal equals names." The numbers on the jerseys of football players constitute a nominal scale of football players of the X team. The names of colors–red, green, and so forth also form a nominal scale. The scale of football players uses numbers as labels, while the color hue scale uses names.

Using numbers for a nominal scale does not mean that the numbers themselves possess any mathematical or arithmetic properties. The lack of the addition property is illustrated with telephone numbers. "If you added 1-800-255-5188 (1-800-CALL-ATT) to 1-800-265-5328 (1-800-COLLECT, from MCI) would you expect to get Candice Bergen (Sprint spokesperson) to answer?" (Person, 1998). Using phone numbers, football players' jersey numbers and social security numbers helps us with identification, but, used in nominal scales, the numbers are just labels and do not possess any numerical properties.

With nominal scales we can arbitrarily relabel, or transform, objects or events providing we use a one-to-one mapping, or relationship, of the labels. A one-to-many or a many-to-one is not permissible; we would generate or lose some elements that constitute the original scale. For example, we can renumber all the football team's jerseys, but we do not give the same number to more than one player. This preserves the one-to-one relationship.

The equality of the scale objects, or events, occurs when the names, numbers or labels are identical. They are not equal in the usual mathematical sense. They are equivalent, one to another.

Nominal scales may not appear to be highly useful. However, they can form the basis of scales of higher types. For example, the standard of colorimetry, the 1931 CIE Two Degree Standard Observer, is based upon the matching of color in the spectrum to a combination of three colored lights: red, green and blue. From these nominal scales, known as the CIE XYZ, tristimulus values, we have boot-strapped the tristimulus values to an interval scale. The most widely used colorimetric interval scale is the CIE L*a*b* system.

4.2.2 Ordinal

An *ordinal scale* uses labels (usually adjectives) or numbers to represent the order of the objects or events. (Remember that "ordinal equals order.") An ordinal scale has a greater than (>), or less than (<), property. As an illustration, consider a size scale of spherical objects that range from marbles, golf balls, tennis balls, and soccer balls, up to and including basketball sizes. On this scale, characteristics such as the volumes or diameters of the spherical objects, possess the property of "greater than" or "less than" depending on the direction one is going with respect to the scale. Notice that the diameters of the objects do not necessarily increase uniformly. The change or difference between the diameter of a marble and a golf ball is smaller than the diameter change from a tennis ball to a soccer ball. From an ordinal scale, all we can state about the diameters of the spheres is that they are greater than the sphere preceding it on the scale.

One could use an ordinal scale in imaging to rank, for instance, samples according to some property, say image quality. All we know about the image quality ranks are that some samples have greater image quality than other samples. Although this knowledge of the sample order in terms of image quality can be very valuable, it does have limitations. The main limitation of an ordinal scale is that we do not know how "close" each sample is to the adjacent samples. An all-too-common practice is to assign numbers to the ranks and average the ranks over the observers and then invoke the properties of numbers to deduce the distance between samples. This is incorrect because the numbers assigned to the ranks have only a "greater-than" property. The distance between samples ranked with a one (first) and two (second) may not be the same as the distance between samples ranked with a nine and a ten. For determining the distance between samples, we need to have at least an interval scale, the next scale type.

4.2.3 Interval

An *interval scale* adds the property of distance to the ordinal scale. Physical scientists and engineers normally think of interval scales when they use numbers for measurements. The Fahrenheit and Celsius temperature scales are interval scales.

Generally, the origin and the multiplier of the interval scale are unknown and arbitrary. In this sense interval scales are on "rubber bands" that linearly stretch and move. They "float." The key property of the interval scale, as far as the Image Quality Circle and psychometric scaling are concerned, is that equal differences in scale values represent equal differences in a "ness" or image quality. This is an extremely valuable property.

A persistent product development question is, "How close?" How close do our images have to be to the specification or to a customer requirement? Knowing the distances between images on some "ness" or image quality scale helps product managers and product development teams set and achieve objectives. An interval scale has the required property to answer the "how close" question, so it is the minimum scale type for Image Quality Circle applications. Interval scales are the essential scale type for generating scales of image quality and customer attributes or "nesses." For this central reason, a substantial amount of this book is devoted to methods for generating interval scales.

Not all "ness" scales are interval scales, since some have a known, fixed zero point. The CIE Lightness scale is one such example. Scales that have a zero point, and are at least interval in nature, are of a higher type called the ratio scale.

4.2.4 Ratio

The *ratio scale* adds an origin to the distance property of the interval scale. Equivalently, a ratio scale is an interval scale with the additive constant, or origin, equal to zero. This origin may or may not be experimentally measurable. Unlike the interval scale, the ratio scale does not "float" with respect to a scale origin. Ratio scales generally differ by a multiplying factor, but the multiplying factor can be quite different for each ratio scale. For example, one unit on a ratio scale of *lightness* is not necessarily equal to one unit on a ratio *colorfulness* scale.

A ratio scale is assumed to have a zero point, which may cause both conceptual and experimental difficulties. For some "nesses" a zero value is easy to conceptualize, but for others it is not so clear. For example, the concept of zero colorfulness, a gray, is intuitively straightforward. What about a "hueness" scale with a hue having a value of zero? How does one go about defining the concept of zero image quality? This difficulty suggests that all "nesses" are not equal when defining them on ratio scales.

Stevens, who was the major figure in developing ratio scaling methodology from about 1938 to his death in 1975, defined two different psychological continua: prothetic and metathetic. *Prothetic continua* are associated with an attribute or "ness" that has *quantity*. Examples of prothetic continua in the imaging field are lightness, brightness, and colorfulness; they possess the idea of "quantity" or "how much." *Metathetic continua* have a qualitative, or *where*, aspect. Stevens' metathetic example was sound pitch (Stevens, 1975). The complete set of colored hues forms a metathetic continuum, although mixtures of two specific hues can be prothetic (Indow and Stevens, 1966).

In practical scaling situations, the distinctions between these two continua are not of major importance. The differences only come to the fore when comparing ratio scales with scales generated by interval scaling techniques. Metathetic continua often show a linear relationship between interval and ratio scales, for the same set of samples, while prothetic continua do not.

There are still unresolved theoretical issues about the role of prothetic and metathetic continua in scaling. For detailed discussions on this topic the interested reader is referred to Stevens (1975), Gescheider (1997), Baird and Noma (1978), and Torgerson (1958).

4.3 Numbers, Numbers

The use of numbers for measurement in physical sciences is almost exclusively associated with either ratio or interval scales: e.g., mass, length, time, and temperature on the Celsius scale. Since most scientists and engineers are familiar with numbers in the context of ratio and interval scales, they are not accustomed to examining the numbers associated with a measurement scale. As mentioned above, when numbers are used as labels in a nominal scale and for position in an ordinal scale, the numbers do not possess the properties we usually associate with numbers.

There are a few examples of numerically based scales that are nominal or ordinal. One of these scales is the CIE tristimulus values, X, Y, and Z, which are nominal scales. This nominal property comes about because the numbers were derived from color matching experiments–experiments to establish the "equality" of colors. In this experiment there was no concept of one color being "greater than" another color. Neither was the concept of the distance between colors part of the original experiments that established the CIE colorimetric system.

Scales derived from CIE XYZ, such as CIE L*a*b*, are widely believed to have at least interval properties. To make the transformation from a nominal scale to an interval scale required another set of psychometric data that had known experimental conditions and an interval scale property. Albert Munsell, an art teacher at the Massachusetts School of Art, developed the *Munsell Book Of Color*, which consisted of color patches arranged in a three-dimensional cylindrical coordinate system (Munsell, 1902). He used interval scaling techniques to determine the distances between the color patches in lightness (called *value* in his system), hue, and chroma. In the early 1940s the color patches contained in the *Munsell Book of Color* were measured using the CIE XYZ system (Newhall, Nickerson and Judd, 1943). From these physical measurements approximate empirical transformations from the CIE XYZ values to Munsell "nesses" of hue, value and chroma were developed. This has further evolved, based on suggestions by Adams (1942) into the now-standardized 1976 CIE L*a*b* color space.

Using models of human judgment to convert from a nominal scale type to a scale type with more mathematical power is common, and forms a basis for data analysis methods described in the chapters that follow.

4.4 Same Data, Different Scales

As a rule, the greater the power of the scale, the greater are the demands placed on the observers who are required to give a response or make judgments. Generating a nominal scale by naming items, or generating an ordinal scale by sorting samples into a "greater than" sequence, are both easy tasks for observers. A ratio scale demands more from observers since they are required to respond with a number for the ratio of the attributes. In concept this is simple, but it is often difficult for observers without some training (Lodge, 1981). Chapter 11 explores study design considerations for ratio scales in more detail.

When communicating results to others, the practitioner is urged to make clear distinctions between the data collection method, the analysis method, and the resulting scale type. Occasionally, the data collection and analysis methods can be mixed and matched so that different scale types result from the same data. For example, different analysis methods can generate either ordinal scales or interval scales. Data collected in category scaling, for instance, can generate an ordinal scale, or with auxiliary models, the same data can be used to generate an interval scale. Given this potential source of confusion, one must be clear and emphatic about data collection method, analysis method, and scale type.

Scales generated using the methods described in succeeding chapters can be used as response variables in a wide array of statistical decision-making procedures to answer specific product development questions. Although the statistical properties of scale values are important in practical applications, covering all statistical analysis methods would take us too far afield, into territory that is heavily trodden. Therefore, in this book, the presentation of statistical tests of scale values will be limited to those that either test underlying models or may not be readily available in introductory statistical texts.

4.5 Multidimensional Scaling

The basic idea of *multidimensional scaling*, or MDS, is to create a multidimensional spatial picture or a map of observer judgments in a psychological space. See Kruskal and Wish (1976) for a very readable introduction to MDS. A recent detailed text on MDS is by Borg and Groenen (1997).

Many computer programs are available to "map" human responses into as many dimensions as the program operator desires. Basically they arrange the points to minimize some distance criterion between the data and the computed spatial representation. MDS has been quite successfully applied to many areas of the social sciences, and remains one of the most widely used scaling tools.

Multidimensional scaling is a very powerful scaling technique, but it is not magic. The major disadvantage of MDS, regarding practical applications, is that it does not direct one to an understanding of either the number of spatial dimensions or the psychological meaning of the picture or map axes. Identification of these dimensions needs an experienced psychometric practitioner.

In spite of its power and popularity, we see no need to cover MDS in this book. Several reasons support this decision. First, it is fraught with uncertainties. There are no agreed-upon methods–standards if you will–by which to compute the spatial configuration from the scaling data. Each commercially available MDS package uses different algorithms and will give slightly different results for the same data set. Additionally, compared with unidimensional scales, there is a paucity of inferential statistical methods by which to test the spatial configuration to determine if it is "correct." Further, there is a lackluster track record of using MDS to discover meaningful attributes in images. Careful examination of the sample set will reveal, more often than not, what "nesses" exist in the images. Finally, the analysis technique almost requires a book of its own for it to be practically useful.

The complete picture of MDS is not at all negative, however. MDS can be a very powerful tool in image quality research. In fact there are many areas where MDS should be applied, particularly in helping to identify the components or "nesses" that result from image processing and compression algorithms. However, examination of the image quality produced by image processing and compression algorithms is more research-oriented compared with the practical product-development focus of this book.

The remaining chapters of this text describe the practical application of scaling techniques useful for the study, analysis and design of imaging systems. Emphasis is placed on methods of generating unidimensional interval scales where the attribute or "ness" lies along one psychological continuum or dimension.

Chapter 5

Thresholds and Just-Noticeable Differences

Two questions that are often important in product development: "What is the value of the 'ness' that is just visible, or just detectable by an observer?" and "What is the minimum value of the 'ness' that is just seen as different from a reference or standard?" The first question asks about the *absolute threshold*, and the second question asks about the difference threshold or *just-noticeable difference (JND).*

Both are equally important, but the emphasis depends somewhat on the level of imaging technology development. The threshold dictates how low a "ness" has to be "pushed" so it is not detectable by observers, and therefore contributes to an image quality judgment. The just-noticeable difference tells how much the "ness" must change so that some fraction of the customers or users actually sees a difference in the "ness."

"Ness" scale values most often possess only interval properties, having an arbitrary constant and multiplier. Manipulating the scale values by adjusting the arbitrary constants does not increase or decrease the underlying psychological precision, nor does it change a psychological zero point. Knowledge of both the absolute threshold and the just-noticeable differences over the full "ness" scale would also be of great practical value in establishing the numerical range of "ness" scale values. For example, the threshold of a "ness" can be set as the zero value of the scale, and the scale increment set equal to the just-noticeable difference at some convenient scale value. Thresholds and JNDs are also valuable in identifying the component "nesses" in an image quality judgment. Any "ness" that is below the absolute threshold cannot be seen and is irrelevant. The number of JNDs describing a "ness" in a sample set is a measure of the range of the "ness" discussed in Chapter 3.

Assigning scale values in terms of absolute thresholds and JNDs is not a fundamental scaling requirement, but it can help in communicating the significance of scale values to scale users. A "ness" scale arranged so a zero value is the threshold and a JND the unit increment, is more interpretable than a scale with an arbitrary origin and multiplier. This property is a nicety, and it is almost never the motivation to pursue such absolute and JND studies.

This chapter describes the basic methods used to find both the absolute threshold and the just-noticeable difference.

5.1 Thresholds, Just-Noticeable Differences and the Image Quality Circle

There are two ways to look at thresholds. First, classical psychophysics views thresholds as the amount of a physical stimulus needed for detection or to evoke a just-noticeable difference. In the classical view, thresholds are expressed as a physical specification of the stimulus, which we would call a Physical Image Parameter in the realm of the Image Quality Circle. The second view is our view. In the Image Quality Circle the threshold or the just-noticeable differences are expressed in terms of the "ness," the Customer Perceptions. This perspective is not unique to the Image Quality Circle. See Baird (1997) for a detailed discussion of just-noticable-differences of "nesses."

This view is a departure from classical psychophysics, but it has the advantage that there are no requirements for a single physical specification (Physical Image Parameter) of the stimulus. Without the requirement to tie into or link to Physical Image Parameters, one can determine thresholds or just-noticeable differences for "nesses" such as graininess (Engeldrum and McNeill, 1985; Dooley and Shaw, 1979) or printed line darkness (Dvorak and Hamerly, 1983), that are combinations of Physical Image Parameters. Taking this view does not preclude applying classical psychophysics. In fact, both can live in harmony within the Image Quality Circle context. One acknowledged disadvantage is that some independent means of measuring the "ness" scale value must be available. In the Image Quality Circle context, this approach requires a sufficiently accurate Visual Algorithm for computing the "ness" from the Physical Image Parameter(s). (See Chapter 2).

5.2 Basic Concepts

The discriminal dispersion or probability density function (discussed in Chapter 8) is the principle behind the concept of just-noticeable differences and thresholds. The observer is asked to respond "yes" or "no" to a "Do you see it?" question or "Is *A* different from *B*?" question. Responses are accumulated over a number of observers. For many reasons, the observers' responses vary even when the stimulus is held constant. This variation is described by a probability distribution, like the discriminal dispersion of Thurstone (1927). The estimation of the probability distribution is the objective of the experimental just-noticeable difference or threshold procedure. Once the empirical probability distribution (cumulative histogram) is established, a psychometric model is fit to the data and some useful parameters are deduced. Details of model fitting and parameter determinations are the topics of this chapter.

Over the last century, three basic methods have evolved to determine absolute thresholds and just-noticeable differences. The three methods are the method of limits, the method of adjustment, and the method of constant stimuli (Baird and Noma, 1978; Gescheider, 1985). They vary in their method of stimulus presentation and, to some extent, data analysis. Both the method of limits and the method of adjustment have been widely used to find the thresholds of light, sound, and other "simple" attributes where the stimulus can be easily controlled. Threshold and just-noticeable difference determination of more complex "nesses," the types common in the field of imaging, are more easily obtained using the method of constant stimuli and its variants.

In the sections that follow, the basic threshold and just-noticeable difference methods are described. Emphasis is on the method of constant stimuli because of its easy application to most types of imaging systems.

5.3 The Psychometric Curve and its Parameters

One might think that the visual threshold for a "ness" is some fixed value. Above the fixed value the "ness" is visible, and below the threshold the "ness" is invisible. In reality, the notion of a threshold is really a statistical concept–the value of the "ness" where the observer says "yes" or "no" is a random variable. This random variable idea is conceptually identical to the discriminal dispersion idea underlying paired comparisons and category scaling. The recurring thread throughout many scaling methods is this idea of a judgment having random variation. It will continue to resurface under various guises in upcoming chapters.

A basic threshold determination consists of presenting a stimulus of a certain level of "ness" and asking the observer if they see the "ness." Observers are instructed to respond with a "yes" or "no," a binary response. Next, the level of the "ness" is changed, and they are asked whether they see it or not. This process is repeated for a range of "ness" levels.

The psychometric curve, sometimes called the frequency-of-seeing curve, describes the proportion of "yes" responses given by observers to various levels of the "ness." Statistically the curve is called a cumulative density function, or sometimes an ogive. A typical curve is shown in Figure 5.1.

The analysis of the empirical proportions essentially consists of determining the threshold and other useful parameters that describe the psychometric curve. For this we need some vocabulary.

The following are some terms used in the field of psychophysics to describe various characteristics of the psychometric curve

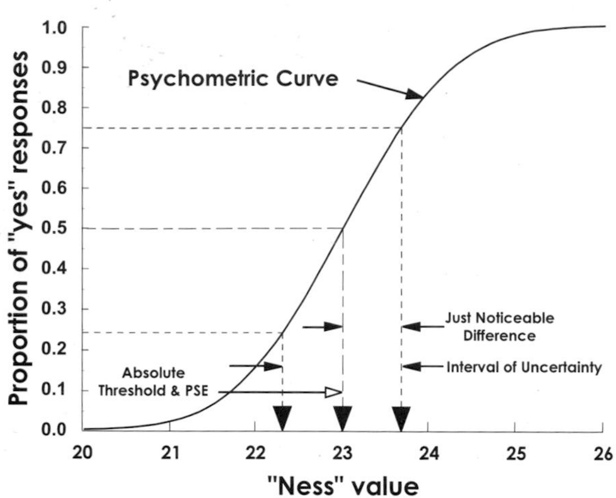

Figure 5.1 - A typical psychometric curve. The axis is the value of a "ness" and the ordinate is the proportion or probability of observers responding "yes." Shown in the figure are the Interval of Uncertainty, the Absolute Threshold and Point-of-Subjective-Equality (PSE) and the Just-Noticeable Difference (JND).

(Gescheider, 1997; Baird and Noma, 1978). Some of these terms apply to determining a threshold, while others are applicable to a just-noticeable-difference determination.

Absolute threshold or *stimulus threshold* is the smallest amount of stimulus "energy," Physical Image Parameter, or "ness" needed to produce an awareness of a "ness." The threshold is usually taken as the point where 50% of the observers see the "ness."

Point of subjective equality (PSE) is used to describe the 0.50 probability point of a psychometric curve from just-noticeable-difference studies. This is the value of the stimulus where 50% of the responses are "yes" to seeing a difference. It is defined in a just-noticeable-difference study as the point where observers find two stimuli equal in the statistical sense. Note that the absolute threshold and the point of subjective equality are the same point on the psychometric curve, but the interpretation depends on the type of threshold that is being determined.

A *stimulus just-noticeable difference (JND)* is the stimulus change required to produce a just-noticeable difference in the perception of the "ness." These are also known as *difference thresholds* or *increment thresholds*. Note that the just-noticeable difference is related to the steepness of the slope of the psychometric curve; a steep slope yields a small just-noticeable difference. In statistical terms, the just-noticeable difference is proportional to the standard deviation of the underlying probability density function used to model the psychometric curve.

Generally, the just-noticeable difference depends on the stimulus level, and is often proportional to the stimulus value. The just-noticeable difference is usually defined as the "ness" value where 75% of the observers see a stimulus with this "ness" value greater than the standard. Although widely recognized, this percentage point is based on convention, and is not a standard. Another value can be used if it is absolutely essential, but a clear statement of the percentage used is mandatory to eliminate confusion.

Interval of uncertainty is the range of stimulus "energy" for which the judgments "can go either way." Marked in Figure 5.1 by the outer set of dotted lines, it is the "ness" or physical image parameter interval corresponding to the range of 0.25 to 0.75 proportion points. The interval of uncertainty is determined by reflecting the two proportions onto the "ness" axis. Most mathematical formulations of the psychometric curve are symmetrical about the threshold, although there are a few exceptions. When symmetry holds, the interval of uncertainty is equal to twice the just-noticeable difference.

5.4 Method of Limits

Both the absolute threshold and the just-noticeable difference can be determined by the method of limits. The basic procedure is to start a sequence of presentations with a sample that does not have the "ness" perceptible, and keep increasing the "ness" amount in the sample until the observer detects the presence of the "ness." At the point of detection, the value of the "ness" is recorded. The presentations are then repeated, starting with the sample having a clearly visible "ness" and decreasing the level of the "ness" until it is no longer visible. The stimulus value is recorded, and after a large number of observers, experimental proportions are estimated. Methodological details are described in the following sections.

5.4.1 Method of Limits–Absolute Threshold

For the determination of the absolute threshold, start with a sequence of closely spaced stimuli exhibiting a single "ness" with known values, x_0, x_1, x_2, ..., x_n. Stimuli of increasing "ness" value are sequentially presented to the observer, in what is called an ascending series. As described above, upon presentation of the stimulus, the observer is asked whether he or she "sees" (detects) the "ness." If the "ness" is not detected, the next stimulus in the sequence is presented and the question is repeated. This process of presenting the sample and asking the question is repeated until the observer responds "yes." When the first "yes" response occurs, the study administrator presents the next stimulus in the sequence to be sure that the observer actually saw the stimuli. If the response is again "yes," the study administrator records the "ness" value that is intermediate between the "ness" value that *was not* detected and the first "ness" value that *was* detected.

The study administrator repeats the process, this time starting with the stimulus with the highest value (descending series), asking the observer if the "ness" is visible or not. Again, when the observer says "no" the "ness" is not visible, the study administrator presents the next stimulus and establishes that the observer has indeed seen a change. As before, the "ness" value that is intermediate between the first "no" and the last "yes" is used as one estimate for the absolute threshold.

Two major sources of observer errors are possible with the method of limits (Gescheider, 1985). The first is called the *error of habituation*. This error occurs when the observer continues to make the same response because the stimulus sequence is monotonic in either an increasing or decreasing direction. Habituation errors tend to inflate the threshold in an ascending sequence, and cause deflation in a decreasing sequence.

The second is called the *error of expectation*. Expectation error occurs because the observer expects the stimulus to change and therefore may respond by saying it has changed when it has not. This error will decrease the threshold in an ascending series, opposite to that of the error of habituation.

Although opposite in effect, for either the ascending or descending series, these two different errors do not necessarily cancel each other out in practical situations. To combat such errors, experimenters vary the starting point of each series and avoid excessively long trials.

A variation on the basic method of limits to reduce these errors is the *up-and-down* or *staircase method.* The up-and-down method was developed in 1943 at the Explosives Research Laboratory, Bruceton PA, to test explosives' resistance to weights dropped on them (Dixon and Mood, 1948). An arbitrary height was selected and a known weight was dropped on a sample of explosive to see if it detonated. If it did, the height was decreased. Conversely, if it did not explode, the height was increased. The critical height, of course, was the height at which the weight just caused the specimen to explode.

The staircase method starts like the basic method of limits with the presentation of either an increasing or decreasing sequence of stimuli. When the observer switches their response from a "no" to a "yes," the value of the "ness" is recorded, and the study administrator immediately changes the direction of the sequence. After a few presentations in the other direction, observers reverse their response again. The study administrator records the "ness" value and switches the sequence direction again. This method quickly "converges" about a value and is stopped after a certain number of reversals. In one respect, this method is analogous to the mathematical summing of terms in an alternating convergent series.

The efficiency in the method lies in the fact that the complete increasing or decreasing sequence is not presented, lessening the burden on the observer. Bakshi and Fuhrmann (1997) used the staircase method in determining the threshold for various image coding schemes by constructing a computer "movie" for stimulus presentation.

Cornsweet (1962) observed that a less-than-honest observer can bias the results. To avoid this possibility, he proposed a refinement on the staircase method called the *double staircase* method. The basic idea is to have two sequences of presentation, one decreasing and one increasing, and randomly switch between them. At some predetermined random time, the study administrator switches from the ascending sequence to the descending sequence, and then at another randomly chosen time interval, switches back. Fundamentally, the idea is to keep the observer "honest" in the sense of reducing the errors of expectation and habituation. Bartleson (1984) described both the single and double staircase methods in detail.

Depending upon the objective, any of the above method of limits procedures can be repeated many times with the same observer. This is called a *trial*, and it measures the absolute threshold for that one observer. The alternative is to conduct the procedure using a group of observers representing an observer population such as the customer population, which would yield an estimate of the threshold for the customer population.

5.4.2 Method of Limits–Just-Noticeable Difference

When a just-noticeable difference is required, the method of limits procedure is changed slightly. First, a sample with a known "ness" value is selected as a standard. Next, a set of stimuli that bracket the "ness" of the standard is selected.

Starting with a "ness" value below the standard, each member of the stimulus sequence increasing in "ness" (ascending sequence) is presented to the observer. The observer is then asked if the sample matches the standard. At the point where the observer says there is a match, the study administrator records the value of the "ness." The descending stimulus sequence, starting from the highest level, is then presented to the observer, one by one, and the observer is asked if the sample matches the standard. Again, at the point where the observer changes response categories, the study administrator records the value of the "ness." To avoid errors, both the standard and test stimuli should be simultaneously presented to the observer.

Variations on the basic method of limits are described in Baird and Noma (1978) and Gescheider (1985).

5.4.3 Method of Limits–Data Analysis

Data analysis for the method of limits is straightforward. If we assume that the data follow a normal or Gaussian distribution (see the discriminal dispersion of Thurstone, Chapter 8), then either the probability density function, histogram, or the cumulative probability function can be completely described by two parameters. These two parameters are the mean, μ, and the standard deviation, σ. The mean, μ, is the 0.50 (50%) probability point of the cumulative density function, and the standard deviation, σ, is proportional to the just-noticeable difference.

For either the absolute threshold or just-noticeable difference, the data consist of a collection of "ness" values, x_j, at the point the observer changes response on both ascending and descending trials. For an estimate of the 0.50 probability point, the mean of the "ness" values can be used. The well known estimate of μ, $\bar{x}$, is given by equation (5.1). Here N = the number of threshold estimates and x_j is the jth threshold estimate. The average "ness" value, $\bar{x}$, is the absolute threshold estimate and is the estimate of the point where 50% of the observers say that the "ness" is just visible.

$$\bar{x} = \frac{1}{N}\sum_{j=1}^{N} x_j \qquad (5.1)$$

In a just-noticeable difference experiment where there is a comparison against a standard, one would expect the "ness" value for the 0.50 probability point to be equal to the standard, but this may not be so. Recall that the "ness" at the 50% point in a just-noticeable difference determination is called the point of subjective equality. This is the point that the observers judge equal to the standard. Ideally, this value should equal the standard, but it may not. In practice, if the point of subjective equality fits within the confidence interval of the standard, it can be considered equal. The usual statistical hypothesis test for the difference in two means is appropriate.

Since the just-noticeable difference is proportional to the standard deviation, we need to estimate the standard deviation. The standard deviation, σ, is just the square root of the variance. Under the normal or Gaussian distribution assumption, the usual unbiased estimator for σ is *s*, and can be calculated from equation (5.2).

(5.2) $$s = \sqrt{\sum_{j=1}^{N} \frac{(x_j - \bar{x})^2}{N-1}}$$

Using the conventional definition of just-noticeable difference, the 0.75 probability point can be computed under the normal assumption by scaling the estimate of the standard deviation, *s*, by a factor. This factor equals 0.67449, and is the number of standard deviations of a unit normal distribution that equal 0.75 probability. Thus the just-noticeable difference, JND, is calculated from equation (5.3).

(5.3) $$JND = 0.67449s$$

If there is concern that the threshold may be different for the ascending and descending series, then the "ness" data can be segmented into two groups. From each group the mean and standard deviation are estimated according to equations (5.2) and (5.3), and the usual t-test for the differences in the means can be performed. The null hypothesis of the t-test is no difference in the means, or thresholds, for the ascending or descending series. Testing the hypothesis that the standard deviations are equal might also be prudent because the just-noticeable difference is derived from this estimate. Any elementary statistics textbook can be consulted for details regarding equal-mean and equal-variance hypothesis tests.

5.4.4 Method of Limits–Considerations

The biggest advantage of the method of limits is its efficiency; a threshold of known precision can be obtained with a few trials. In any practical application of the method, there are a few factors that the study administrator needs to consider. Cornsweet (1962) suggested procedural tactics in four key areas.

1) Where to start the "ness" sequence.
2) Initial "ness" step size.
3) When to stop collecting data.
4) Modification of step sizes.

Where to Start the "Ness" Sequence–For maximum efficiency, the study administrator needs to have a good idea of the threshold or just-noticeable difference, since the series needs to be started near and should surround the threshold or just-noticeable difference. Of course, if the threshold were known, there would be no need to collect the data.

An approximate threshold or just-noticeable difference estimate can be obtained by conducting a pilot experiment with only a few observers. Knowledge of the threshold is not critical for the method, for after a few trials the observer starts to hover around that value, assuming no adaptation effects. What is critical is the stimulus set must bracket the threshold, and this may be difficult for image "nesses" that are not easy to control.

Initial "Ness" Step Size–A step interval that is too small will require a great many trials, while a too-large interval will not enable sufficient precision in the threshold estimate. Arguments suggest that the "ness" interval should be equally spaced logarithmically, but these arguments are based on classical psychophysics and there is nothing to suggest that logarithmic spacing should be a requirement for image "nesses." A linear "ness" step size or increment is often used for image "nesses" (Hamerly, 1983; Hamerly and Dvorak, 1981; Zwick, 1975). The optimum step interval is the just-noticeable difference (Dixon and Massey, 1948).

When to Stop Collecting Data–Knowing when to stop the data collection series contributes to the efficiency. The more trials, the better the threshold estimate, but data quality may be compromised if observer fatigue and boredom take over. Establishing the number of response changes to be used as the stopping criterion before starting the study is the simplest and most rudimentary method. Maintaining the number criterion during the study is also important because it affects the threshold estimate. More sophisticated and more complex approaches are available. Wetherill and Levitt (1965) provided additional alternative stopping rules that can be used for estimating percent "yes" responses other than 50%.

Modification of Step Sizes–As the observer converges on the threshold value, modifying the step size under some circumstances is possible. Initial steps may be large, but as the threshold is approached (as indicated by the change in response category), the interval may be decreased.

If automating the threshold determination task is possible, sophisticated procedures incorporating the considerations given above are available. PEST (Parameter Estimation by Sequential Testing), is an adaptive procedure proposed by Taylor and Creelman (1967). An improved version is called the Best PEST by Lieberman and Pentland (1982), who also provide a simple BASIC computer program. The PEST methods are quite efficient and use the statistical procedure called maximum likelihood to estimate the threshold.

QUEST (Watson and Pelli, 1983), a method similar to PEST, uses Bayesian statistics to compute the threshold. It makes optimal use of all the data to both estimate the threshold and stop taking data when the estimate is within a certain confidence interval. A rudimentary BASIC program is provided to carry out the necessary calculations as the stimuli are being presented.

Comparing the PEST and QUEST statistical threshold estimation techniques via computer simulation, Emerson (1986) concluded that the Bayesian method produces a threshold that has a smaller bias and lower variance. However, his simulations were limited with respect to the parameter space that he explored, so this is not the last word on the topic.

For the serious user of method of limits, implementation of either the simple Best PEST or the QUEST adaptive technique is recommended. No MathCad® sheets for these procedures are provided.

5.5 Method of Adjustment

The *method of adjustment* goes under several pseudonyms: method of average error, method of reproduction and method of equivalent stimuli. Basically the method of adjustment is very similar to the method of limits, except the observer adjusts the "ness" by turning a knob, moving a slider, or using another control method.

First, a random value of the "ness" is selected by the study administrator. Next, the observer adjusts the "ness" of the sample until it is just visible (for an absolute threshold determination), or until it matches the standard (when determining a just-noticeable difference). At this point the test administrator records the "ness" value, and then randomly selects a new "ness" value.

Like the method of limits, this procedure can be repeated many times by one observer or once by many observers. The number of observers depends on the precision of the threshold needed.

Applying the method of adjustment to imaging situations requires the "ness" to be continuously adjustable by the observer. For complex "nesses," the method of adjustment has a major drawback, namely the difficulty of changing the "ness" instantaneously in response to an input from the observer. The method of adjustment has been used to identify thresholds of light and sound levels, but few reported studies have used the method of adjustment for typical imaging system "nesses." However, as computer power increases and knowledge of the Physical Image Parameters comprising "nesses" becomes more comprehensive, the method of adjustment will find more widespread application.

A particular advantage of the method of adjustment over the method of limits is the active involvement of the observer. Actively engaging the observer raises interest, reduces boredom and tediousness, and generally improves the quality of the data.

5.5.1 Method of Adjustment–Data Analysis

Data analysis for the method of adjustment follows the same course as the method of limits. The data to be analyzed consists of the "ness" control setting (the "ness" value) obtained either during the threshold adjustment experiment or an adjustment-to-standard experiment. All the data analysis methods in Section 5.4.3 can be applied here.

5.6 Method of Constant Stimuli

In the *method of constant stimuli* for determining an absolute threshold and just-noticeable difference, the "constant" is a selected set of samples (stimuli) that remain fixed throughout the experiment. This contrasts to the varying nature of the stimuli used in the method of limits and method of adjustment. The set of samples is usually chosen such that the sample member with the lowest level of "ness" *is never* selected by the observers and the sample with the highest "ness" level *is always* selected by all of the observers. Usually a pilot study must be run to identify the never-selected and always-selected samples. A typical sample count is between five and ten.

Unlike the method of limits and method of adjustment, the method of constant stimuli collects data that can be analyzed as a psychometric curve.

5.6.1 Method of Constant Stimuli–Absolute Threshold

Table 5.1 Data Summary for Method of Constant Stimuli

Sample ID	"Ness" Value	Proportion, $p_i = f_i/N$
A	x_1	f_1/N
B	x_2	f_2/N
C	x_3	f_3/N
...	...	...
K	x_k	f_k/N

Instead of responding to a standard or reference, the observer is asked to indicate if the "ness" is detected in each sample. Samples of the set are presented to the observer in a random sequence, and a response is requested during each presentation. If the observer answers "yes" to the "can you see the ness" question, the study administrator increments the frequency counter opposite the sample "ness" value. The data is recorded in a form like that in Table 5.1. In this table the left-hand column is the sample or stimulus identification. The middle column is the "ness" value of the sample, x_i, determined independently by way of a Visual Algorithm connecting the "ness" to the Physical Image Parameters. The third column is the total number of observers responding "yes" when the sample was presented, f_i. Division by the total number of observations, N, yields the proportion, or fraction, of "yes" responses.

At the end of the data collection process, the study administrator has the samples with the known "ness" values and the proportion of times that the "ness" was seen or detected by the group of observers. This data is plotted as a curve like that shown in Figure 5.1, where the axis is the "ness" values, x_i, and the ordinate is the corresponding f_i/N. This plot is the experimental data from which the psychometric curve and its parameters will be estimated.

5.6.2 Method of Constant Stimuli–Just-Noticeable Difference

For determining just-noticeable differences, the observer is given the reference or standard and a sample. The observer's task is to compare each sample with the reference sequentially and indicate if the sample has more of the "ness" than the reference. A "yes" response is recorded in the data sheet by incrementing the frequency counter.

5.6.3 Psychometric Models–Basic Data Analysis

When the observer makes a "yes" response, a one is scored for sample x_i, and nothing is scored when the response is "no." The proportion, p_i, of "yes" responses for sample x_i is just the sum of the responses divided by the total number of observers, N, that judged that specific stimulus, f_i/N.

Two data vectors are available, the known values of the "nesses" and the proportion of "yes" responses for each sample. To analyze the data, we need a suitable model of observer response. In the context of absolute thresholds and just-noticeable differences, these models are called psychometric models, psychometric functions, or psychometric curves.

For all psychometric models, the dependent variable is the fraction or percent of "yes" responses. A "yes" response can mean either the stimulus was detected, or a sample was judged greater than a standard. These data are empirical estimates of probabilities.

The general estimation problem is to determine the value of the "ness" at some fixed probability or proportion of a "yes" response. By convention, the fixed percentage point, the criterion, for a just-noticeable difference is the 0.75 or 75% percentage, which is halfway between pure chance, 0.50, and perfect, 1.00 (Torgerson, 1958). Recall that the just-noticeable difference is the "ness" distance equivalent to the difference between the 0.50 and 0.75 proportion points. The 0.75 proportion is a convention and is strongly recommended. The criterion point of threshold estimation is the 0.50 point.

A plot of the empirical probabilities or proportions versus the "ness" value is called a psychometric curve, or sometimes the frequency-of-seeing curve (see Figure 5.1). If many observers are used, the data will follow a smooth curve. With few observers–a common occurrence–the plot of the empirical proportions may vary considerably from a smooth curve.

One could draw a smooth psychometric curve through the data and estimate the criterion "ness" value, but such an estimate may not be very precise. A quantitative alternative is to hypothesize a model, or a functional form for the psychometric function, and fit this function to the experimental data. Knowing the functional form of the psychometric curve enables a reliable estimate of the "ness" value for the absolute threshold or just-noticeable difference.

Models or techniques called linear probability models, logit and probit models, and logistic regression analysis provide the tools for estimating the parameters of the psychometric function. These techniques are extensively used in areas where the response to a question either is binary (yes/no) or limited to a few categories.

The basic idea of linear probability models is to determine empirically what factors account for the probability of a "yes" response by fitting a model to empirical data. An excellent series of monographs (Aldrich and Nelson, 1984; Liao, 1994; Menard, 1995) is available from Sage Publications that discusses these models and techniques in more detail.

A strong connection exists between the functional forms of the psychometric curve and the models of indirect scaling covered in later chapters. The psychological process of deciding if two samples are different in a paired comparison situation is not conceptually different from the process of deciding if a sample is just-noticeably different from some standard. In fact, Gaussian and logistic functions are two functions used extensively as models for psychometric curves and indirect scaling, as we will see in later chapters.

(5.4) $$P_{js} = F(\alpha_s + \beta_s x_{js})$$

Formally, equation (5.4) states that P_{js}, the probability that sample (stimuli) j is judged to have more of the "ness" than the standard s, is some linear function, $F(\,)$, of the "ness" value, x_{js}. This formulation is also called a linear probability model. The function $F(\,)$ distinguishes the type of psychometric, or linear probability model.

Two popular psychometric models–Gaussian and logistic–and methods to estimate the parameters α and β of equation (5.4) are described in the next sections.

5.6.3.1 Gaussian Psychometric Model

The function $F(\,)$ for the Gaussian model is shown in equation (5.5), and denoted for convenience as $\Phi(\alpha_s + \beta_s x_{js})$.

(5.5) $$P_{js} = F(\alpha_s + \beta_s x_{js}) = \frac{1}{\sqrt{2\pi}} \int_{-(\alpha_s + \beta_s x_{js})}^{\infty} e^{-\frac{u^2}{2}} du = \Phi(\alpha_s + \beta_s x_{js})$$

The solution to equation (5.5) is just the inverse, $\Phi^{-1}(P_{js}) = \alpha_s + \beta_s x_{js} = z$ and is called the *probit* in some contexts and *z-value* in others. No closed form for the inverse Gaussian probability function is known, so the inversion requires either tables or numerical computer routines for a solution.

The simplest solution method, although not necessarily the best from a statistical point of view, is to estimate α_s and β_s as follows:

1) Convert the proportions, P_{js}, to standard normal z-values via a table of normal probability giving $z = \alpha_s + \beta_s x_{js}$. Note that the x_{js} are the known or measured values of the "ness". Proportions of 1.00 and zero correspond to indeterminate z-values. One solution that substitutes $1/2J$ for the zero proportion and $1 - 1/2J$ for the unity proportion can be applied here. (This technique is used again in Chapter 9.) However, if the data includes more than one adjacent zero or one proportion, Bock and Jones (1968) suggest applying the above rule only to the first value in the sequence and eliminating the remaining zeros and ones from the analysis.

2) Use a linear least squares-fit (linear regression) to find the best line for $z = \alpha_s + \beta_s x_{js}$, thus yielding estimates of the slope, β_s, and the intercept, α_s.

Once the parameters of the psychometric curve have been estimated, other values of interest need to be determined: the threshold and/or the just-noticeable difference, and the point of subjective equality.

1) The absolute threshold is the "ness" value corresponding to z = 0, or where the probability of detection is 50%. For a Gaussian function, it can be determined from $\alpha_s + \beta_s x_{js}, = 0$, giving $x_{thrsh} = -\alpha_s/\beta_s$ as the absolute threshold estimate. In a just-noticeable difference experiment where a standard is used, the point of subjective equality (PSE) is also the "ness" value corresponding to z = 0, and ideally should equal the "ness" value of the standard. If it does not, this error is called the Constant Error, CE, and is defined as CE = PSE("ness") - standard("ness").

2) The just-noticeable difference is normally defined as one-half the average of the "ness" interval between the 0.25 and the 0.75 probability points. For the normal distribution, the z-values for these probability points are ±0.67449. The upper (0.75) proportion point, $x_{u,}$ is computed using $(0.67449 - \alpha_s)/\beta_s$ and the lower (0.25) proportion point, x_l, is computed using $(-0.67449 - \alpha_s)/\beta_s$. The average just-noticeable difference is computed using $(x_u + x_l)/2$. If the "ness" values have not been transformed, say by taking the logarithm, then the Gaussian psychometric model is symmetrical with respect to $z = 0$. When the Gaussian psychometric model is symmetrical, it is sufficient to take $x_u - x_{PSE}$ as the estimate for the just-noticeable difference.

The basic criticism of this least squares approach is that it minimizes the squared deviations about the z-values, not the experimental proportion values, P_{js}. Bock and Jones (1968), Aldrich and Nelson (1984), and Liao (1994) described other computational techniques such as weighted least squares, minimum chi-square, and maximum likelihood, with different minimization objectives.

With today's capable data analysis packages, carrying out a nonlinear least squares-fit to minimize the squared deviations about the proportions is very convenient. Other considerations include goodness-of-fit of the psychometric model to the data and confidence intervals for the point of subjective equality and the just-noticeable difference. The confidence interval on the parameters will be addressed later in this chapter.

MathCad® sheet `jndg1.mcd` provides a least squares solution to the Gaussian psychometric model.

5.6.3.2 Logistic Psychometric Model

The logistic model has its roots in toxicology, but has been applied recently in the social sciences and psychophysics areas. Equation (5.6) describes the logistic psychometric function.

(5.6) $$Pjs = F(\alpha_s + \beta_s x_{js}) = \frac{1}{1+e^{-(\alpha_s+\beta_s x_{js})}} = \frac{e^{(\alpha_s+\beta_s x_{js})}}{1+e^{(\alpha_s+\beta_s x_{js})}}$$

The lower equation on the far right-hand side of equation (5.6) is the definition commonly found in the social science literature. The one above this is often found in the psychophysics literature, no doubt because of its compactness.

Expanding the exponent(s) of equation (5.6) to include other factors in linear combinations, yields what are called linear probability models. These models do not seem popular with psychophysicists, but for modeling "nesses" that are combinations of two or more Physical Image Parameters, they offer some additional possibilities. A linear probability model could be used to establish a "ness" threshold in terms of the relevant set of Physical Image Parameters if the Visual Algorithm is known (Engeldrum, 1998).

(5.7) $$\ln\left(\frac{P_{js}}{1-P_{js}}\right) = \alpha_s + \beta_s x_{js}$$

Equation (5.6) can be solved directly for $\alpha_s + \beta_s x_{js}$, which yields equation (5.7).

The quantity $ln[P_{js}/(1 - P_{js})]$ is called the *logit,* and this formalism is often called the logit model. Note from equation (5.7) that the logit is a linear function of the "ness" values, and is related to the "nesses" in the same conceptual way as the Gaussian model.

Logistic parameter estimation proceeds similarly as with the Gaussian psychometric model:

1) Convert the number of positive ("yes") responses, r_{js}, to logits, l, using $\ln[(r_{js}+ ½) / (J - r_{js} + ½)] = \alpha_s + \beta_s x_{js}$. Note that the x_{js} are the measured values of the "ness," from, say a Visual Algorithm, and J is the number of observers that responded to that particular sample. Adding the ½ factor in the above equation reduces the slight bias in the logits that result from taking the simple ratio of r_{js}/J as the estimate of the proportions (Anscombe, 1956). An added advantage of the ½ factor is that it eliminates the zero and 1.00 proportion problem.

2) Use a linear least squares-fit (linear regression) to find the best fit for $l = \alpha_s + \beta_s x_{js}$, thus yielding estimates of the slope, β_s, and the intercept, α_s. An alternative option is to use nonlinear least squares estimation software to fit equation (5.6) directly.

Once the parameters of the psychometric curve have been estimated, we need to compute the threshold and/or the just-noticeable difference, and the point of subjective equality, (PSE). (In the field of toxicology the threshold in a logistic psychometric model is also known as the "lethal dose.")

1) The *threshold*, or point of subjective equality, is the value where logit, $l = 0$, or where the probability of detection is 50%. This value can be determined from $\alpha_s + \beta_s x_{js} = 0$, giving $x_{js} = -\alpha_s/\beta_s$ as the threshold estimate. Note that this estimate

is identical to the estimate using the Gaussian psychometric function.

2) The *just-noticeable difference* is normally defined as the average of the "ness" interval between the 0.25 probability and the 0.75 probability points. For the logistic model, the values for these probability points are ±1.0986. The upper, Dl_u, is computed using $(1.0986 - \alpha_s)/\beta_s$ and the lower, Dl_l, is computed via $(-1.0986 - \alpha_s)/\beta_s$. The just-noticeable difference or ΔS estimate is computed by $(Dl_u + Dl_l)/2$. Because of the symmetry of the logistic function, working with either the upper or lower probability points will suffice, providing the "ness" scale has not been nonlinearly transformed.

Other computing options are available for determining the parameters of the logistic function (Bock and Jones, 1968; Aldrich and Nelson, 1984; and Liao, 1994). The distinction among the methods is the variance in the estimates of α_s and β_s. In a study comparing maximum likelihood and minimum chi-square estimation procedures, Berkson (1955) could find no compelling reason for one method over another. The differences in the results from the two estimation methods hinge on the symmetry of the "ness" values around the point of subjective equality, and how the zero and unity proportions are treated (Bock and Jones, 1968). For "ness" values symmetrical about the 0.50 proportion point, and proportions in the 0.05 to 0.95 range, all the methods produce essentially equivalent results. However, the maximum likelihood method is very popular, and is available in many popular computer statistics packages.

A least squares solution for the logistic model can be found in the MathCad® sheet `jndll.mcd`.

$$P_{js} = 1 - e^{-\left(\frac{x_{js}}{\alpha}\right)^{\beta}} \tag{5.8}$$

5.6.3.3 Other Psychometric Models

The Gaussian and logistic models are not the only ones available. Watson (1979) describes the use of the Weibull (1951) distribution. Watson also provides a maximum likelihood method for estimating the parameters. The general form of the Weibull probability is given by equation (5.8), where α and β are parameters to be estimated. A more general form that includes guess rates and "finger error rates" is described by Watson and Fitzhugh (1990).

As we will see in the section on confidence intervals, and in later chapters on indirect scaling, it is extremely difficult in practice to choose the "correct" psychometric model. The standard assumption is to use the Gaussian psychometric model; without some theoretical assumptions or a large number of observers, little rationale exists for selecting others.

5.6.4 Variations on the Method of Constant Stimuli

Variations on the basic method of constant stimuli are available and can be applied in many practical circumstances. They are all equivalent, in that they all generate data for fitting a psychometric curve. Selection of a particular method is largely a matter of practical working conditions and time available for data collection. Some of these additional methods are described next.

5.6.4.1 Paired Comparison Variation

One useful variation on the method of constant stimuli is standard paired comparisons with some additional steps (Guilford, 1954; Culler, 1926). It is assumed that a set of closely spaced stimuli is available, and the "ness" values of this set are known. The paired-comparison method is a sequence of two-sample comparisons. The frequency or proportion data matrix forms the basis of scale value determination (see Chapter 8). Inherent in the paired-comparison data collection method is the method of constant stimuli, where each sample serves, in effect, as a standard. There are several differences in both the method of sample presentation and of data collection between the standard paired-comparison data collection method and paired comparisons with constant stimuli.

First, all combinations are presented to the observer with "left-right" order tracked, which will average out position effects. A comparison of pair A-B, with A on the left and B on the right, is assumed to be different from the comparison of pair B-A. The major consequence of this change is the increase in the number of comparisons to $n(n-1)$ from $n(n-1)/2$, resulting in a doubling of observer effort. If pairs of identical samples are available, then like samples can be compared: A-A for example. These self-comparison results can be used to estimate observer guessing rates. With this addition, the full n^2 number of comparisons is required.

Secondly, in the standard paired-comparison methodology, when the observer selects the member of the pair that has more of the "ness" or is preferred, one is added in the column of the frequency matrix when the observer chooses the column sample over the row sample (see Chapter 8). Standard paired-comparison methodology also assumes that the comparison of A-B is the same as B-A, and that in an A-A or a B-B comparison, one sample will be selected over itself 50% of the time. A result of the last two assumptions is that only $n(n-1)/2$ comparisons need be made, and that the proportion matrix is symmetric; that is, $p_{i,j} + p_{j,i} = 1$.

Finally, the analysis of the data in this variation proceeds in quite a different manner than in standard paired-comparison scale development. The objective in standard paired comparison is to generate scale values, but the goal of this constant stimuli variation is to estimate the psychometric function.

A real advantage of this method is that a psychometric function, and therefore the just-noticeable difference, can be determined for each of the n samples used in the paired comparison. This may offer real convenience and time savings in some applications.

5.6.4.1.1 Data Collection

Application of the paired-comparison method to the determination of absolute thresholds or just-noticeable differences requires two modifications to the standard paired-comparison data collection procedure:

1) All pairs are presented to the observer, a total of $n(n-1)$ comparisons. This means there is a distinction between the "left" and "right" in a pair, and both pairs are presented. If exact duplicate samples are available, then perform the comparison of the sample with itself, for a total of n^2 comparisons. This will yield estimates for $p_{ii,}$ rather than using an assumed 0.50 probability. These estimates can be used as probabilities in correcting for observer guessing (see Section 5.9).

2) Upon presentation of sample pair *ij*, ask the observer to select the one sample that has the highest visible "ness." Add one to the frequency data matrix, ***F***, at location *ij,* row column notation. Recall that sample *i* is on the "left," or the first presented, and sample *j* is on the "right" or the second one presented. The pair *ji* is the space-reversed pair; i.e., *j* is on the left and *i* is on the right.

3) Repeat the process for *J* observers. See Section 5.8 on the number of observers for an appropriate selection of *J*.

5.6.4.1.2 Data Analysis

The generation of a psychometric curve for each sample (stimuli) proceeds as follows:

1) Take the *n* by *n* frequency matrix of data, ***F***, and divide each entry by the number of observers that observed each combination. This yields an *n* by *n* proportion matrix, ***P***, that has values from zero to 1.00.

2) Form two data vectors, ***x*** and ***y***. The ***x*** vector contains the physically measured "ness" values. The *n* ***y*** vectors are the columns of the proportion matrix, ***P***. The two vectors are the empirical data that comprise the axis, **x,** and ordinate, **y,** values, describing the *n* psychometric curves.

3) Use any of the methods described in Section 5.6.3.1 to fit each psychometric curve and determine the absolute threshold or the just-noticeable difference. Either Gaussian or logistic psychometric curves are applicable.

Generally, an excessive data collection effort is required to use this technique. Yet under some circumstances it may be useful, particularly when no specific standard is available for a comparison. Often in imaging applications, standard samples cannot be generated with precisely known values of "nesses."

Incorporating paired comparisons into the method of constant stimuli can reduce bias, as well. After multiple presentations with a fixed reference, even though left-right may be randomized, it is possible when using the standard method of constant stimuli for the observer continually to select the reference, essentially guessing. In this paired-comparison variation, the presentation of all possible pairs effectively "randomizes" references, so the observer will be less likely to give a biased response.

5.6.4.2 Sorting

Sorting stimuli according to some criteria is an easy task for most observers. This is a variation on category scaling, except the number of categories is two–"see a ness," or "not see a ness."

The task is to have the observer sort a set of stimuli into two piles according to whether the "ness" is present (detected) or not present (not detected).

For absolute threshold determination, the observer puts each sample into a pile marked "no ness" if the "ness" is not visible, and the remainder goes in a second pile marked "yes ness." The above is repeated many times by one observer, or performed once by many observers.

For determining just-noticeable differences, there is slight variation in the experimental procedure. Typically there is a comparison standard, and the observer is asked to put the stimulus into the "greater than the standard" pile if the stimulus is judged to have a "ness" value greater than the standard. The second pile collects samples with "equal to or less" of the "ness" than the standard.

5.6.4.2.1 Data Collection

Using the sorting method, data is recorded in the following manner. On the data sheet two columns are constructed, one that contains the "ness" values of each sample, and a second that contains the response data. If a sample is judged by an observer to have the "ness" in question (a "yes"), a one is added to the number in the second column opposite the sample. Over a large number of observers, there are an increasing number of "yes" responses as the "ness" value increases. Dividing the number (frequency) of "yes" responses by the total number of observers (or observations if it is one observer) gives the proportion (probability) for each value of "ness." This is the basic psychometric curve data.

5.6.4.2.2 Data Analysis

Once the proportions are generated, any of the methods described in Section 5.6.3 can be applied to compute the psychometric curve parameters, threshold and just-noticeable difference.

5.6.4.3 Triangle or Three-Sample Method

The previous method of constant stimuli variation used two samples (sample stimuli and the standard or reference) in a comparison. There are some cases where a "ness" may not be clearly defined, but determining an absolute threshold or a just-noticeable difference is required. The three-sample procedure (Bock and Jones, 1968) and the triangle tests (Meilgaard, Civille and Carr, 1991) provide alternatives in these situations.

As the name implies, three stimuli or samples are used in the judgment. Two of the three samples are the same, and one is different. The observer's task is to pick the one that is different: the odd stimulus. For threshold determination, two of the three samples would have a "ness" value of zero and would appear in all trios. In a just-noticeable difference determination, two samples of the trio would be the reference sample. Suppose the reference, or no-"ness" sample, is designated x_0, and the set of samples $x_j, j = 1...k$. The samples are presented in the sequence x_0, x_0, x_j, with the spatial or temporal position of x_j randomized in each presentation (Bock and Jones, 1968).

An advantage of the three-sample method is the ability to decide if the observer is "correct" in selecting the sample. If the study administrator knows the correct answer, then it is possible to detect when the observer is guessing and apply a correction (see Section 5.9). This type of paradigm is called a three-alternative-forced-choice. With two samples it is called the two-alternative-forced-choice.

One possible disadvantage to this technique for imaging applications is the requirement of duplicate samples at each level of the "ness." Making exact duplicates of images is possible with some imaging technologies, but often it is not. When it cannot be assured that two of the samples are identical, this method is not appropriate for threshold or just-noticeable difference determination.

5.6.4.3.1 Data Collection

Tabulating the response data for the three-sample method is slightly different. The basic data arrangement of Table 5.1 is used. Here, the counter is increased only when *the correct response is given*. The correct response is known by the location, or position, of the stimulus. For example, if the "odd" sample was the first in a row of three and the observer selected the first sample, this would be a correct response. The selection of any other stimulus is incorrect. A zero, or no increase in the counter, is tabulated when an incorrect response is given.

5.6.4.3.2 Data Analysis

Analysis of the frequencies of correct response proceeds as with other scaling exercises. Each frequency is divided by the number of judgments yielding the proportion of correct responses, P_{js}. These proportions are then corrected for guessing using equation (5.9) (see Section 5.9 for details).

(5.9) $$P'_{js} = \frac{3P_{js} - 1}{2}$$

If an observer just guesses, then there is a 1/3 probability that a correct response will be given. Thus the lower limit on the proportions is 1/3 and the upper limit is 1.00. Note that the corrected proportions, P'_{js}, are bounded by zero and one.

The corrected proportions from equation (5.9) can be used in calculating the psychometric function parameter estimates as described in Section 5.6.3.

5.7 Confidence Intervals on Estimates

Once the absolute threshold and the just-noticeable differences are estimated, a further consideration is the precision of these estimated values. A simple method is presented here based on the usual assumption that the observers' responses are drawn from a binomial distribution.

After the parameters α_s and β_s of either the Gaussian or Logistic models are estimated, the shape and location of the psychometric curve is considered known in relation to the "ness." For computing the confidence intervals on the proportions, we accept the estimated parameters as defining the psychometric curve. Once the upper and lower proportions, π_{upper} and π_{lower}, are determined, these are converted to "ness" scale values using the fitted psychometric model. Confidence intervals for any other proportion can also be determined using this method.

The usual approach is to solve the binomial distribution, given the number of "yes" responses and number of observations, for the probability p of the distribution (Bock and Jones, 1968). This is a little cumbersome, and a simpler method giving the exact confidence interval is available using the F-distribution (Sachs, 1984; Bock and Jones, 1968).

Let r = the number of "yes" responses, J = the number of observers, α = the tail probability or risk, and $F_{\gamma,\upsilon 1,\upsilon 2}$ the F distribution with tail probability γ and degrees of freedom $\upsilon 1$, $\upsilon 2$. Note that since the number of observers, J, is known, the number of correct responses, r, can be estimated for any specific proportion from the relation r = *proportion* times J. This enables confidence interval estimation for any proportion that results from integer r and J. The following equations (5.10) give the upper and lower proportions, π_{upper} and π_{lower}, as the $1\text{-}\gamma$ confidence intervals.

(5.10) $$\pi_{upper} = \frac{(r+1)F_{1-\frac{\alpha}{2},2(r+1),2(J-r)}}{J-r+(r+1)F_{1-\frac{\alpha}{2},2(r+1),2(J-r)}}$$

$$\pi_{lower} = \frac{r}{r+(J-r+1)F_{1-\frac{\alpha}{2},2(J-r+1),2r}}$$

Once π_{upper} and π_{lower} are determined from equations (5.10), the upper and lower confidence limits on the "ness" for the Gaussian model are determined by solving equation (5.5), $\Phi^{-1}(\pi_{upper}) = \alpha_s + \beta_s x_{upper}$, for x_{upper}, and solving $\Phi^{-1}(\pi_{lower}) = \alpha_s + \beta_s x_{lower}$, for x_{lower}. For the logistic model, the appropriate equations are, $ln[\pi_{upper}/(1 - \pi_{upper})] = \alpha_s + \beta_s x_{upper}$, for x_{upper}, and $ln[\pi_{lower}/(1 - \pi_{lower})] = \alpha_s + \beta_s x_{lower}$ for x_{lower}.

In all practical experiments, the number of observers, J, is a finite, usually small number. One significant consequence is that the proportions are quantized to values that are multiples of $1/J$. For example, if there are twenty observers, then the proportions can only have values that are increments of $1/20 = 0.05$. This means that when using equation (5.10) to estimate the confidence limits, the intervals are tied to the number of observers; J and r are integers. When computing the confidence intervals for the proportion of 0.75, the convention for a just-noticeable difference, it may not be possible to compute the confidence intervals for exactly 0.75. If, for example, only 19 observers were used in a study, then the proportions are quantized at $1/19 = 0.0526$ increments, and the closest values to the 0.75 proportion are $14/19 = 0.7368$ and $15/19 = 0.7895$. One could choose the closest proportion from which to compute the confidence limits: $14/19 = 0.7368$ in this case. Another possibility is to compute both the upper and lower confidence limits for the two closest values and then compute a weighted average, weighting according to the difference to the desired proportion.

5.8 Number of Observers

The number of observers and the confidence limits are two sides of the same coin. Knowing a threshold or a just-noticeable difference to high confidence, small error, requires a large number of observers. Alternatively, if the objective is to find the absolute threshold or just-noticeable difference of an individual observer (not a common situation in product development), the judgments are replicated about fifty to one hundred times by a single observer. For n samples this means $100n$ total judgments from one observer!

In practical cases, interest lies in the threshold or just-noticeable difference of a population–specifically, the population of customers. It may or may not be easy to obtain one hundred or so observers, so practicality dictates the actual number to be used in such studies.

The number of observers can be computed directly once one knows the desired confidence interval. However, this assumes that we know the precision on the proportions. The exact solution is to solve equations (5.10) for N, with π_{upper} and π_{lower} assumed known. This is tedious, so a good approximation is in order.

Using the normal approximation to the binomial distribution, a simple approximation can be developed for the number of observers, J, assuming a known confidence interval on the proportions, π, π_{upper} and π_{lower} (Sachs, 1984). This approximation is given in equation (5.11).

$$J \approx \frac{4z^2_{\alpha}\pi(1-\pi)}{(\pi_{upper} - \pi_{lower})^2} \quad (5.11)$$

In equation (5.11) z = the z-value from a table of the normal distribution, for 95% confidence, $z = 1.96$. This approximation is quite good for proportions around 0.50, the absolute threshold. At high and low proportions, equation (5.11) is not as accurate because of the poor approximation of the binomial distribution. The range of useful proportions for using equation (5.11) is about 0.20 to 0.80. In equation (5.11) the maximum value of J occurs when $\pi = 0.5$, and (5.11) reduces to $[z_\alpha/(\pi_{upper}-\pi_{lower})]^2$, a conservative estimate for J.

(5.12) $$J \approx \left(\frac{z_\alpha \sqrt{2\pi}}{\beta_s \Delta x}\right)^2$$

If the slope of the psychometric curve β_s, is known by some previous experiment, then the number of observers, J, can be estimated in terms of the confidence interval on the "ness," Δx. Equation (5.12) gives a conservative approximation for J.

Both equations (5.11) and (5.12) give observer estimates that are often higher than required. If a precise estimate of observers is required, the rough value can be fine tuned by substituting the computed value of J into equation (5.10) and estimating the confidence limits about the selected proportions. Iterating between equations (5.11) and (5.10) will improve the estimate of J.

5.9 Correcting for Observer Guessing

There is a distinction between the different variations of the method of constant stimuli or method of limits, and the standard method. The distinguishing feature is that the study administrator knows when the observer is "correct" in the standard method. Two ways for the study administrator to know if the observer makes the correct selection are to present the stimulus in a known spatial (or temporal) location, or present the stimulus with other stimuli that are "blanks." For threshold studies, the spatial location is common, while the "blank" method is more applicable to just-noticeable difference investigations. If the observer selects the wrong location or the blank, the study administrator knows the observer made an error. This construct enables a determination of observer error, guessing, and is called a two-alternative-forced-choice paradigm. This is contrasted with the typical method of limits and method of constant stimuli techniques that are "yes/no" methods and usually do not offer an estimate of observer error, or "guessing rate."

When observers cannot decide which sample to choose in the judgment task, they may guess. Observers may also be instructed to guess if they cannot readily determine which sample to choose. In fact, a guessing strategy that always selected the reference sample would lead to an erroneous 0.50 correct proportion.

In a threshold determination where there are no extraneous influences on the observer, one would expect the proportions of "yes I see the ness" to drop to zero when the "ness" reaches some small value, and climb to 1.00 when the "ness" reaches some high value. If in fact the proportion of "yes" responses *does not* drop to zero for very low "ness" values, it is an indication that the observer is resorting to guessing. In some situations the proportions of "yes" responses follow the expectation of the observer that the stimulus will appear.

One effect of guessing is that the proportion (probability) of correct responses estimated from the number of correct responses may not be accurate. This is a consequence of a forced-choice experiment. A simple correction for guessing can be made, as the following analysis illustrates (Frieden, 1983).

Let *P(correct)* = the probability of a correct decision, *P(correct | detects)* = the probability that the observer gives the correct response given that he detects a "ness" or a difference in the samples, *P(detects)* = the probability that the observer actually detects a "ness" or a difference, *P(correct | guesses)* = the probability that the observer gives the correct response given that he guesses there is a "ness" or a difference in the samples, and *P(guesses)* = the probability the observer guesses. The *P(correct)* is represented by equation(5.13).

$$P(correct) = P(correct|detects)P(detects) + P(correct|guesses)P(guesses) \tag{5.13}$$

It is reasonable to assume that if the observer detects a "ness" or a difference, a correct response will always follow, so *P(correct | detects)* = 1.00. Over many observations, it seems rational to suppose that, on average, the *P(correct | guesses)* = ½. One last assumption is that the observer always guesses when there is no detection of the difference, so *P(guesses)* = *1-P(detects)*. Substituting these assumptions into equation (5.13) and solving for the probability that the observer detects a difference between two samples or stimuli, yields equation (5.14).

$$P(detects) = p* = \frac{P(correct) - \frac{1}{2}}{1 - \frac{1}{2}} = 2P(correct) - 1 \tag{5.14}$$

This result can be generalized for M-choice methods, such as the three sample method, (M = 3) yielding equation (5.15).

$$P(detects) = p* = \frac{MP(correct) - 1}{M - 1} \tag{5.15}$$

The corrected probability values, p^*, given by equation (5.15) are used as the proportion values to estimate the parameters of the psychometric models described in Section 5.6.3.

In the practical application of the guessing correction, defined by equation (5.14), some problems arise. First, it is over many observations that the probability of a correct response given the presence of a "ness" is expected to be 0.50 *(P(correct | guesses) = 0.50)*. For any observer, the proportion can be greater or less than its expected value. Second, the above analysis assumes that the observer always guesses when there is no detection of the "ness" or a difference, so *P(guesses) = 1 - P(detects)*. For each decision or trial, the observer may not abide by this rule. Because these probabilities are in fact random variables, for any given experiment the computed *P(detects)*, according to equation (5.14), may be negative or greater than 1.00. Bock and Jones (1968) suggest that for *P(correct)* $\leq$ *1/M* the value *1/M* + *1/MJ* be substituted, where *J* = number of observers. For *P(correct)* > *1*, substitute *1 - 1/MJ*. These are somewhat arbitrary, but rational, substitutions in these situations.

A reasonable assumption for one observer is that their guessing strategy would be constant, and correcting the empirical proportions might be prudent if the experimental conditions allow. On the other hand, when using a group of observers, a realistic assumption is that their individual guessing strategies are highly variable and a correction for guessing is not needed.

Although the methods in this chapter are described in terms of a "yes/no" paradigm, recasting them into a two-alternative-forced-choice method is possible. By using space (location) or time to vary the display of the reference stimulus, the study administrator knows the correct answer, and can use the guessing model described here to correct the empirical proportions. These corrected proportions can then be used in the psychometric curve estimation procedures described in Section 5.6.3.

More sophisticated psychometric models with parameter estimation methods that include guessing and other factors, are available (Watson, 1979; Watson and Fitzhugh, 1990).

5.10 Imaging Thresholds and Just-Noticeable Differences

A limited amount of information exists in the literature on thresholds or just-noticeable differences for imaging "nesses." The lack of Visual Algorithms to be used in calculating the "nesses" is at the root of this paucity. Some work has been done, though, in the study of graininess thresholds in the context of a linear probabilty model (Engeldrum, 1998), and colorimetric tolerances for image reproduction (Stokes, Fairchild and Berns, 1992).

Generally, threshold and just-noticeable difference efforts have focused on physical image parameters. Threshold determinations are available for the following physical image parameters:

- Line and edge boundary variations (Hamerly and Springer, 1985).
- Sinusoidal reflectance variations, "banding" (Burningham, 1994).

A few physical image parameter just-noticeable differences have also been reported:

- Text character optical density, font line width, line boundary variation (Dvorak and Hamerly, 1983).
- Edge gradient extent, and line profiles extent (Hamerly and Dvorak, 1981).
- Uniform areas having line and random non-uniformities (Hamerly, 1983).
- Color granularity (Zwick and Brothers, 1975).

Additional work is needed in this area using both conventional methods, like the ones described here, and more sophisticated models of thresholds and just-noticeable difference such as signal detection theory. Both these paths will be enhanced when there are more of the Image Quality Circle components in place–notably Visual Algorithms.

5.11 Advanced Methods–Signal Detection Theory

The most significant criticism of the conventional threshold and just-noticeable difference methods, and indeed the whole threshold concept, is the empirical evidence showing that these values depend on an observer's criterion (Gescheider, 1997; Swets, 1996; Macmillian and Creelman, 1991; Baird and Noma, 1978).

Fortunately, a comprehensive theory accounts for an observer's criterion, guessing ("false alarms"), and other practical issues associated with thresholds and just-noticeable difference studies. It is called signal detection theory (theory of signal detection), and it was developed in the 1950s from ideas in the fields of communication, radar detection, and statistics. In fact, a basic notion of signal detection theory is equivalent to statistical hypothesis testing (Macmillian and Creelman, 1991).

Signal detection theory will not be covered in this text, simply because it is beyond our scope. There seem to be no reported applications of signal detection theory in the field of conventional imaging, although it has been applied to the assessment of medical imaging systems. Other obvious applications could include assessment of color differences, and criterion-free estimates of observer sensitivity to small changes in "nesses."

A good overview of the successful applications of signal detection theory in a number of diverse fields is provided by Swets (1996), a pioneer in the application to the field of psychology. Gescheider (1997) provides several highly readable introductory chapters on the topic. The most comprehensive reference on signal detection theory, in a scaling context, is the text by Macmillian and Creelman (1991).

Chapter 6

Ordinal Scaling

From the perspective of an observer, ordinal scaling studies are simple tasks, which may be why they are so widely used. However, it is often not appreciated that, without additional theoretical assumptions, ordinal scales only reveal the "greater-than" property of samples. In some applications, this greater-than property is sufficient and clearly warrants the use of these techniques. Unfortunately, for Image Quality Circle applications such as formulating Image Quality Models and Visual Algorithms, an ordinal scale will be found lacking, and an interval scale is a minimum requirement.

Among the most common ordinal scaling methods are the ranking method, the paired-comparison method, and category scaling.

6.1 Rank Order Method

Asking observers to rank samples is perhaps the simplest ordinal scaling method to administer. The observer is asked to rank the image samples in order, from best to worst, along an attribute defined by the instructions, such as text darkness. If there are n samples, where n can be quite large, then the ranks go from one to n, where n is usually assigned to the greatest amount of the attribute. The usual stratagem is to get rankings from J observers, assign a number to the ranks and calculate an average of the ranks. Recall that this scale only gives information about the sequence of image samples that have a greater amount of the "ness" than the preceding sample. In Chapter 9, we will show how these ranking data can be transformed into an interval scale by adding some additional theory.

6.1.1 Observer Instructions

This prototype for the rank order scaling method is modeled after Bartleson (1984). The observers' task is to arrange a series of samples in order of some "ness." This instruction prototype has the sample with the lowest "ness" on the left, and the highest "ness" on the right.

> "Here is a set of stimuli (samples). Please place them in order of how much ('...ness') they have. The sample with the smallest amount of ('...ness') is placed on the left and the

sample with the greatest amount of ('...ness') is placed on the right. You may move the samples around and rearrange them until you are satisfied that they are ordered from left to right according to ('...ness')."

Try these instructions in a pilot study before doing extensive word smithing.

6.1.2 Data Collection–Observer-by-Observer

Two possible methods for data collection for rank order scaling are available. Both methods generate the same scale values, but represent the data in two different ways.

Table 6.1 Illustration of data matrix, ***R***, from a ranking study

	Sample number				
Observer	1	2	3	...	n
1	3	1	n	...	6
2	2	3	n-1	...	5
3	3	1	n-2	...	6
...	...	...	...	...	...
J	4	1	n	...	7

The first option is to form a data matrix, ***R***, with a column representing each sample, numbered *1* to n in Table 6.1. Each row of this data matrix contains the responses of an observer (recorded as numbers from *1* to n), representing the rank of each sample, recorded in the column for that sample. Observers are identified in the first column, numbered *1* to J in our example. For each observer, we record the rank given by the observer for the stimuli identified by the column. For example, in Table 6.1, observer one ranked sample one in third position, sample two in first position, sample three in the nth position, and sample n in sixth position. The data matrix, ***R***, is of size J rows by n columns.

This method of data presentation is convenient for converting the ranking data into a proportion matrix, and is therefore the preferred method. Once the proportion matrix is available, other techniques can be used to generate an interval scale, as we will see in Chapter 9.

6.1.3 Analysis–Observer-by-Observer

The scale consists of the average rank of each sample and can be calculated by equation (6.1).

$$AvgRank_1 = \frac{1}{J}[1 \;\; 1 \;\; 1 \;\; \dots \;\; 1_J]\boldsymbol{R} \qquad (6.1)$$

The row vector of 1's in equation (6.1) is of length J. Equation (6.1) computes the column sum and divides the result by the number of observers, yielding the average rank for each stimulus or sample. The vector AvgRank_1 has length n, the number of image samples.

6.1.4 Data Collection–Histogram Method

The second method collects the data as a histogram matrix. As with the observer-by-observer method, the columns are the samples. With the histogram method, the rows are the ranks, *1* to n. Each cell of the data matrix, ***H***, contains the number of times the sample was judged to have the rank specified by the row, as shown in Table 6.2.

Table 6.2 Illustration of the histogram data matrix, ***H***, from a ranking study

	Sample number				
Sample Rank	1	2	3	...	n
1	10	0	0	...	6
2	31	2	0	...	1
3	27	27	1	...	5
...	...	...	...	...	...
r	0	1	5	...	0

Data matrix ***H*** should have as column sums the number of times each sample was ranked. For example, in the cell representing the rank of one for sample one (row one, column one), we find the entry

"10." Sample one was ranked number one by ten observers. The next row entry for sample one is "31," so sample one was ranked number two 31 times. The remainder of the table is filled out similarly.

6.1.5 Analysis–Histogram Method

The data matrix is in the form of a histogram, with a row for each rank, a column for each sample, with cells containing the frequency of rank selection. If each entry in the data matrix is divided by the number of times the sample was ranked, then we have an estimate of the probability of the sample being assigned the rank. The average rank for each sample is computed by multiplying this probability estimate by the rank and summing over all ranks. This can be computed from equation (6.2).

$$AvgRank_2 = \frac{1}{J}[1 \quad 2 \quad 3 \quad \ldots \quad n]\boldsymbol{H} \tag{6.2}$$

The row vector in equation (6.2) has the integer values of the ranks from *1* to n, and $\boldsymbol{H}$ is the n by n histogram matrix. The number of observers, J, divides the results to give the average rank as the scale value. Equation (6.2) is easily recognized as the expected value (average), of a scale of integer numbers (the ranks).

Recall that the ranks calculated by these two methods only possess the greater-than property of an ordinal scale. When observers rank samples, they do not produce an interval scale. No knowledge of the distance between the samples on the "ness" scale is available. In other words, the distance on the "ness" scale between an average rank of, say, 2.50 to 3.50 and 6.50 to 5.50 is generally not the same, in spite of what may be implied by the arithmetic. The only statement that can be made is that, on average, one sample is ranked higher or lower than another sample on the "ness" scale. No significance should be attributed to the fact that the average rank of two samples is, say, 3.56 and 3.58, and a second pair may have values 5.00 and 9.00. Conclusions for both pairs are the same; the samples with the average rank of 3.58 and 9.00 have a greater amount of the "ness" than the samples with the average rank of 3.56 and 5.00.

6.1.6 Variations

Instead of a straight rank order, other methods exist for having observers put samples in order of increasing or decreasing "ness." The next two variations are really computer-sorting algorithms performed by observers. The observer acts as the comparator and decides whether the sample has more or less of the "ness." Based on this decision, the observer moves the sample.

6.1.6.1 Human Bubble Sort

This is a version of the computer bubble sort. It is not efficient, because for n samples it can require of the observer, at most, n^2 comparisons. A set of 50 samples could require as many as 2,500 comparisons! Only the most dedicated observer will complete such a large task.

The method is as follows:

1) The study administrator randomly lays out the samples on a table from one to n.
2) The observer starts at the first or "left"-most position and compares samples one and two. If the samples are in increasing order of the "ness," or image quality, then the samples are left in order; otherwise they are reversed.
3) Next, the observer compares samples two and three. Again, if the samples are in increasing order of the "ness," or image quality, then the samples are left in order, otherwise they are reversed.
4) This process is repeated until the observer makes one pass through the n samples.
5) After the first pass the observer continually repeats the process until all n samples are rank ordered.

A variation of this is called the *insertion sort*, which is what a card player does when ordering the cards according to suit and rank within the suit. At worst, it still requires n^2 effort by the observer. However, this is conservative because human observers can see patterns and groups, and can arrange samples in groups larger than one.

If the observer is a "perfect comparator," then the samples are guaranteed to be in rank order according to the "ness." All the samples are visible and the observer has the ability to fine-tune the order.

Other computer-sorting algorithms can be used, such as Shell's sort or the very efficient heapsort (Press *et. al.*, 1986). However, these methods can result in a complex task for the observer, negating the advantage of the rank order data collection procedure.

Data is tabulated according to Table 6.1, and equation (6.1) is used to compute the average ranks.

6.1.6.2 Human Quick Sort

If physical space for laying out the samples is limited, and the number of samples is large, say 50 or more, then the human quick sort may be the answer. The idea is to sort a "pile" of samples into "high" and "low" piles of the "ness" or image quality. This is repeated for each pile the observer generates until the sort is reduced to one or two samples.

The method goes like this:

1) All the samples are given to the observer with the instructions to look through the "pile" to get an idea of the range of the "ness."
2) The observer then sorts the "pile" into a high1 "ness" pile and a low1 "ness" pile.

3) Next the observer sorts the high1 "pile" into a high2 "ness" pile and a low2 "ness" pile. This is followed by a sorting of the low1 "ness" pile into a high3 and low3 "ness" pile. This sorting is not unlike generating a binary tree.
4) The process is repeated until about four to eight samples remain in each pile. At this point, the observers simply rank order the remaining samples in each pile. All the rank orders of each pile are brought together for the rank order of all the samples.

One disadvantage of this method is the possible shift in the observer's criterion. Once the piles are generated the observer does not have convenient access to the samples in other piles to stabilize the criterion.

In large-sample and small-space scaling study environments, the advantages are quite compelling. Space is only needed for the piles, a small number, and the number of sorted piles is $log_2(n)$ at most. Such large sample numbers are rarely required, but when large numbers are essential, the human quick sort is recommended.

Data is tabulated according to Table 6.1, and equation (6.1) is used to compute the average ranks. This is the preferred method because the data can be used to develop a proportion matrix from which an interval scale can be computed. Chapter 9 describes this method.

6.2 Paired-Comparison Method

The technique of paired comparisons is attributed to Gustav Fechner, who described it in 1860 (Torgerson, 1956; David, 1988). Paired comparisons are rarely used for ordinal scale generation because the procedure is so time-consuming. The real utility of paired-comparison methodology is the ability to generate, with some additional theory, an interval scale from such data. Generating interval scales from paired-comparison data will be explored in detail in Chapter 8.

Suppose we have a set of n color image samples and we wish to scale their colorfulness. The samples are presented to an observer in pairs and the observer responds by selecting the sample that has the greatest amount of colorfulness. This pairwise presentation is repeated for all possible $n(n-1)/2$ pairs, the number of all possible combinations of n objects taken two at a time. For a few samples there are few pairs to be judged, but for, say, 20 samples, the number of judgments climbs rapidly to 190, a task that can become tiresome for the observer.

6.2.1 Observer Instructions

The observer's task is to choose one out of the two samples presented that has the characteristics the study administrator has focused on. For example, an observer may be directed to "Choose the sample that has more sharpness." Paired comparison is a method sometimes used where a preference question is asked; i.e., "Choose the one you prefer." To be sure a "ness" scale is created, the observer must be explicitly instructed to respond to the "ness." A question about preference only gives an answer to the observer's preference.

The following are some prototype observer instructions. The first one is used to gather a response about a "ness," and the second asks a preference question.

> "I will present to you pairs of stimuli (samples, pictures, images). Please tell me (select) which one of the pair has the greatest ('...ness,' image quality)."

> "I will present to you pairs of stimuli (samples, pictures, images). Please tell me (select) which one of the pair you prefer."

The Paired Comparison method can often be completely automated, where the observers' selection process is indicated by a mouse click or a keystroke on a computer keyboard. The exact phrasing in the observers' instructions should reflect the actual method of data collection.

6.2.2 Data Collection–Paired Comparison

Data is collected as a matrix, $\boldsymbol{F}$, with both columns and rows identified to represent each sample. If the observer selects sample j over i, $j>i$, we put a one in the jth column and the ith row of the data matrix $\boldsymbol{F}$. Following this procedure for J observers we can accumulate a data matrix that has in each location the number of times the sample in the jth column was chosen over the sample in the ith row.

6.2.3 Analysis–Paired Comparison

An average rank can be calculated from this data matrix, $\boldsymbol{F}$, by computing the column average given by the following formula, equation (6.3).

$$AvgRank_3 = \frac{1}{J}[1 \quad 1 \quad 1 \quad \dots \quad 1]\boldsymbol{F} \tag{6.3}$$

AvgRank$_3$ is a 1 by n vector that contains the average rank of the n samples. The row vector of ones is n elements in length, $\boldsymbol{F}$ is an n by n matrix, and J is the number of observers used to gather the paired-comparison data in $\boldsymbol{F}$.

If each element in the $\boldsymbol{F}$ matrix is divided by the number of observers who contributed to the datum, then the new matrix, $\boldsymbol{P}$, is an estimate of the proportion (probability) that the column stimulus was chosen over the row stimuli. This interpretation will be used in Chapter 8 to develop an interval scale from this proportion matrix.

6.3 Category Scaling

Although category data collection methods can produce interval scales, the most common data collection method used can only be guaranteed to yield an ordinal scale, so a brief description is appropriate here. Chapter 10 contains a comprehensive discussion of using category scaling methodology to generate interval scales.

6.3.1 Data Collection–Category Scales

Category scaling requires the observer to place samples in categories. These categories can be labeled with names like "good," "better," and "best," or with numbers (1 to 5), or names for ranks (first, second, third). Data is collected as a matrix, $\boldsymbol{K}$, with the n rows being the samples and the $m+1$ columns the categories. Each element in the $\boldsymbol{K}$ matrix is the frequency that the sample (row) was placed in the category (column). Each row of $\boldsymbol{K}$ is a histogram.

In a typical application of category scaling, the observer is instructed to make the categories equal intervals, the method of *equal-appearing intervals*. However, with this method observers tend to use each category equally often, independent of the distribution of the attribute in samples (Gescheider, 1985 and Guilford, 1954). Also, there is no way to decide, using this method, if the observer is following the "equal-interval" instructions. This can introduce scale distortion, in that the categories are assumed to have equal "width" on the "ness" dimension, but they may not. So the scale is ordinal at best.

Under some situations, observers can easily put samples in equal interval categories, and Bartleson (1984) gives an example of scaling colorfulness using color chips as stimuli. When observers can easily construct equal intervals, a direct interval scale is possible by computing the average category for the samples. This is only valid if the equal interval properties of the categories are confirmed. Details on using category scaling to generate interval scales can be found in Chapter 10, and it is highly recommended that the chapter be read before using this method.

6.3.2 Analysis–Category Scales

Generating a scale requires numbers for the categories. If categories are numbered, these may be used directly. For named categories, we need to assign arbitrary values, or weights, to the categories to compute an average.

(6.4) $$AvgCat = \frac{1}{J} K \,[1 \quad 2 \quad 3 \quad \ldots \quad m+1]^T$$

Usually the first category is given the value *1*, the second *2*, and so forth, up to $m+1$ categories. The scale consists of the average category of each sample and can be calculated by equation (6.4).

The row vector in equation (6.4) is of length $m+1$, the number of categories. Equation (6.4) computes the average category for each stimulus or sample. If the same number of observers did not judge all the samples, then each row should be divided by the $\boldsymbol{K}$ matrix row sum.

The vector of scale values (AvgCat), has length n (the number of image samples).

Worked examples of these ordinal scaling techniques can be found in the file `ordscal1.mcd` on the MathCad® disk.

Chapter 7

Direct Interval Scaling

Interval scaling can be put into two basic classifications: direct (or partition) scaling, and confusion (or indirect) scaling (Stevens, 1960). The appropriate choice of the technique for any given scaling study depends on the characteristics of the samples, or stimuli, to be scaled. The key criterion is how "close together" the levels of the attributes, or "nesses" are in the sample set.

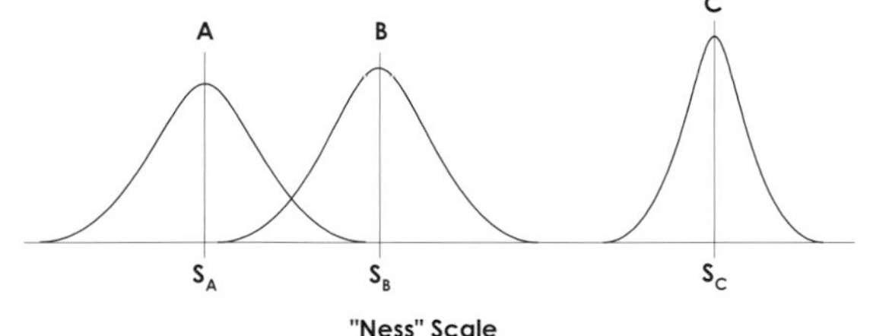

Figure 7.1 Discriminal Dispersions for Three Samples.

Figure 7.1 illustrates three hypothetical distributions representing "ness" judgments of many observers for three samples, A, B, and C. The mean value of each distribution, S_A, S_B, or S_C, is the psychometric or scale value of the "ness." The width or standard deviation of these distributions, the *discriminal dispersion* as Thurstone (1927) called it, describes the variation in responses by the observers.

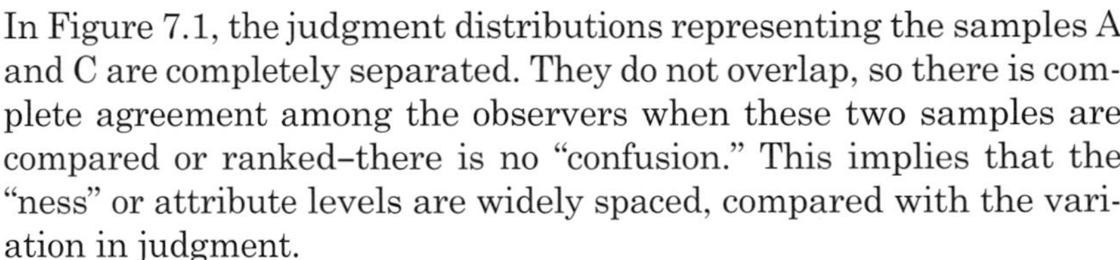

In Figure 7.1, the judgment distributions representing the samples A and C are completely separated. They do not overlap, so there is complete agreement among the observers when these two samples are compared or ranked–there is no "confusion." This implies that the "ness" or attribute levels are widely spaced, compared with the variation in judgment.

Using *indirect interval scaling*, with wide spacing of distributions and therefore no confusion or overlapping of distributions for adjacent samples, the theoretical challenge is to decide exactly where on the "ness" dimension the samples lie.

The distributions representing samples A and B in Figure 7.1 display a level of "confusion" between the two samples. Since the distributions overlap, observers do not universally agree on the scale values. S_B, the mean scale value from sample B, is greater than S_A, the mean scale value for sample A. However, the overlapping tails of the distributions suggest that in some small fraction of judgments, the sample A would have been judged to have more of the "ness" than sample B.

Thurstonc's Law of Comparative Judgment, covered in Chapters 8 and 9, provides a theoretical foundation for accommodating such confusion when generating interval scales. If the samples possess only small differences in the "ness" and there is much confusion in the judgments, the paired-comparison data collection method combined with the Law of Comparative Judgment is preferred to direct interval scaling. In situations where no confusion exists among the samples, there are two reasons for not using confusion-based scaling methods. The first reason is the fact that the paired comparison data collection method is very inefficient in the number of judgments required of the observer. Secondly, with no confusion among samples, scale values cannot be determined. A better approach would be to use one of the direct interval scaling techniques described below.

7.1 Graphical Rating Scale Method–With Anchors

The underlying concept of the graphical rating scale method requires the observer to equate a physical distance to the distance between samples on the "ness" scale. Numerous experiments have demonstrated that over short distances, observers use physical distance to express a distance on a "ness" dimension. (See Chapter 11 on Ratio Scaling for more applications of this interesting property.) Two methods of this technique–the line and the ruler–are in wide use (Bartleson, 1984; Zwick, 1984; Jones and McManus, 1986).

7.1.1 Line

In one technique, the observer is given a card with a line of about 5" to 6" in length. At the ends of the line there are adjectives describing the amount or strength of the "ness." For example, at the left end of the line there might be a label, "No graininess," and at the right end the label might read, "Very extreme graininess." The task for the observer is to indicate, by a mark on the line, the amount of the attribute in each sample. Physical distance on the line is taken as the distance of the stimuli on the attribute or "ness" scale. The end-point adjectives can be thought of as anchors in that they provide two reference points. Lines on cards are not essential to this method; any convenient method of collecting distance, such as the movement of a cursor on a computer screen over a distance selected by the observer, would be equally acceptable.

7.1.2 Data Reduction–Line

Data reduction for this method consists of computing the average distance of the mark on the line for each sample. The distance can be referenced from the end of the line and then normalized relative to the length of the line or any other convenient distance increment. Normalizing relative to the length of the line is permissible because the interval scale is "floating" with respect to an additive constant and a multiplication factor. Formally, the data is tabulated in a J by n matrix, $\boldsymbol{D}$, where the columns are the samples, and the rows are the observers. A row vector, *1* by J, of 1's multiplies the data matrix. The sum or average of the columns provides an interval scale value for each sample, as shown in equation (7.1).

$$S = \frac{1}{J}[1 \quad 1 \quad 1 \quad \ldots \quad 1_J]\boldsymbol{D} \tag{7.1}$$

The disadvantages of this technique are the time-consuming sequential presentation of each stimulus, and the possibility of the criterion for judgment shifting during the data collection session.

7.1.3 Ruler

A variation of the graphical rating scale method with anchors is to use a large ruler, 4 feet to 5 feet in length, with tick marks along the ruler (Engeldrum, 1991; Engeldrum and McNeill, 1985). A tape measure may also be used. The ruler may or may not have numerals at appropriate intervals, but a numbered ruler makes data collection somewhat easier. At intervals of say 15% and 85% of the full length, are placed reference samples called anchors. These samples, usually drawn from the sample set, are the approximate "best" and "worst" samples. By placing the anchors at 15% and 85% of the ruler ends, the observers are allowed to make judgments greater and lesser than the anchor values, if they so desire. Often the best and worst samples are obvious, but not always. To eliminate the possibility of unintended bias in the selection of anchors, a small-scale ranking study can be conducted. The samples that are consistently ranked the lowest and highest by observers should be selected as anchors. Do not be overly concerned about correct selection. By not placing the anchors at the ends of the ruler, provision is made for any observer that may not agree with the anchor selection.

Each observer is asked to place the sample on the ruler, varying the distance according to the amount of the "ness" it has compared with the reference or anchor samples. The task can become unwieldy if there is a large number of samples, but experience suggests that a set of 20 to 25 samples on a large ruler is workable. This technique allows the observer to see all the samples simultaneously, and untrained observers seem to have little difficulty.

7.1.4 Data Reduction–Ruler

The generation of scale values uses the same equation used for the line technique, equation (7.1). The column means produce scale values directly. Besides the column mean, the column variance can also be computed from the data matrix.

These two parameters, combined with standard statistical techniques, can be used to assess the precision of the scale values and the significant differences between the samples. See Klockars and Sax (1986) and Toothaker (1993) for some important statistical considerations when comparing the scale values.

7.1.5 Observer Instructions

Prototype observer instructions for the graphical rating scale method using a ruler with anchors follow. Notice the instruction at the end reinforcing the idea that this is not a test and that the observer's opinion on the samples is what is wanted.

> "In front of you is a scale (ruler) with values from (X) to (Y) that will be used to determine your ratings of (...'ness,' image quality). [Two samples have already been placed next to the scale at values (A) and (B). These are reference points.] A higher number on the scale indicates more (...'ness,' image quality). Please place the samples on the ruler so the distance between the samples on theortional to the difference in the (...'ness,' image quality). If two or more samples have the same (...'ness,' image quality) place them above the other(s). There are no right or wrong answers. We are seeking your opinion."

If there are no references, or anchors, eliminate the two sentences within the brackets, [ ], from the instructions.

Instructions for a graphical rating scale using marks on a reference line to indicate the judgments follow (Bartleson, 1984):

> "You will be shown each, in turn, of a series of colored samples. We would like to know how much colorful('ness') each of these samples has. A paper will accompany each sample. The paper contains a line running from 'No Colorfulness' to 'Very Colorful.' Please use the pencil that you will be given to place a mark on the line at the position where you think the colorfulness of the sample belongs. You may place marks at the ends of the line but not off the line beyond the ends."

For a computer-controlled data collection procedure where a "slider" is used as an indicator, change the pencil and paper references.

7.2 Graphical Rating Scale Method–No Anchors

Sometimes using anchors with the graphical rating scale method is either impractical or inconvenient. Anchors require two samples, usually drawn from the sample set, which may not be available. One must also be concerned that arbitrarily selecting the anchors, essentially fixing the scale between the anchors, may inadvertently bias the results. For these and possibly other reasons, forgoing the use of anchors may be desirable in some instances.

The no-anchor method is identical to the line-and-ruler methods, except there are no references or anchors of any form: either visual, verbal, or printed words. If anchors are not used, then there is no guarantee that each observer will use the line, or ruler, the same way. For example, they may not use the full length of ruler or place the samples on the same portion of the ruler.

The consequence of observers using the scale any way they wish is that each observer's ratings are on a "rubber band" with respect to every other observer's ratings, and the rubber band may be shifted about some origin. To be sure, the rubber band is finitely expanded or contracted, but nonetheless the section of the ruler used by each observer is different. An interval scale has two arbitrary constants, a multiplier and some additive constant, so this effect does not violate the interval scale assumptions. Without some accounting for this rubber band effect, the variance of the scale value calculated over all observers can be expected to be larger than the "with anchors" case.

7.2.1 Data Analysis–No Anchors

The solution to the rubber band effect to is to put each observer on a common scale after data collection; in essence, we expand or contract and relocate the rubber band for each observer so they all coincide. Two common methods to accomplish this normalization of observers are available.

The best-known method is to compute the mean and variance of the rating scale values of each observer for all the samples. The variance or its square root, the standard deviation, is a measure of spread, or how much of the total ruler the observer used. A centering value for the observers' ratings is the mean rating scale value that is an estimator of the central location of the scale for each observer. If the rating data is organized as a matrix with the rows as observers and the columns representing the samples, these calculations are performed for each row or observer. With the standard deviation as the estimate of the length of the ruler the observer used, and the mean as the estimate of what part of the ruler was used, we can adjust the data to a common rating scale for each observer. This can be accomplished by subtracting the mean value from each observer's rating and dividing the result by the observer's rating scale standard deviation. In this way all observers have a mean scale value of zero and a spread, standard deviation, of unity. The calculations are given in equation (7.2), where $\boldsymbol{A}$ is the normalized rating data, $\boldsymbol{D}$ is the raw rating data matrix, $mean_i$ is the row mean and $std.\ dev_i$ is the row standard deviation. Interval scale values can now be calculated using equation (7.1).

$$A_{ij} = \frac{D_{ij} - mean_i}{std.\,dev._i} \tag{7.2}$$

A second method for data adjustment uses a linear transform for each observer that adjusts each observer's raw data so that, on average, it is equal to the group average. The first step is to calculate the column means of the $\boldsymbol{D}$ matrix using equation (7.1), which gives a set of group average scale values. The next step is to find the slope and intercept of a linear equation that can be used to adjust each observer's raw data so that it equals the average scale value (determined in the first step), in a least squares sense. If we have J observers, we need J pairs of slopes and intercepts, one for each observer. Here we treat the group mean scale values as dependent variables and each observer's set of ratings as the independent variable. If we let b_{0i} and b_{1i} be the intercept and the slope of the linear transform for the ith observer, then the adjusted rating data matrix, $\boldsymbol{A}$, is calculated according to equation (7.3). The column means of the adjusted matrix $\boldsymbol{A}$ can be computed, according to equation (7.1) to yield the scale values of the samples.

$$A_{ij} = b_{0i} + b_{1i} D_{ij} \tag{7.3}$$

Frequently, the normalizing techniques described above will reduce the estimated standard deviation of a sample scale value. Of course, within any given sample set some scale values may have an increased standard deviation. Also, in any given scaling study, the reductions in the standard deviations or variances of the scale values using any of the above normalizations may not all be statistically significant. Reduction in the scale value standard deviation is important if scale values are used as response variables in a statistically designed experiment, or if statistical conclusions must be drawn regarding scale value differences.

MathCad® sheet `grs1.mcd` implements the methods described by equations (7.1-7.3).

Chapter 8

Indirect Interval Scaling–Case V and Paired Comparison

The previous chapter described methods in which the observer is asked to estimate the amount of a "ness" or image quality attribute and equate that estimate with distance. In this sense, the observer gives a direct estimate of the "ness" scale value. Although indirect scaling may be simpler in data collection, it is more complicated in data analysis and requires additional theory or models for scale generation.

We start the topic of indirect scaling with the well-known and widely used technique of paired comparisons. The psychological theory for converting paired-comparison data to an interval scale has been around for nearly a century, but is often a confusing method to new users. The method of data collection using paired comparisons was mentioned briefly in Chapter 6, which covers ordinal scaling methods. As described in Chapter 6, using a proportion data matrix without additional theory limits paired comparison to ordinal scaling.

This chapter provides a descriptive approach to the method of paired comparison combined with Thurstone's Law of Comparative Judgment to generate an interval scale. A more comprehensive treatment of the paired-comparison method is given by David (1988) and Bock and Jones (1968). Some statistical tests of significance for paired-comparison data are described by Starks and David (1961, 1988).

8.1 Paired-Comparison Data Collection Method

We introduced this data collection method in Chapter 6 on ordinal methods, but for clarity the method is repeated here.

The basic method of paired comparisons consists of sequentially presenting pairs of samples to an observer and asking the observer which one of the pair has the greatest amount of the "ness." If, upon presentation of a pair of samples, the observer selects sample j over i,

$j>i$, as having more of the attribute or "ness" in question, we put a *1* in the jth column and the ith row of the data matrix.

Using all of the J observers, we accumulate a data matrix, the frequency matrix, $\boldsymbol{F}$, that has in each location of the matrix the number of times the sample in the jth column was chosen over the sample in the ith row.

The next step is to form the proportion matrix, $\boldsymbol{P}$, by dividing each element by the number of observers that judged the pair. If all the observers did not judge each pair, then the proportions can be determined from the frequency matrix by the relationship: $p_{ij} = f_{ij}/(f_{ij}+f_{ji})$. Most often, J observers will judge all pairs, so all the frequency data matrix elements are divided by J to calculate the proportion. Only the upper or lower triangle above or below the diagonal of the proportion matrix needs to be calculated. This is because the proportions always sum to unity, $p_{ij} + p_{ji} = 1$, and so either half can be computed from the other. This proportion matrix, $\boldsymbol{P}$, is the starting point for one of several models used to generate an interval scale value.

8.2 Thurstone's Law of Comparative Judgment

Leon Lewis Thurstone was a notable psychophysicist in the first half of the 20th century. Interestingly, like Gustav Fechner, the physicist-turned psychologist, Thurstone started his career as an engineer (Stevens, 1959). In his now-classic 1927 paper (Thurstone, 1927) he formalized a model for the judgment process, enumerated different cases of the model, and identified the assumptions needed for determining scale values.

Imagine one observer repeatedly comparing a set of samples on some "ness" dimension, psychological dimension or the *psychological continuum*, as Thurstone (1927) called it. For various reasons, an observer may vary his or her response for the same two samples, resulting in a distribution of responses like those illustrated in Figure 7.1 of the previous chapter. In the years since Thurstone's work, the vocabulary used in judgment theory has changed. Thurstone called the process by which we make judgments of samples the *discriminal process*. In today's nomenclature, we call the discriminal process a random variable (Luce, 1994). (It is also possible to consider Thurstone's discriminal processes as analogous to the membership functions of fuzzy logic theory.)

Thurstone (1927) assumed that the discriminal process was a random variable whose probability density function follows a Gaussian or normal function on the psychological continuum or "ness" scale. Since Thurstone expressed the scale in terms of the probability density function, the mean value of the probability density function is the scale value. Thurstone called the standard deviation, σ, or spread of the observers' responses, the *discriminal dispersion*. Today we would say that the discriminal dispersion is just the standard deviation of the responses.

The problem for which Thurstone provided the model was the generation of the scale values of the samples from the proportion matrix, ***P***, which is experimentally determined via the paired-comparison technique. Thurstone observed that the proportion of times that stimulus A was judged greater than B, A>B, was an *indirect* measure of the distance on the "ness" scale between A and B. From statistical theory, the average, or expected value, of the difference of two random variables is just the difference in the expected values. This result is independent of the distribution of the discriminal process. For samples A and B, the average value is just the difference in the scale values, S_A-S_B.

(8.1) $$z_{A-B} = \frac{S_A - S_B}{\sqrt{\sigma^2{}_A + \sigma^2{}_B - 2\rho\sigma_A\sigma_B}}$$

The square of the standard deviation of the probability density function describing the difference between the two samples, the variance, $\sigma^2_{A\text{-}B}$, is well known and is given by: $\sigma^2_{A\text{-}B} = \sigma^2_A + \sigma^2_B - 2\rho\sigma_A\sigma_B$, where ρ is the correlation between stimuli A and B and has values that range from *-1* to *+1*. The difference in the mean scale values can be normalized by dividing by the standard deviation, giving results in terms of well-known z-values. Equation (8.1) formalizes this result.

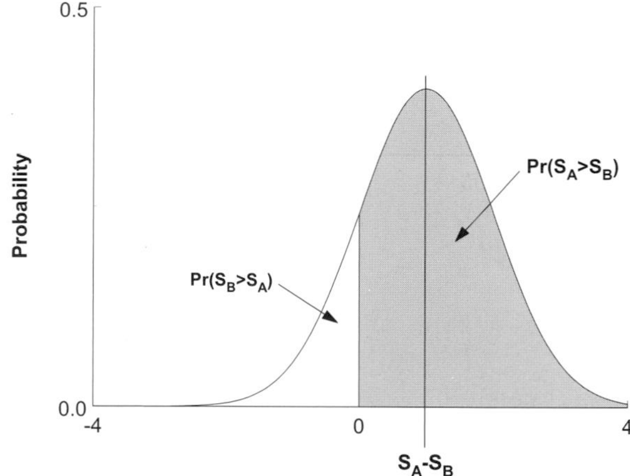

Figure 8.1 The shaded area shows the proportion of time that sample A is chosen over sample B; Pr($S_A > S_B$). The unshaded area is equal to the fraction of time sample B is chosen over sample A; Pr($S_B > S_A$).

Thurstone's assumption that the discriminal difference follows a normal or Gaussian distribution lets us use the shaded area in Figure 8.1 to describe the relationship between the experimentally determined proportion, or the probability of S_A preferred to S_B, and the difference in the scale values. This is formally given by equation (8.2).

(8.2) $$P(S_A > S_B) = \frac{1}{\sigma_{A-B}\sqrt{2\pi}} \int_0^{+\infty} e^{-\frac{1}{2}\left(\frac{t-(S_A-S_B)}{\sqrt{\sigma^2{}_A+\sigma^2{}_B-2\rho\sigma_A\sigma_B}}\right)}$$

Equation (8.2) establishes a relationship between the empirical proportions, or probability, and the parameters of the scale difference, $\Delta S = S_A\text{-}S_B$, probability density function. Substituting equation (8.1) into (8.2) and changing the variable of integration will be convenient for later work. This yields equation (8.3).

(8.3) $$P(S_A > S_B) = \frac{1}{\sqrt{2\pi}} \int_{-(S_A-S_B)}^{+\infty} e^{-\frac{t^2}{2}}\, dt$$

Given the experimentally determined proportion for each element in the ***P*** matrix, we need to determine the differences in scale value, S_A-S_B that satisfy equation (8.2). Using equation (8.1), Thurstone developed an expression for the scale value difference in terms of z-values, the variances and the correlation coefficient. This model is shown in equation (8.4).

(8.4) $$S_A - S_B = z_{A-B}\sqrt{\sigma^2{}_A + \sigma^2{}_B - 2\rho\sigma_A\sigma_B}$$

Thurstone's complete Law of Comparative Judgment is defined by equation (8.4), but there is no known general solution. To solve the problem, some simplifying assumptions about the sample variances and the correlation coefficient must be made. Thurstone organized the assumptions into five cases that are summarized in Table 8.1. Cases I and II are virtually identical, and require knowledge of all the parameters in equation (8.4) for a solution. Case III makes the simplifying assumption that the correlation between the observers' responses is zero. Case IV assumes that the variances for the two discriminal processes, σ^2_A and σ^2_B, are approximately equal. This assumption reduces the problem of finding the scale values to a linear problem that has a solution described later. A Case IV solution gives both the scale values and the discriminal dispersions. Case V, by far the most widely applied, uses the assumptions of Case IV plus

Table 8.1 Thurstone's Six Cases of the Law of Comparative Judgment

Case	Correlation Coefficient	Discriminal Dispersions	Model Equation
I - Replication over trials for single observer	$0 \le \rho \le +1$	$\sigma^2_A \ne \sigma^2_B$	$S_A - S_B = z_{A-B}\sqrt{\sigma^2_A + \sigma^2_B - 2\rho\sigma_A\sigma_B}$
II - Replication over observers	$0 \le \rho \le +1$	$\sigma^2_A \ne \sigma^2_B$	$S_A - S_B = z_{A-B}\sqrt{\sigma^2_A + \sigma^2_B - 2\rho\sigma_A\sigma_B}$
III	$\rho = 0$	$\sigma^2_A \ne \sigma^2_B$	$S_A - S_B = z_{A-B}\sqrt{\sigma^2_A + \sigma^2_B}$
IV	$\rho = 0$	$\sigma^2_A \approx \sigma^2_B$	$S_A - S_B = \frac{z_{A-B}}{\sqrt{2}}(\sigma_A + \sigma_B)$
V	$\rho = 0$	$\sigma^2_A = \sigma^2_B$	$S_A - S_B = z_{A-B}\sigma\sqrt{2}$
Va	$\rho = k$	$\sigma^2_A = \sigma^2_B$	$S_A - S_B = z_{A-B}\sigma\sqrt{2(1-k)}$
VI	$\rho = 0$	$\sigma_A = a + bS_A$ $\sigma_B = a + bS_B$	$\ln(S_A) - \ln(S_B) = z_{A-B}$

the added supposition that the two variances are indeed equal. Case V enables the practical application of the Law of Comparative Judgment.

In 1951 Mosteller (1951a) showed that assuming a correlation of zero is not necessary for Case V, only that it is a constant. This less-restrictive assumption is often called Thurstone's Case Va. No particular distinction is made, in practice, between Case V and Case Va. The reason is that both cases describe a scale value with an arbitrary unknown multiplier, so it is practically impossible to distinguish between them.

Later, Stevens (1959) added what he called Case VI. In Case VI, the standard deviations are assumed to be proportional to the scale values, and the correlation between the sample scale values is assumed to be zero. Under Case VI assumptions, the discriminal dispersion is now assumed to be the lognormal distribution, which results in a scale that is linear on a logarithmic basis. Another interpretation is that the empirical proportions are related to a ratio of the scale values, and are therefore equivalent to the differences in logarithms (Helm, Messick and Tucker, 1961).

There are few reported uses of Case VI, but in at least one instance it has been shown superior to Case V (Jones, 1967). The solutions are identical to Case V where the scale value is now logarithmic, not linear. No *a priori* reason exists to know or assume that the "ness" scale is logarithmic, and there are no external criteria to help in invoking the Case VI assumptions for practical scaling applications. However, when developing visual algorithms, it might prove useful to consider the "ness" scale to be logarithmic.

The parameter assumptions and model equations for the six cases of the Law of Comparative Judgment are summarized in Table 8.1. The most practical and useful cases of the Law of Comparative Judgment are Case IV, V, Va. In this chapter, we will focus mostly on Case V, leaving the other cases for Chapter 9.

Scale values generated using Thurstone's Law of Comparative Judgment are interval scales, and they can be multiplied by an arbitrary constant. It is common practice when using Case V and Va to assume that all the multipliers of the z-value in the right-hand column of Table 8.1 equal unity. Still, this is an arbitrary scale factor, which can be adjusted according to the use of the scale.

8.2.1 Case V Solution

Case V of the Law of Comparative Judgment is most extensively used because the scale values can easily be determined from the proportion matrix using the paired-comparison data collection method. In describing this solution for the scale values, a general approach is taken that will lay a foundation for introducing and applying non-Gaussian discriminal dispersions.

(8.5) $$S_A - S_B = z_{A-B}\sigma\sqrt{2}$$

The model equation for Case V, from Table 8.1, shows that the scale value difference, S_A-S_B, is equal to the standard normal z-value times a constant according to equation (8.5).

(8.6) $$P(A > B) = H(S_A - S_B)$$

(8.7) $$S_A - S_B = H^{-1}[P(A > B)]$$

Recall that the empirical proportion is used as the estimate of the probability of one sample selected over the other sample. This is formally stated in equation (8.6) where P(A>B) is the probability that sample A being chosen over B, S_A and S_B are the scale values, and *H( )* is the cumulative density function that transforms the scale differences into probabilities. In principle we can invert equation (8.6) and solve for the differences in the scale values using equation (8.7).

Usually, *H( )* can be any suitable cumulative probability density function. Different *H( )* functions represent different models of the judgment process, some of which will be described in the next chapter. Note that the inverse function in equation (8.7) is equal to the unit-normal z-values of equation (8.4), where we have set the parameter σ times the square root of two equal to unity. In practice one can use a table, a spreadsheet, or another means of calculating the z-values for a unit-normal distribution.

Sometimes the experimental proportions are either one or zero; in fact if a one exists in the proportion matrix, a corresponding zero also exists, so there is always an even number of ones and zeros. For these cases, the scale values of the differencalues, take on values of $\pm\infty$ and are not suitable for scale computation. Right now this can be ignored, since we will assume no unanimous agreement. However, this and other practical problems will be explored more fully later in this chapter.

$$S = \begin{bmatrix} S_1 - S_1 & S_2 - S_1 & \dots & S_n - S_1 \\ S_1 - S_2 & S_2 - S_2 & \dots & S_n - S_2 \\ S_1 - S_3 & S_2 - S_3 & \dots & S_n - S_3 \\ \vdots & \vdots & \dots & \\ S_1 - S_n & S_2 - S_n & \cdots & S_n - S_n \end{bmatrix} \tag{8.8}$$

After using the inverse of equation (8.3), to transform each element in the ***P*** matrix, we have a matrix, ***S***, of scale value differences, as illustrated in equation (8.8). The actual numerical values in the matrix are the z-values, but we use the scale value difference to illustrate the Case V solution clearly.

The least squares solution for the scale values for Case V can readily be determined from the column sums and some auxiliary assumptions (Mosteller, 1951; Noether, 1960). Note that the sum of the first column of the ***S*** matrix divided by the number of samples is $\frac{1}{n}\sum_{i=1}^{n}(S_1 - S_i) = (S_1 - \overline{S})$. If we set the arbitrary constant of the scale so that the average of all the scale values is zero, $\overline{S} = 0$, then the column sums give the scale values directly; S_1 - 0 = S_1. According to Noether (Noether, 1960), this least squares solution is independent of the function, *H( )*, used to transform the proportion data to scale value difference data. Note also that the row sums yield an inverted but valid scale that is the negative of the scale values when summing over columns.

Case V assumptions–namely zero correlation between the samples and equal variance or discriminal dispersions–are not as limiting as they would appear. Mosteller (1951b) has shown that if the discriminal dispersions or variances are constant except for some samples, then the samples that follow the assumptions will be correctly spaced; the violators will not. It is difficult to know, *a priori*, which samples have different discriminal dispersions, but at least the other scale values are not affected by these deviant samples.

The MathCad® sheet that illustrates the Case V solution of Thurstone's Law of Comparative Judgment can be found in file `pc1.mcd`.

8.2.2 Test of the Law of Comparative Judgment

To guard against a situation where the Case V model is inadequate due to unequal variances and the possibility that the correlation coefficient is not zero, Mosteller (1951c) proposed a chi-square test on an arcsine transformation of the reconstructed matrix of proportions. The arcsine transformation changes the proportions into normal deviates, assuming many observers, that has a mean value of zero and a constant variance of *1/J*. The following formulation of Mosteller's test is by David (1988):

$$\hat{z}_{ij} = S_i - S_j \tag{8.9}$$

1) Form the estimate of the ***Z*** matrix from the scale values, *S*, according to equation (8.9). If the scale values have been multiplied by a factor and a constant has been added, they must be transformed back to the original z-values before computing the elements of the ***Z*** matrix.
2) Convert the z_{ij} to probabilities, p'_{ij}, using a table of normal deviates, equation (8.3).These proportions are what is expected if the Case V model is correct.

3) Transform both measured proportions, p_{ij}, and the computed proportions, p'_{ij}, to an angle in radians, θ_{ij} and θ'_{ij}, using the arcsine transformation given by equation (8.10). This is a well-known transformation that converts the binomially distributed proportion to an asymptotically normal (Gaussian) random variable, $N(\theta, 1/J)$, for large J (Wilks, 1962).

(8.10) $$\theta'_{ij} = \sin^{-1}(2p'_{ij} - 1)$$

4) Form the χ^2 variable according to equation (8.11), where J = the number of observers or replications.

(8.11) $$\chi^2 = J\sum_{i<j}(\theta_{ij} - \theta'_{ij})^2$$

The degrees of freedom, df, for the χ^2 test are: $df = (n-1)(n-2)/2$, where n = the number of samples.

Mosteller (1951c) reports that when using this chi-square test there may be a tendency to accept the hypothesis that the model fits the data, when the hypothesis should be rejected. In other words, the model often appears better than it really is. Bock (1958), and Bock and Jones (1968) have suggested that this is due to the inherent correlation in the observers' responses because there are common samples in the scale value estimate. Such correlation in observers' responses is a statistical sampling issue and should not be confused with the correlation of the discriminal dispersions of Thurstone's Law of Comparative Judgment. The solution proposed by Bock (1958, 1968) is to "correct" the χ^2 value according to equation (8.12).

(8.12) $$\chi^2_{corr} = \frac{\chi^2}{1-2\rho}$$

A major practical difficulty arises because the value of ρ is generally unknown. However, in Bock's analysis (1958, 1968), the value of the correlation coefficient, ρ, was shown to vary from a maximum of one-third for scale estimates with a common sample, to a minimum of zero for scale estimates with no common sample. These two bounds enable some approximate model testing, but an area of indecision remains. Note that by substituting $\rho = 1/3$ and $\rho = 0$ into equation (8.12), the two values of χ^2_{corr} become $3\chi^2$ and χ^2. If the adjusted χ^2_{corr} is not significant when assuming $\rho = 1/3$, $\chi^2_{corr} = 3\chi^2$, then one can reasonably assume that the Case V model represents the data. Alternatively, if the unadjusted χ^2 is significant, then the model does not fit the data. When the correlation coefficient lies between zero and one-third, the situation is more complex, and the interested reader can see Bock (1968) for more information.

Note that it is the angular transformation of the proportion that leads to equation (8.12), not the Gaussian model underlying Thurstone's Case V. Using the revised χ^2 test of equation (8.12) for the Gaussian model, or any of the models described in the next chapter, should not cause any serious errors providing the proportions lie within the range of 0.05 to 0.95.

Failure of Thurstone's Case Va or V model can have several causes. A basic assumption of this model is that the "ness" being scaled is unidimensional and lies along one psychological dimension. Circular triads or intransitivity may suggest that the unidimensional assumption is not correct. A *circular triad* is a logical inconsistency in an observer's ordering of the samples. For example, if an observer prefers A over B and B over C, logically A should be preferred over C. If this logical ordering does not occur, it is called a circular triad. Scaling study administrators should take such inconsistencies as clues that the attribute may not be unidimensional. Statistical tests of significance for the number of triads can be found in Kendall and Gibbons (1990). Be aware, though, that observing a few circular triads does not necessarily suggest lack of unidimensionality. Depending on the particulars, that is, the mean and standard deviation of the discriminal process, there may be a non-zero probability that a circular triad should occur.

The Case V model can fail if the assumption of equal discriminal dispersions is inappropriate, in which case the use of Case IV may be more appropriate. Case IV requires the estimation of both the scale value and discriminal dispersion for each sample, and a different scale estimation procedure must be used. Using Case IV as a model has not been popular, possibly because of the extensive computations–which will be described in Chapter 9–and lack of awareness that a reasonably simple solution exists.

The calculations for Case V of the Law of Comparative Judgment, along with Mosteller's χ^2 test of proportions, can be found in the MathCad® file `pc1.mcd`

8.2.3 Confidence Interval and Sample Size

Bock (1968) proposed a confidence interval for the *difference* between two scale values, ΔS, based upon the arcsine transform, equation (8.10), and the limiting, large n, normal (Gaussian) distribution. This critical difference can be computed according to equation (8.13).

$$\Delta S = z_{1-\alpha/2}\sqrt{2\left[\frac{1+\rho(n-2)}{nJ}\right]} \tag{8.13}$$

Here z is the *(1-α/2)* value from the table of normal probabilities, n is the number of samples, J is the number of observers and ρ is the correlation coefficient, $0 \le \rho \le 1/3$. Equation (8.13) can be solved for J, the number of observers, in terms of the confidence interval z-value, the difference between two scale values, ΔS, and the number of samples, n. The solution for the number of observers is given by equation (8.14), where a value of $\rho = 1/3$ is used to give an upper bound value for J.

$$J = \frac{2}{3}\left(\frac{z}{\Delta S}\right)^2\left(\frac{n+1}{n}\right) \tag{8.14}$$

This method can be used to decide, for example, how many observers are needed to achieve a 95% confidence interval in the difference of two sharpness scale values of, say, 0.25. Assume the number of samples, n, is *7* and a 0.95 confidence interval is desired: $(1-\alpha) = 0.95$ and therefore $\alpha = 0.05$. The z-value from a table of normal probabilities can be determined by looking for the z-value that gives a probability of $(1-\alpha/2) = 0.975$. This z-value is 1.96. Substituting these values into equation (8.14) readily yields the number of observers, about 47. If one is willing to assume that $\rho = 0$, the number of observers shrinks to about 18. This can be readily verified from equation (8.13).

8.3 Reducing the Work

Using the paired-comparison method for samples that are not close on the "ness" dimension is inefficient. Comparisons of pairs that are far apart result in unanimous judgments, which leads to a zero or one in the proportion matrix. The obvious strategy is to avoid comparing pairs that are widely spaced on the "ness" dimension. Suggesting avoidance is an easy statement to make, but knowing which samples are far apart implies the scale values are known. Then there would be no need to perform the scaling! If there is some idea of the samples that are far apart, then these comparisons are not performed, and the scale can be generated using the incomplete matrix methods of Chapter 9.

8.3.1 Sample Subgroups and Scale Merging

When the paired-comparison scaling method must be used but the number of samples is quite large, making all $n(n-1)/2$ comparisons may be impractical. One comparison-reduction method is to divide the samples into subgroups. The subgroups are selected so that within each subgroup there are no unanimous choices. Since the subgroups are smaller, the overall number of comparisons is smaller. However, there is a bit of circular reasoning in this logic–one needs to have some knowledge of the scale values to construct the subgroups, so some preliminary experiments may be needed. A small ranking study will suggest which samples lay at the extremes of the scale, and will provide an order for the samples.

With a strategy for dividing the samples into more-manageable subgroups, one must also have a strategy for reuniting the subgroups into a single group. Each subgroup scale is an interval scale with an arbitrary multiplication factor and an arbitrary additive constant, usually zero. The task is to stitch each subgroup scale together into a continuum. Stitching the scales is accomplished by computing a linear transformation of adjacent subgroups to map one scale to the next adjacent scale. To make one continuous interval scale, two or more "end" samples of one subgroup must appear in the next (adjacent) subgroup, so the linear transformation can be computed. The rank order of the complete sample set can be used to identify adjacent or "end" samples in each subgroup.

At least two samples are needed to estimate two parameters, the slope and intercept of the transformation. In practice, a pilot experiment may be needed to ensure that the two or more samples that appear in the two subgroups do not suffer from the unanimity of agreement. This scale-stitching technique was used by Stevens and Volkman in 1940 (Stevens and Volkman, 1940) to build an auditory pitch scale from scaling temporal frequency stimuli, and more recently by Burningham and Ng in constructing an image quality scale of printers (Burningham and Ng, 1992). Torgerson (1958) also suggested methods of reducing the number of comparisons.

(8.15)
$$S_{12} = b_0 + b_1 S_{11}$$
$$S_{22} = b_0 + b_1 S_{21}$$

The mathematical procedure for combining two scales with at least two common samples is as follows. Assume the scale value of sample 1 on scale 1 (denoted S_{11}), sample 2 on scale 1 (denoted S_{21}), sample 1 on scale 2 (denoted S_{12}), and sample 2 on scale 2 (denoted S_{22}), are all known. From these known values two coefficients, b_0 and b_1, of a linear transformation that relates the values on scale one to the values on scale two, are determined by solving equations (8.15).

(8.16)
$$b_1 = \frac{S_{12} - S_{22}}{S_{11} - S_{21}}$$
$$b_0 = S_{12} - b_1 S_{11}$$

The solution to b_0 and b_1 for two overlapping samples is given by the set of equations (8.16).

(8.17)
$$\begin{bmatrix} S_{12} \\ S_{22} \end{bmatrix} = \begin{bmatrix} 1 & S_{11} \\ 1 & S_{21} \end{bmatrix} \begin{bmatrix} b_0 \\ b_1 \end{bmatrix} = [\boldsymbol{S}_2] = [\boldsymbol{S}_1][\boldsymbol{b}]$$

Least squares techniques can be used to estimate the parameters b_0 and b_1 if three or more overlapping samples are available. In matrix notation we can rewrite equation set (8.16) as matrix equation (8.17).

(8.18)
$$\boldsymbol{b} = \left(\boldsymbol{S}_1^T \boldsymbol{S}_1\right)^{-1} \boldsymbol{S}_1^T \boldsymbol{S}_2$$

The least squares solution for the coefficient vector, $\boldsymbol{b}$, for any number of samples greater than two, common to the sets, is given by equation (8.18).

Reducing the overall number of comparisons using a sample subgroup method is recommended if the full set of samples covers a wide "ness" range, and/or the sample set is large. Breaking a large sample set into smaller subgroups reduces the number of pairs to compare, reduces the stress on the observers, and can eliminate the incomplete matrix problem. However, a penalty for using this technique is that one must determine the approximate scale values so appropriate subgroups can be constructed.

8.3.2 Sorting

Subgrouping a large number of samples for use with paired comparisons is not the only method to reducing the observer work. Whaley (1979) proposed an interesting solution using a computer sorting algorithm. (Sorting algorithms for rank ordering samples were discussed in Chapter 6.) Using a sorting algorithm yields three advantages: 1) it reduces the average number of comparisons because it has a tendency to compare samples that are close; 2) it does not make many comparisons of samples far apart and; 3) the sorted list is the rank order of the samples.

All sorting algorithms require a test of inequality: for example, is A>B? Whaley's approach is to use the observer as the inequality tester instead of using the computer. The computer sorting algorithm would present the observer with the pair to evaluate and the observer would enter the judgment to the computer.

Whaley's example used the shell-sorting algorithm that requires an average of $n^{3/2}$ comparisons, worst case (Press, *et. al.*, 1986). Any efficient sorting algorithm can be used: for example, the Heapsort that requires only $n\log_2(n)$ comparisons, worst case (Press, *et. al.*, 1986). The break-even point for the shell sort is six samples (seven samples for the Heapsort), so when scaling six or fewer samples these algorithms offer no advantage. Be cognizant that some popular sorting algorithms, such as the Quicksort and Bubblesort, require in worst case situations n^2 comparisons, which always exceeds $n(n-1)/2$ comparisons for standard paired comparison. Also, because all comparisons are not made, the frequency matrix will not have the same sum for all the $\boldsymbol{F}_{ij} + \boldsymbol{F}_{ji}$ elements and care should be exercised when computing proportions.

Using sorting algorithms appears like a "quick fix" for large numbers of samples, but it has its down side. The major disadvantage is that there is a tendency to present one sample of a pair twice in a row; that is, the same sample appears in two sequential pairs. This violates the basic principle of keeping a common sample maximally separated in time (Torgerson, 1958), and could give biased results.

8.3.3 Proportions From Ranking Data

The process of ranking a set of n samples from 1 to n along a "ness" dimension is inherently a comparison of all samples with each other (Thurstone, 1931). Thus a set of ranks of n samples contains the same data as a paired-comparison experiment, but it is gathered in a different way. A considerable saving of experimental labor is possible by converting ranking data to a proportion matrix.

Thurstone (1931) described an exact method–but in 1931, without computers to do calculations, this method was laborious. Thus, Thurstone was forced to develop a practical approximation. With computers to do the work, there is no need to use the approximation. The following explanation of the exact method is close to Thurstone's original work (1931), but also benefits from Bock and Jones (1968).

For illustration, assume four samples: A, B, C, and D. For these four samples there are $n(n-1)/2$ or six possible comparisons. Suppose the four samples are ranked B, D, A, and C by the first observer. Taking the rankings pairwise, from left to right gives, B>D, B>A, B>C, D>A, D>C, and A>C, for a total of six comparisons of one sample over another. The greater-than symbol, >, is taken to mean that the left member is selected over the right member of the pair. What remains to be done is to convert these rankings into a frequency matrix, $\boldsymbol{F}$.

Starting at the first of the six comparisons (B>D), and using the usual convention of the column preference over the row, add one to the count in the cell of the $\boldsymbol{F}$ matrix at the intersection of column B and row D. The next addition to the cell counter goes at the intersection of column B and row A, and so forth. The beginning of an algorithm to convert ranking data to a frequency matrix starts to emerge. Instead of using labels for the samples; e.g. A, B, C, D, we use numbers, and collect the ranking data so the number in the column is the rank (position) assigned to that sample.

To apply this technique, the data are collected using any of the rank order methods described in Chapter 6. Generally, these methods have the observer rank the samples in order of increasing "ness," with the lowest amount of "ness" on the left and the highest on the right. The raw data in each element of matrix $\boldsymbol{R}$ is the rank awarded the sample (column) by the observer (row) with *1* equal to the lowest value and n equal to the highest or greatest amount of the "ness."

The algorithm to convert the ranking data to a frequency matrix proceeds similarly:

1) Start with the first observer and begin with the first sample, column one, and compare the number in the second column to the number in the first column. If the number in the first column is greater than the number in the second column, then the first sample is preferred to the second sample and the counter is incremented in location $\boldsymbol{F}_{1,2}$ of the frequency matrix, $\boldsymbol{F}$; otherwise the counter in $\boldsymbol{F}_{2,1}$ is incremented.
2) The next comparison is column one to column three, and the same test is performed. All other columns are tested against the first column.
3) Start the same sequence of comparisons at column two. At the end of the comparison sequence, comparisons of columns *2-3*, *2-4*, *etc.* up to *2-n* are complete.
4) Start the same process with column three and repeat the test with each subsequent pair in the row. The process is continued until the last comparison is between column *(n-1)* and n.
5) At this point the frequency matrix is complete for the first observer. Iterating over all the observers gives the complete frequency matrix for the ranking experiment.

Another, probably clearer, way to describe the algorithm is to write it in so-called pseudo-code. Start with an n by n frequency matrix, $\boldsymbol{F}$, that has zeros in all its cells and the rank order data matrix $\boldsymbol{R}$. The following "for" loops are the embodiment of the previous five step description:

```
for i = 1 to number_rows_of_R
    for j = 1 to number_of_columns_of_R-1
        for k = j + 1 to number_of_columns_of_R
            if Rij > Rik then
                    Fjk = Fjk + 1
                else
                    Fkj = Fkj + 1
            endif
        endfor
    endfor
endfor
```

At the end of this process, the n by n matrix $\boldsymbol{F}$ has the number of times the column sample was preferred to the row sample. Division of each element of $\boldsymbol{F}$ by the number of observers, J, converts the numbers into an n by n proportion matrix, $\boldsymbol{P}$.

A MathCad® sheet, file `rnk2pro.mcd` contains a program to convert ranking data to a proportion matrix, along with an example.

8.4 Paired Comparison Variations

All of the methods described thus far are based on the application of Thurstone's Law of Comparative Judgment. There are other ways to generate an interval scale from paired-comparison data collection techniques that do not invoke the Law of Comparative Judgment, but often involve other assumptions. The rubric under which these methods fall is called non-Thurstonian scaling, and we will describe two here. The *Scheffé method* assumes that the seven categories are spaced at equal intervals, that is, that the "ness" distance between the categories is the same. Chapter 10 explores this issue more fully, so it is recommended that Chapter 10 be read before using the Scheffé method. The second method uses paired comparisons, with a twist; the observer is asked to indicate on a numerical scale how different the two samples are. As described in "Chapter 11: Ratio Scaling," the observer may or may not use numbers according to the difference in the sample "ness." Nevertheless, this method can be used to estimate interval scales, but not without some mathematical manipulation.

8.4.1 Paired Comparison Plus Category

The motivation for the development of this technique by Scheffé (1952) was his interest in developing an analysis of variance technique for paired comparison. His method uses a seven-point scoring scale by which to judge the difference between the pairs. In this respect the technique is a combination of a seven-point category rating scale and paired comparison. The idea is to have the observer estimate the difference in the pair and assign a number to this difference. One of seven values is assigned to the pair according to the expression of difference by the observer, using the following set of descriptors.

+3 = strongly prefer sample *i* to sample *j*.
+2 = moderately prefer sample *i* to sample *j*.
+1 = slightly prefer sample *i* to sample *j*.
0 = no preference.
-1 = slightly prefer sample *j* to sample *i*.
-2 = moderately prefer sample *j* to sample *i*.
-3 = strongly prefer sample *j* to sample *i*.

One can consider this method to be a named-category scale within a paired-comparison experiment. See Chapter 10 for more discussion on assigning numbers and adjectives to categories.

8.4.1.1 Data Collection and Scale Generation

Scheffé's (1952) original method made a distinction between an *ij* and a *ji* sample presentation. The reason for this distinction was that he wanted to estimate the effects of sample presentation order on scale value. The method described here does not include this ordering effect, and so it is more in line with classic paired-comparison methods.

In a comparison of sample i to sample j, the observers' response (+3 to -3), is added to the number in the n by n frequency matrix, $\boldsymbol{F}$, at location i,j. The complementary number is added to the numberin location j,i in the frequency matrix. For example, if the observer "moderately prefers" sample *2* to sample *5*, a +2 is added to the frequency matrix at $\boldsymbol{F}_{2,5}$ and a -2 is added to the frequency matrix at $\boldsymbol{F}_{5,2}$. The elements of the frequency matrix accumulate the number of "points" assigned to the sample pair. A check on the frequency matrix is possible by noting that $\boldsymbol{F}_{i,j} + \boldsymbol{F}_{j,i} = 0$. A scale value can be computed for each of the n samples by taking the column sum of the frequency matrix, $\boldsymbol{F}$.

The categories using this method are not limited to seven–a larger number can be used. In fact, Scheffé (1952) proposed the addition of two more categories because he found that observers "jammed" the scores at each end when there were no further extreme categories for their judgments. What has been described here are categories of "preference," but for "ness" or image quality scaling these categories need to be relabeled. Chapter 10 has some suggestions on the number of categories and the labels.

8.4.2 Paired Comparison Plus Distance

The implied assumption in this method is that a physical distance selected by the observer represents a "ness" or image quality distance between samples or stimuli. This is the same assumption made when using the graphical rating scale method described in Chapter 7. Upon presentation of a pair of samples, the observer selects one of the pair and gives an estimate of the difference between the samples. This difference estimate may be a ±3 point scale, without descriptive adjectives associated with the numbers, or a 0 to 10 scale, say, for characterizing the difference from "no difference" to "extreme difference."

Another possibility is to use a piece of paper, asking the observer to draw a line indicating distance. Similarly, a slider on a computer monitor interface can be positioned to show distance. Again, the ruler may be anchored via adjectives, or can be merely a numerical range. Note that the paired-comparison-plus-distance method is just a graphic rating scale method implemented on a pairwise basis.

8.4.2.1 Data Tabulation and Scale Generation

As one would expect, the tabulation of the observers' response data is different when distance is considered along with paired comparisons. One way to arrange the data matrix is to have the rows represent the observers, *1 to J*, and the columns represent all possible paired comparisons. If there are n samples there will be $n(n\text{-}1)/2$ columns of the data matrix, $\boldsymbol{D}$. Labeling the top of the columns as i-j to represent the pairs under consideration is useful. As an illustration, suppose there are four samples: A, B, C, and D. For the column headings write all possible pairs; for example, A-B, A-C, A-D, B-C, B-D, and C-D. The reason for writing them this way, and in this order, is to make the analysis clearer.

In the data collection step we need to keep track of the choice and distance, and assign an appropriate sign to the distance for the analysis. The distance between two objects is always positive, but by incorporating a sign at this stage of analysis, we can call the distance a directed distance. For example, if the sign is positive, the observers' response is in the "positive direction."

Suppose sample pair B-D is given to the kth observer for a judgment. The observer chooses D and estimates the difference between sample B and D, on a scale of 0 to 10, to be, say, four. The study administrator puts the "sign of D times distance" into the row of the kth observer and the column B-D in the data matrix ***D***. In this instance a -4 is put in the data matrix. Had the observer chosen B, instead of D, the administrator would have put a +4 in the same location. The algorithm to set the sign of the distance is simply the sign of the sample letter (identification) in the column heading. At the completion of the experiment matrix ***D*** contains J rows, one for each observer, $n(n-1)/2$ columns headed by the pair identifications, and the entries are the signed distances between the two samples given by the observer.

One cannot assume that each observer will use the number scale the same way, so each observer's raw scale values are computed from the array of distances. For example, one person's four is another person's eight for the same sample.

1) Form a column matrix from each observer's row of data; this is just the transpose.
2) Construct a coefficient matrix (sometimes called "contrasts" by statisticians) that forms a series of linear equations representing the data. For each observer, the left column vector in equation (8.19) is identical to the row vector of the data sheet, which is the column of signed distance numbers, except in symbolic form for this illustration. The matrix ***X***, is a coefficient matrix that forms the difference (distance) for all the pairs. The last row in the data vector and the ***X*** matrix forces the sum of the distances, or scale values, equal to zero for each observer. We expect the range of the score values to be different for each observer because observers do not use the numbers in the same way. Equation (8.19) in matrix notation is equation (8.20).

$$\begin{bmatrix} A-B \\ A-C \\ A-D \\ B-C \\ B-D \\ C-D \\ 0 \end{bmatrix} = \begin{bmatrix} 1 & -1 & 0 & 0 \\ 1 & 0 & -1 & 0 \\ 1 & 0 & 0 & -1 \\ 0 & 1 & -1 & 0 \\ 0 & 1 & 0 & -1 \\ 0 & 0 & 1 & -1 \\ 1 & 1 & 1 & 1 \end{bmatrix} \begin{bmatrix} A \\ B \\ C \\ D \end{bmatrix} \tag{8.19}$$

$$\boldsymbol{d} = \boldsymbol{XS} \tag{8.20}$$

In equation (8.20) ***d*** is the column vector of signed distances between the sample pairs, of length $n(n-1)/2+1$; ***X*** is the coefficient matrix, $n(n-1)/2+1$ by n; and ***S*** is the vector of scaled values of length n. The least squares solution of equation (8.20) for the vector of scale values $\boldsymbol{S}$ is given by equation (8.21).

$$\boldsymbol{S} = \left(\boldsymbol{X}^T \boldsymbol{X}\right)^{-1} \boldsymbol{X}^T \boldsymbol{d} \tag{8.21}$$

3) Equation (8.21) gives the scale values for only one observer, so the equation must be solved repeatedly for all J observers. Recall that the sum of the scale values is zero, but the range of values for each observer will be different because they used the distance scale differently. To reduce this "rubberband" effect, each observer's data needs to be multiplied by a constant. (Recall that the same problem was encountered with the graphical rating scale method in Chapter 7.) A simple way to align the scores of all the observers to a common reference is to divide each observer's scores by their score's standard deviation. The sequential combination of computing the score and dividing by the standard deviation gives each observer's scale a zero mean and unit standard deviation. This process reduces the scale variance due to each observer's unique use of the number scale in estimating the distance between samples.
4) At this point a standardized interval scale for each observer exists, and appropriate statistical analysis can be performed. A simple averaging of the observers' scores for each of the n samples yields a scale value for the sample.

The MathCad® sheet `pcdist.mcd` illustrates the computation of scale values starting with the data matrix $\boldsymbol{D}$.

This chapter has focused only on Thurstone's Case V or Va of his Law of Comparative Judgment. If this case applies, the scale values can be tested statistically. Yet what does one do if Case V is found *not* to apply to our scaling data? The next chapter, Chapter 9, looks at solutions to other cases, discusses additional practical details, and generalizes Thurstone's model.

Chapter 9

Indirect Interval Scaling–Generalization of Thurstone's Case V

In the previous chapter, we explored Thurstone's Case V model of the Law of Comparative Judgment in its most widely used application: with paired-comparison data. In this chapter, we will examine Thurstone's Case IV model, which is rarely used by researchers. In addition, Chapter 9 will present methods to deal with the problem of scale estimation with the zeros and ones that often appear in the proportion matrix. Recognizing that experimental data has inherent variability, the final section in this chapter looks at the bias and variance of computed scale values, and suggests tactics for reducing them.

9.1 Other Thurstonian Case V Models

The "ness" is a random variable whose probability density function is widely assumed to follow a normal or Gaussian model. Although Thurstone's Law of Comparative Judgment is most often applied to Case V and paired-comparison data, conversion of experimental proportions to scale value differences can be accomplished with other models or theories. In a series of papers, Yellot and coauthors (1977, 1978, 1979) show the equivalence of Thurstone's Case V to other so-called "choice and utility" models. Their work lets us apply the Law of Comparative Judgment in the broader context of choice and utility theory, as opposed to simple scaling theory (Baird and Noma, 1978).

The function or model associated with any of these theories is the cumulative distribution function, which is the integral of the probability density function that characterizes scale value differences. For independent, identically distributed random variables (Case V only), the scale value difference probability density function results from the self-convolution of Thurstone's discriminal process probability density function. Various assumptions about the discriminal process probability density function can yield different models. Five such models are summarized in Table 9.1 (David, 1988; Baird and Noma,

Table 9.1 Summary of Thurstonian Case V Models
(After Baird and Noma, 1978 and David, 1988)

Model Name	Discriminal Process PDF	Scale Value Difference PDF	Model, $H(S_A\text{-}S_B)$ CDF
Gaussian (Thurstone Case V)	$y=\frac{1}{\sqrt{2\pi}}e^{-\left(\frac{x-S_A}{2}\right)^2}$	$y=\frac{1}{\sqrt{2\pi}}e-\left(\frac{S_A-S_B}{2}\right)^2$	$H(S_A-S_B)=\frac{1}{\sqrt{2\pi}}\int_{-(S_A-S_B)}^{\infty}e^{-\left(\frac{x^2}{2}\right)}dx$
Logistic Bradley-Terry Luce, BTL)	$y=e^{-(x-S_A)}e^{e-(x-S_A)}$	$y=\frac{1}{4}sech^2\left(\frac{S_A-S_B}{2}\right)$	$H(S_A-S_B)=\int_{-(S_A-S_B)}^{\infty}sech^2\left(\frac{x}{2}\right)dx$ $=\frac{1}{1+e^{-(S_A-S_B)}}$
Exponential (Noether)	$y=\begin{cases}e^{-(x-S_A)} & for\ x\geq S_A\\ 0 & for\ x<S_A\end{cases}$	$y=\frac{1}{2}e^{-\lvert S_A-S_B\rvert}$	$H(S_A-S_B)=\frac{1}{2}\int_{-(S_A-S_B)}^{\infty}e^{-\lvert x\rvert}dx$ $=\frac{1}{2}e^{(S_A-S_B)}\quad for\ (S_A-S_B)\leq 0$ $=1-\frac{1}{2}e^{-(S_A-S_B)}\quad for\ (S_A-S_B)>0$
Angular Transformation		$y=\frac{1}{2}cos(S_A-S_B)$ $for\ -\frac{\pi}{2}\leq(S_A-S_B)\leq\frac{\pi}{2}$	$H(S_A-S_B)=\frac{1}{2}\left[1+sin(S_A-S_B)\right]$
Uniform Distribution	$y=\frac{1}{w}\ for\ \lvert x\rvert\leq S_A\pm\frac{w}{2}$	$y-\frac{1}{w}\left(1+\frac{S_A-S_B}{w}\right)for\ -w\leq S_A-S_B\leq 0$ $y=\frac{1}{w}\left(1-\frac{S_A-S_B}{w}\right)for\quad 0\leq S_A-S_B\leq w$	$H(S_A-S_B)=\frac{1}{2}+\frac{S_A-S_B}{w}$ $-sign(S_A-S_B)\left[\frac{(S_A-S_B)^2}{2w^2}\right]$ $for\ -w\leq(S_A-S_B)\leq w$

1978). Note that the Angular Transformation model listed in Table 9.1 does not provide a probability density function for discriminal process or judgment errors. Thus the Angular Transformation model does not, strictly speaking, follow the classical Thurstone Case V Law of Comparative Judgment. An extensive discussion is beyond this book's scope, but see Yellot (1977) and Baird and Noma (1978) for an interesting examination of applying Thurstone's Law of Comparative Judgment in cases without probability density functions.

As Bartleson (1984) has remarked, in most applications there is little to choose among, given real-world experimental data. Often, the number of observers is insufficient to enable statistical selection of a particular model. In practice, the choice of model relates more to the underlying assumptions one is willing to make regarding the "discriminal process" than anything else. Of all the discriminal process probability density functions listed in Table 9.1, the normal or Gaussian model used in Thurstone's Case V seems the most plausible, lacking any additional information. Perhaps this is why it is so widely used.

The selection of a particular function to transform the proportion data has theoretical implications. As an example, the discriminal process (probability density function), associated with the logistic function is known as the extreme value or Gumbel distribution. This density function is not symmetrical about the mean value, and has a tail that extends to positive values. For Case V, choosing the logistic transformation theoretically implies that the observers' discriminal processes are positively skewed, which may or may not be true. An important underlying theoretical point is that each transformation function implies something about the observers' judgment process. To view the choice of transformation as a function fitting problem ignores these theoretical assumptions. However, as with all theories, one is free to choose a theory that is appropriate. Unfortunately, the selection criteria used most often is how well the model fits the data.

Selecting the appropriate model is made more complicated because each model varies in the basic shape of the transformation equation, and real-world realities mean that we work with a finite number of observers. For example, it is known that around the 0.50 proportion point the models are approximately linear, so all transformation models in Table 9.1 give virtually identical results around this point. This is illustrated in Figure 9.1, where the transformation curves have been scaled so the probabilities match when S_A-S_B = ±1.00. Note that over the range of S_A-S_B = ±1.00, there is little difference in the probabilities or proportions among the various models; the curves are virtually identical. The differences become apparent when S_A-S_B exceeds 1.00, or when extreme proportions occur.

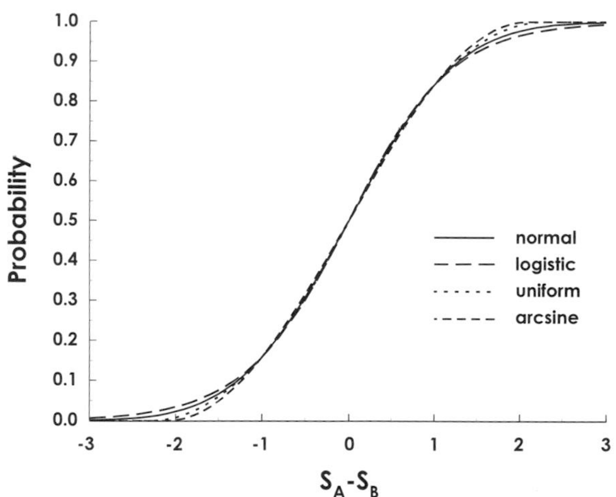

Figure 9.1 Comparison of four transformations: normal, logistic, uniform, and arcsine.

Recall that the basic data set for application of a Thurstonian model is the frequency that one of a pair is chosen over another, provided as a number. The sum of the frequencies for the *ij* and *ji* pair is equal to the number of observers that judged the pair. Division of these two frequencies by the total gives an estimated proportion of one sample chosen over the other. Since the number of observers is finite, there are a finite number of proportions. In fact, for proportions other than zero and one, they occur in increments of *1/(number of observers)*. For example, if $J = 5$ observers judge a sample, the proportion increments occur at every $1/J$ or 0.20: 0, 0.20, 0.40, 0.60, 0.80, and 1.00, and there are exactly $J+1$ possible proportions. There are no other values. Ignoring the unanimous proportions, zero and one, the smallest possible proportion is *1/(number of observers)* and the largest *1-1/(number of observers)*. This quantization of the proportion values limits the practical range of the models to the central region, unless the quantization is reduced by using a very large number of observers. To complicate the model selection issue further, appropriateness is also affected by the statistical method of scale estimation, such as least squares or maximum likelihood.

Hohle (1966) compared the Gaussian distribution, Thurstone Case V and the logistic (Bradley-Terry-Luce, BTL) models (Table 9.1) using maximum likelihood methods of scale estimation. He concluded that the logistic model offered a marginally better fit of experimental data. Jackson and Fleckenstein (1957) tested the logistic and Gaussian models, among others, and concluded that the logistic model represented the data slightly better than the Gaussian model; however, there were enough caveats about violations of the assumptions to cloud the conclusion.

9.2 Case IV Solution

By supposing Case V holds, one assumes that the observed proportion matrix is unaffected by discriminal dispersions (variances) or correlations. Mosteller (1951b) has shown that only the samples whose discriminal dispersions(s) are different from the group will have errors in scale values. If one is willing to accept some error in computed scale values of samples that violate the Case V assumptions, it reduces the motivation for considering the more complicated Case IV. Also, using Case V makes the analysis or scale-generation problem much easier. Whether Case V is the appropriate model can be tested. If Thurstone's Case V model fails using Mosteller's test described in Section 8.2.2 (Mosteller, 1951c), the next possible step in the analysis is to consider Case IV.

Thurstone's Case IV (Thurstone, 1927) is based on the assumption that the discriminal dispersions (variances) for all the samples are *approximately* equal and the correlations between samples are zero. The assumption of approximately equal discriminal dispersions reduces the square root of the sum of the variances, in the general Law of Comparative Judgment, to the sum of two standard deviations (see Table 8.1). This approximation makes estimating the scale values and the discriminal dispersions a linear problem.

Surprisingly, Case IV is almost never invoked in practice. One reason for lack of use is that the prevailing method of solution, a variation on Thurstone's (1932) original method, is only an approximation (Torgerson, 1958). However, Gibson (1953) worked out a least squares solution of Case IV that gives both the scale values and the discriminal dispersions for each sample. We have not seen use of Gibson's method reported in the literature, possibly because of two problems. First, there is a minimum 10-by-10 matrix to invert, clearly a non-trivial matter in 1951. Secondly, there is an apparent error in his formulation. The matrix issues are of no practical consequence with today's computers, so the next section describes Gibson's method with a correction to "make it work."

9.2.1 Gibson's Solution for Case IV

For Case IV, Thurstone (1927) assumed that the correlation coefficient between two samples equals zero and the discriminal dispersions, σ, are approximately equal. He specifically assumed that $\sigma_i = \sigma_j + \Delta$, where Δ is a small value. The derivation will not be repeated here, but basically the approach is to expand, in a series, the square root term in Case III, which yields the defining equation (9.1) for Case IV.

$$S_A - S_B = \frac{1}{\sqrt{2}} z_{AB}(\sigma_A + \sigma_B) \quad (9.1)$$

The Case IV problem is to estimate S_A, S_B, σ_A, and σ_B. Gibson (1953) recognized that Case IV was a linear problem and solvable by well-known methods. His contribution was to put the set of equations in a usable form for a practical solution.

Solving equation (9.1) for n samples uses two constraints: 1) $\Sigma S_i = 0$ and 2) $\Sigma \sigma_i = n$. Defining the sum of the scale values to be zero establishes the interval scale constant, and represents the usual Case V practice. The second constraint establishes the overall "scale multiplier" of the interval scale, and is equivalent to making the average discriminal dispersion equal to unity. Both are arbitrary constants and are permitted operations on an interval scale.

Gibson proposed two methods of solution. The second method, described here, uses the two constraints described above and requires a minimum of five samples for solution. Derivation of the method of solution proceeds as follows. For each pair of samples, there is one equation like (9.1) above. To each equation add the scale values S_1 through S_n on the left-hand side (LHS). Since the sum of these values is zero, it does not change the balance of the equation. The next step is to scale the set of equations by multiplying each side by $z_{AB}/\sqrt{2}$ and then add the sum of the σ's to the LHS and n times $z_{AB}/\sqrt{2}$ to the right-hand side (RHS). Collecting terms yields a system of ten equations and ten unknowns: the five scale values and the five discriminal dispersions. This results in a system of equations given by (9.2).

$$
\begin{aligned}
2S_1+0+S_3+S_4+S_5+\frac{1}{\sqrt{2}}z_{12}\left(0+0+\sigma_3+\sigma_4+\sigma_5\right)&=\frac{1}{\sqrt{2}}nz_{12}\\
2S_1+S_2+0+S_4+S_5+\frac{1}{\sqrt{2}}z_{13}\left(0+\sigma_2+0+\sigma_4+\sigma_5\right)&=\frac{1}{\sqrt{2}}nz_{13}\\
2S_1+S_2+S_3+0+S_5+\frac{1}{\sqrt{2}}z_{14}\left(0+\sigma_2+\sigma_3+0+\sigma_5\right)&=\frac{1}{\sqrt{2}}nz_{14}\\
2S_1+S_2+S_3+S_4+0+\frac{1}{\sqrt{2}}z_{15}\left(0+\sigma_2+\sigma_3+\sigma_4+0\right)&=\frac{1}{\sqrt{2}}nz_{15}\\
S_1+2S_2+0+S_4+S_5+\frac{1}{\sqrt{2}}z_{23}\left(\sigma_1+0+0+\sigma_4+\sigma_5\right)&=\frac{1}{\sqrt{2}}nz_{23}\\
S_1+2S_2+S_3+0+S_5+\frac{1}{\sqrt{2}}z_{24}\left(\sigma_1+0+\sigma_3+0+\sigma_5\right)&=\frac{1}{\sqrt{2}}nz_{24}\\
S_1+2S_2+S_3+S_4+0+\frac{1}{\sqrt{2}}z_{25}\left(\sigma_1+0+\sigma_3+\sigma_4+0\right)&=\frac{1}{\sqrt{2}}nz_{25}\\
S_1+S_2+2S_3+0+S_5+\frac{1}{\sqrt{2}}z_{34}\left(\sigma_1+\sigma_2+0+0+\sigma_5\right)&=\frac{1}{\sqrt{2}}nz_{34}\\
S_1+S_2+2S_3+S_4+0+\frac{1}{\sqrt{2}}z_{35}\left(\sigma_1+\sigma_2+0+\sigma_4+0\right)&=\frac{1}{\sqrt{2}}nz_{35}\\
S_1+S_2+S_3+2S_4+0+\frac{1}{\sqrt{2}}z_{45}\left(\sigma_1+\sigma_2+\sigma_3+0+0\right)&=\frac{1}{\sqrt{2}}nz_{45}\\
S_1+S_2+S_3+S_4+S_5+\sigma_1+\sigma_2+\sigma_3+\sigma_4+\sigma_5&=n
\end{aligned}
\tag{9.2}
$$

The last equation is just a formalization of the two constraints: the sum of the scale values equal zero and the sum of the discriminal dispersions equal the number of samples. Gibson's formulation without this final equation yields a matrix of insufficient rank. This system of equations can be readily put in matrix form given by equation (9.3).

$$E = BG \tag{9.3}$$

In equation (9.3) $\boldsymbol{E}$ is a column vector of the known z-values multiplied by a constant, $nz_{ij}/\sqrt{2}$. $\boldsymbol{B}$ is a $(2n+1)$ by $2n$ matrix of coefficients of the S's, and σ's, $\boldsymbol{G}$ is a column vector of unknowns, the scale values, S_i, $1...n$, followed by the discriminal dispersions, σ_i, $1...n$. The least squares solution for the vector $\boldsymbol{G}$ is given by equation (9.4).

$$\left(B^T B\right)^{-1} B^T E \tag{9.4}$$

From equation set (9.2) it can be seen that there are $2n$ unknowns, n scale values plus n discriminal dispersions, so at least $2n$ equations are necessary. For paired comparisons a total of $n(n-1)/2$ data points are available. The minimum number of samples, n, can be determined by equating the two constraints, $2n = n(n-1)/2$, and solving for n. Thus, at least five samples are necessary to use this method.

Using Gibson's method when there are ones and zeros in the paired-comparison proportion matrix is also possible. Recall that if there is complete agreement among the observers, the proportion will be either a one or a zero, and the z-values will be indeterminate. The strategy for coping with this problem is to leave the equation with the one or zero proportion out of the system of equations. This is only possible with enough samples, where we have more equations than are required for a solution, or "excess" equations. The number of excess equations, δ, can be determined by solving $2n - n(n-1)/2 = \delta$ for δ. This yields Table (9.2), which displays the number of samples and the excess number of equations.

Table 9.2 Number of "Excess" Equations Using Gibson's Case IV Solution

Number of Samples	Number of Comparisons	"Excess" Number of Equations
5	10	0
6	15	3
7	21	7
8	28	12
9	36	18

According to Table 9.2, if there are only five samples then there is no possibility of excluding an equation because there are no excess equations. However, as the number of samples increases, there is a substantial possibility of eliminating equations. If one's study uses six samples, Table 9.2 shows that up to three equations could be eliminated with enough equations remaining for calculating a least squares solution for the scale values and discriminal dispersions. Recall, though, that for every zero in the proportion matrix there is also a one; they come in pairs, so full advantage cannot be taken unless the number of available excess equations is even.

9.2.2 Case IV as an Approximation to Case III

Case IV, compared to Case V, is one step closer concerning model parameters to Thurstone's complete Law of Comparative Judgment. The next step "up" is known as Case III, where the parameters or factors to be estimated are the square root of the sum of the variances. In this sense, Case III is closer to the full Law of Comparative Judgment, as it has only the assumption of zero correlation in its formulation.

On the surface it appears that Case IV, where the sum is used instead of the square root of the sum of the squares of the discriminal dispersions, is a poor approximation to Case III. An analysis readily reveals that the Case IV approximation, the sum of the discriminal dispersions divided by the square root of two, is numerically identical to Case III if the dispersions for the two samples are equal. The approximation error increases as the differences, or Δ, increases. We can form the fractional error, ε, by taking Case III as "correct," and find that it depends on the ratio σ_2/σ_1. The derivation will not be given here, but we state the result in equation (9.5), where $R = (\sigma_2/\sigma_1) - 1$.

$$\varepsilon = \frac{1+\frac{R}{2}}{\sqrt{1+R+\frac{R^2}{2}}} - 1 \tag{9.5}$$

From equation (9.5) several things can be seen. First, the error in Case IV compared to Case III is always negative, meaning that the Case IV approximation always underestimates the square root of the sum of the squares. Secondly, when R is zero the error, ε, is zero, as it should be. The range of R is determined by the assumptions made in deriving Case IV. This range is $-1 \leq R \leq 1.81$. When $R = -1$ the maximum error is -29.3%. If, on the other hand $-0.5 \leq R \leq 1$, implying that the discriminal dispersions can stand in up to a 2:1 ratio, then the error in using Case IV parameters is only -5.1%. Therefore, under highly practical circumstances, Case IV is a very good approximation to Case III when combined with Gibson's simple least squares method for estimating scale values and discriminal dispersions.

An example of Gibson's Case IV method is found in the MathCad® file `pciv1.mcd`.

9.3 The Zero-One Proportion Matrix Problems

When one works with paired comparisons and Thurstone's models, the basic data takes the form of a proportion matrix; the proportion of the time sample A is chosen over sample B. It often happens that some matrix cells will have ones and zeros, or they are blank. In most practical imaging applications, the diagonal cells are blank because the sample is rarely compared with itself. A one or zero occurs in the matrix when there is unanimous agreement among observers for a particular sample pair. Early in Chapter 7, we observed that when the distributions or discriminal dispersions of responses do not overlap, there is no "confusion" about the samples (see Figure 7.1). In other words, the samples are too far apart on the "ness" scale to yield differences of judgments.

Using any of the models presented in section 9.1 to transform a probability or proportion of one or zero results in a z-value of $-\infty$ or $+\infty$, which makes practical computation impossible. Cells without data, on the other hand, are caused by pairs not being judged, for whatever reason, which results in an incomplete data matrix. Since these situations occur frequently in practice, some solution is required.

The strategies for dealing with this problem fit broadly into two different categories. Either get the data matrix "right" by adding observers, or make the best estimate of the scale values using the existing data. Selection of the most appropriate strategy depends on practical and philosophical considerations.

9.3.1 More Observers

The most obvious technique is to use more observers. Since only one observer is needed to change the proportions to something less than one and greater than zero, recruiting observers is, essentially, betting that someone will eventually make the contrary judgment and break the unanimity. If in fact the samples are very far apart on the "ness" dimension, an observer with a contrary judgment may never be found. There are practical and economic limits to the number of observers, so this is not a realistic strategy for solving the zero-one proportion problem.

9.3.2 Zero-One Data Substitutions

Data "fixing" methods substitute the ones or zeros of the data matrix with another value. Guilford (1954) recommended setting the maximum or minimum proportions to 0.977 and 0.023. This corresponds to z-values of ±2, using the Thurstone (Gaussian) model. Such arbitrary substitutions can bias the scale. Noether (1960) had a less arbitrary suggestion. He recognized that the proportions are in fact quantized data, which is quantized in increments of *1/number of observers*. The ones and zeros are converted to a proportion that is the difference between the last quantized value before one, or the first quantized value after zero. Thus $p = 0$ is set to $1/(2n)$ and $p = 1$ is set to $1-1/(2n)$. Noether's tactic addresses the arbitrariness of Guilford's suggestion, and it reduces the bias in the scale value. There are other methods that are found in the literature that promote the addition of a suitable constant to numerator and denominator before calculating an experimental proportion. On the surface these factors also "solve" the zero-one proportion problem, but they were not designed to do so. Their main purpose is to reduce the bias and variance in the estimated scale value, and when used they should be used for all proportion estimates. Bias and variance of the estimated scale values is a topic of Section 9.4.

All of these data substitution schemes are rather arbitrary, and there is no compelling reason to employ any one of them. The preferred method is the least squares solution, described next, which does not use the zero and one proportion data to estimate the scale values.

9.3.3 Morrisey's Incomplete Matrix Solution–Case V

The one-zero problem can be handled as an incomplete-matrix problem by ignoring the cells with the ones or zeros. In the late 1950s both Morrisey (1955) and Gulliksen (1956) independently proposed a least squares solution to this problem. Morrisey, who worked for the Eastman Kodak Company and was interested in using scaling to solve problems related to image quality, published his work in the *Journal of the Optical Society of America*, the preeminent optical journal of the day. Gulliksen, a professor at Princeton and consultant to the Educational Testing Service, published his work a little over a year later in *Psychometrika*, the preeminent psychometric journal, apparently unaware of Morrisey's work. The following description of the method follows Morrisey (1955).

The key to both methods is to recognize that there is an incomplete set of equations that relate the scale value difference to the transformed values, or z-values, determined from the proportions. For any of the Case V models described in Table 9.1, a linear relationship exists between the scale value difference and the z-value for each judged pair. For sample one and sample two we have equation (9.6).

(9.6) $$z_{12} = S_1 - S_2$$

There are no equations for the missing pairs or unanimous (zero-one proportion) pairs. A set of linear equations can be written for the measured sample pairs in a vector format, where the elements of the $\boldsymbol{z}$ column vector are the z_{ij}*-values* of the judged pairs, equation (9.6). We form a matrix, $\boldsymbol{X}$, sometimes called the *design matrix* by statisticians, where the columns correspond to the samples and the rows represent the judged pair. Recall that in a complete matrix there are $n(n\text{-}1)/2$ rows, but because the proportions are incomplete, the design matrix will be $(k+1)n$, where k is less than $n(n\text{-}1)/2$. The entries of the $\boldsymbol{X}$ matrix consist of $+1$ and -1 in the columns of the pair that has been compared. In the n by 1 column $\boldsymbol{S}$ vector are the unknown scale values. To assure that $\boldsymbol{X}$ not be singular, we increase the rank of $\boldsymbol{X}$ by adding the usual constraint that the sum of the scale values is equal to zero; thus the last row of $\boldsymbol{X}$ has all 1's as entries and the last element of the $\boldsymbol{Z}$ vector has a 0. So, we have the following matrix formulation in equation (9.7).

(9.7) $$\begin{bmatrix} z_{12} \\ z_{13} \\ z_{24} \\ \vdots \\ 0_{k+1} \end{bmatrix} = \begin{bmatrix} 1 & -1 & 0 & 0 & \cdots & 0_n \\ 1 & 0 & -1 & 0 & \cdots & 0_n \\ 0 & 1 & 0 & -1 & \cdots & 0_n \\ \vdots & \vdots & \vdots & \vdots & \vdots & \vdots \\ 1 & 1 & 1 & 1 & \cdots & 1_n \end{bmatrix} \begin{bmatrix} S_1 \\ S_2 \\ S_3 \\ \vdots \\ S_n \end{bmatrix}$$

Note that there must be valid data for at least n judged pairs to use this method and $k \geq n$. Usually, there will be more equations than unknowns so a least squares solution, equation (9.8), is used to solve for the $\boldsymbol{S}$ vector of scale values.

(9.8) $$\boldsymbol{S} = \left(\boldsymbol{X}^T\boldsymbol{X}\right)^{-1}\boldsymbol{X}^T\boldsymbol{z}$$

The standard error of the least squares fit to the scale values has been given by Jackson *et. al.* (1957) as equation (9.9).

(9.9) $$e_s = \sqrt{\frac{(\boldsymbol{z}-\boldsymbol{XS})^T(\boldsymbol{z}-\boldsymbol{XS})}{k-n}}$$

The method of Gulliksen (1956) is slightly different, and constructs both the $\boldsymbol{X^TX}$ matrix and the $\boldsymbol{X^TZ}$ matrix directly. Let $\boldsymbol{M} = \boldsymbol{X^TX}$ and construct $\boldsymbol{M}$ according to the following algorithm:

1) Enter a 1 in $\boldsymbol{M}$ for each cell entry in the transformed proportion matrix, $\boldsymbol{Z}$, where the proportion is either a zero or a 1.
2) Enter zero in all other off-diagonal cells.
3) For the diagonals of $\boldsymbol{M}$ enter the number of data points in each column of the proportion matrix, including the comparison of the sample with itself.
4) The matrix $\boldsymbol{D} = \boldsymbol{X^Tz}$ is just the vector of column sums of the $\boldsymbol{Z}$ matrix.
5) With these two matrices the solution for the least squares scale values, $\boldsymbol{S}$, can be obtained by using equation (9.10).

(9.10) $$\boldsymbol{S} = \boldsymbol{M}^{-1}\boldsymbol{D} = (\boldsymbol{X}^T\boldsymbol{X})^{-1}\boldsymbol{X}^T\boldsymbol{z}$$

Using Gulliksen's treatment, there is no $\boldsymbol{X}$ matrix to estimate the standard error, but this is moot if Mosteller's (1951c) χ^2 test, equation (8.11), is used to test the proportion matrix.

This least squares method is a superior alternative to data-fixing methods because it ignores the zero or one proportions and uses the balance of the data to make the best estimate of the scale values. It is highly preferred for this reason.

This solution method, incomplete least squares, can be found in the MathCad® file `pc2.mcd`.

9.3.4 Different Scaling Method

If none of the previous solutions to the zero-one problem is acceptable, then consider modifying the study by using a different scaling technique. The one-zero problem comes about because the samples are spaced far apart on the "ness" dimension, and using a confusion scaling technique is not appropriate. A better approach is to use a direct technique such as the graphic rating scale method described in Chapter 7. Be aware of the tendency to cling to a "favorite" method when it should be abandoned in favor of a more appropriate one.

Experience suggests that the fewer assumptions that need to be made to generate the scale, the better. Paired-comparison methods require several assumptions–including assumptions for the linear model and for the scale estimation methods–in order to construct an interval scale.

9.4 Statistical Bias and Variance in Scale Estimates

Statistics describing the scale and discriminal dispersion estimates get very little attention in most scaling literature. A desirable attribute of scale values using any of the Thurstonian models of Table 9.1 is what statisticians call *minimum variance unbiased estimators*. Overall, most of the estimators for both scale values and discriminal dispersion are biased, and do not have a constant variance. All hope is not lost, for there exist methods of calculation, called estimators, that can be used to minimize both the bias and variance in the scale estimate. Other than Bock and Jones (1968), we have seen no reports of scaling studies using the bias-correction approach in practical applications of paired comparison.

In all the paired-comparison methods, an experimental proportion is converted to a z-value using one of the Thurstonian models described in section 9.1. These experimental proportions, p, are the frequencies, f, that one sample is selected over another sample, divided by the total number of observers, J, that evaluated that particular sample pair: $p = f/J$. Statistically, f is a random variable usually assumed to come from a binomial distribution with parameter p^*: the true probability of choosing one sample over another. A minimum variance unbiased estimate of p^* is in fact f/J, so as far as proportion estimates go, this is a good estimator.

Conceptually, a problem arises because every time the experiment is repeated, a new value of f/J is calculated. This is called sampling, and the underlying sampling distribution is assumed to be the binomial. However, this is not the complete picture for Thurstonian models. All proportions undergo some form of nonlinear transformation to z-values from which the scale values and discriminal dispersions are calculated. A significant consequence of the combination of an underlying binomial proportion distribution with a nonlinear conversion of p to z-values is the introduction of a bias and variance in the computed scale values, loosely called *sampling errors*. Not confusing the parameters of the Law of Comparative Judgment and nonlinear models in Table 9.1 with these sampling errors is important. They are very different.

The next section provides an outline of the bias and variance in scale values, and offers tactics for correction. This treatment is brief because it is beyond the scope of this book, and a thorough discussion would take many chapters. The interested reader is referred to Bock and Jones (1968).

9.4.1 Bias and Variance Corrections

The most detailed investigation available of the bias and variance in the scale value for several Thurstonian models is reported by Bock and Jones (1968). They showed that the bias and variance can be reduced by using bias correction factors like those outlined in Table 9.3. Figure 9.2 (next page) illustrates the bias in the transformed z-value as a function of the true proportion, for a different number of observers. For the curves illustrated here, the Gaussian Thurstonian model was used and a factor of 3/8 was added to the numerator and 3/4 to the denominator before calculation of the proportion. The bias with the correction is very small–essentially zero for mid proportions–but increases as the proportion approaches the extremes. Notice that the maximum bias occurs at the last quantized proportion and it is essentially independent of the number of observers. Note that these curves are for a single proportion.

Table 9.3 Bias Corrections for Proportions and Thurstonian Paired–Comparison Models

Model Name	Bias Correction Formulas for Proportions
Gaussian	1) $p_{ij} = \dfrac{f_{ij} + \frac{3}{8}}{f_{ij} + f_{ji} + \frac{3}{4}}$ 2) $p_{ij} = \dfrac{1}{2J} \; for \; \dfrac{f_{ij}}{f_{ij} + f_{ji}} = 0$ $p_{ij} = 1 - \dfrac{1}{2J} \; for \; \dfrac{f_{ij}}{f_{ij} + f_{ji}} = 1$ (Bock and Jones, 1968)
Logistic	1) $z_{ij} = \ln\left(\dfrac{f_{ij} + \frac{3}{8}}{J - f_{ij} + \frac{3}{4}}\right)$ 2) $z_{ij} = \ln\left(\dfrac{f_{ij} + \frac{1}{2}}{J - f_{ij} + \frac{1}{2}}\right)$ $for \; f_{ij} = 0 \; or \; J \; use \; \frac{1}{4} \; instead \; of \; \frac{1}{2}$ (Anscombe, 1956)
Angular	1) $p_{ij} = \dfrac{f_{ij} + \frac{3}{8}}{f_{ij} + f_{ji} + \frac{3}{4}}$ (Anscombe, 1948) 2) $p_{ij} = \dfrac{f_{ij} + \frac{1}{4}}{f_{ij} + f_{ji} + \frac{1}{2}}$ (Anscombe, 1956)

The variance as a function of true proportion, using the same bias correction as that used in the calculations shown in Figure 9.2, is illustrated in Figure 9.3 (next page). The peak variance occurs at the true proportion value of 0.50 and decreases as the proportion departs from this value. Increasing the number of observers flattens and depresses the peak so the variance is relatively flat over the central region, having a value of about 0.12 for fifteen observers. Recall that these are variances, the squares of the standard deviations, and are much smaller numerically. As can be seen from Figure 9.3, the variance of a single pair is quite dependent on the number of observers. Increasing the count of observers will reduce the variance almost everywhere.

At first glance it would appear that there is substantial bias and variance in the computed scale values for any type of Thurstonian scaling model. However, these values are for one comparison pair,

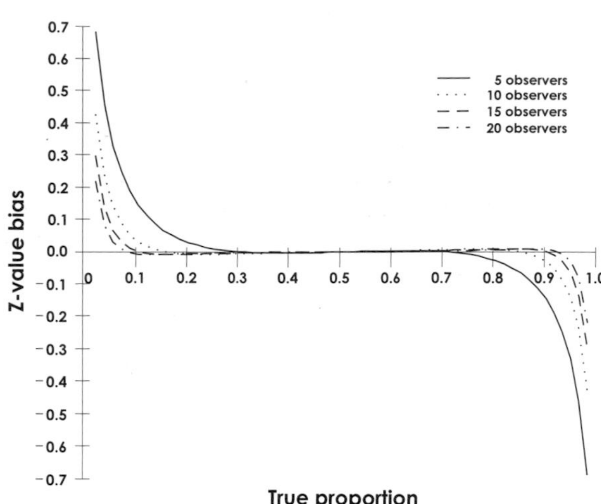

Figure 9.2 Z-value bias for a Gaussian discriminal dispersion model and the bias correction in Table 9.3.

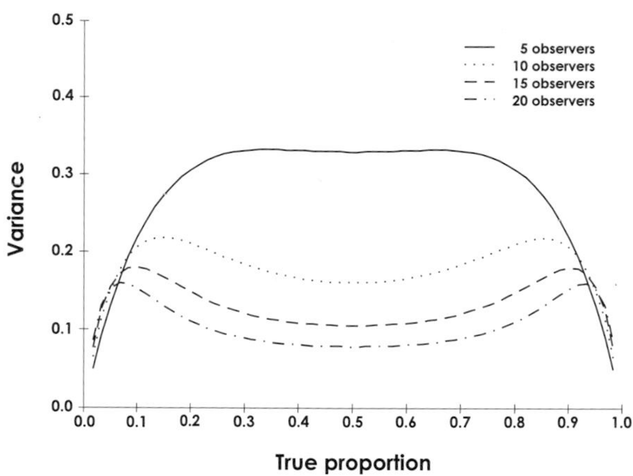

Figure 9.3 The sampling variance for the Gaussian discriminal dispersion when using the bias correction in Table 9.3.

and scale values are typically estimated by taking an average, which would be the column average of z-values for Case V. This averaging process reduces both the scale bias (the biases are often positive and negative and tend to cancel) and the variances.

Remarkably, the highly recommended "cure" for the zero-one proportion problem, substituting $1/2J$ for the zero proportion and $1\text{-}1/(2J)$ for the unity proportion, is also a useful estimator for reducing the variance and bias. Better solutions are described in Section 9.3.3 that ignore the pairs that have the zero-one proportions.

Historically, the analytical emphasis on bias reduction has been to consider only the logistic and angular transforms because they are mathematically tractable (Anscombe, 1948). The simplest corrections have been to add small constants to the numerator and denominator of the f/J fraction. According to Bock and Jones (1968) these bias corrections also serve to reduce the variance in the scale value. Numerical analysis, the same performed to calculate the curves in Figure 9.2 and 9.3, illustrates that there exists a "universal" bias corrector that also reduces the sampling variance. This correction, which the analysis shows will work for nearly all the transformations in Table 9.1, is simply the addition of a small fraction to the numerator and denominator. The simplest and most general correction consists of adding 3/8 to the numerator, f, and 3/4 to the denominator, J. These fractions can be analytically derived for the logistic and angular transformations (Anscombe, 1948), but not for Case V-Gaussian combinations. (Appreciate that a greater reduction in the bias and variance can be obtained by increasing the number of observers than by a mathematical correction.) Table 9.3 summarizes suggested bias correction methods for some popular Thurstonian models. These bias corrections are often promoted as methods for *correcting* the zero-one proportion problem, but they are conceptually completely different. Although they do, in fact, "solve" the problem for zero and one proportions by preventing their occurrence, this method is not recommended.

One major benefit to using the corrections in Table 9.3 is the reduction in bias for extreme z-values and the variance reduction for z-values about zero (Bock and Jones, 1968). Since there is no compelling reason not to correct for known bias effects in scale estimation, it should be incorporated as standard practice when estimating proportions that will be subsequently transformed to z-values.

The MathCad® sheets accompanying this book offer the option to use these bias and variance reduction techniques.

9.4.2 Other Applications Untried

Paired comparison is not the only scaling method that uses proportions as the basic building block for scaling. In the next chapter the method of category scaling called the Law of Category Judgment will be described; it also uses proportions but with one important change. This method of deriving a scale from category scaling data uses the sum of proportions before transforming to z-values. Yet there does not seem to be any literature on bias and variance reduction techniques for this scaling method.

Applying these bias and variance reduction techniques to other scaling methods might seem reasonable. However, broader application may not be appropriate simply because these have been developed specifically for paired comparison applications and are not necessarily correct for others. More work needs to be done before any universality can be claimed for these bias reduction estimators.

Chapter 10

Indirect Interval Scales–Category Scaling Methods

Category scaling is probably the most widely known of all scaling methods. Anyone who has attended school is all too familiar with letter grades describing academic performance, with "A" standing for excellent work, "B" being the grade for good work, and so on. (I always wondered what happened to the letter grade "E?" Perhaps it was never used because it might be confused with "excellent.")

Category scaling is popular for two principal reasons. First, data collection is simple. Second, when adjectives are used for category labels, scale meaning is easily understood. It has remained popular in the social sciences, but use has waned somewhat in psychophysics. The one notable exception to this trend has been the Recommendation ITU-R BT.500-7 (1995), *Methodology for the Subjective Assessment of the Quality of Television Pictures*. This international recommendation (standard) provides several category techniques for scaling the quality of television images.

The discussion of category scaling in this chapter will focus on two well-established methods. One data analysis method, called *Equal-Appearing Intervals*, behaves like an ordinal scale, which limits its usefulness for Image Quality Circle applications. The method of *Successive Categories or Intervals* combined with Torgerson's Law of Categorical Judgment, on the other hand, is a true interval method.

10.1 Equal-Appearing Intervals

The general category data collection method requires the observer to place samples in categories of equal-appearing intervals. *Equal-appearing* is equivalent to saying the categories are of equal width, except of course for the end categories. In practice, the assumption of equal-width intervals is somewhat tenuous. Categories are labeled with names like "good," "better," and "best," or with just numbers (for example 1 to 5), or simply a rank ordering. Data is collected as a matrix, ***K***, with the n rows being the samples and the $m+1$ columns the categories. Each element of the data matrix is the number of times the sample (row) was placed in the category (column). These basic methods are reminiscent of ordinal scaling described earlier in Chapter 6. As with ordinal scaling, this method of data collection does not directly yield an interval scale without additional assumptions or models.

At first glance, the equal-appearing intervals data collection method seems straightforward. However, observers tend to use each category equally often, independent of the amount of the "ness" in the samples (Gescheider, 1985; Guilford, 1954). This results in scale distortion, because the underlying assumption is that the categories have equal "width" on the "ness" dimension. Experienced observers can put samples in equal interval categories under certain conditions. Bartleson (1984), for instance, gives an example of equal interval category scaling of the colorfulness of color chips.

The number of categories available to the observer is a key consideration in equal interval scaling. The practice suggested by Bartleson (1984) and Meilgaard, *et. al.* (1991) is to have an odd number of category adjectives (points), usually from five to eleven. In a study of the quality of projected photographic transparencies, Bartleson and Woodbury (1965) found optimum relative precision of judgments and category utilization with eleven categories when experienced observers were used. Typically, highly skilled observers are more effective at using many categories than "average" or moderately skilled observers (Bartleson and Woodbury, 1965).

Average human human observers typically distinguish only about seven different categories (Miller, 1956; Norwich, 1981), so additional categories may contribute very little "scale information." Many categories require the observer to make fine intervals of discrimination among the categories, while a smaller number does not. Since having many categories does not necessarily increase the "resolution" of the scale, study designers should strive to keep the number of categories in the range of five to eleven.

10.1.1 Category Labels

Adjectives are often used instead of numbers to label each category. If an interval scale is required, then these labels should be perceived by the observer as having equal intervals on the "ness" dimension. A "quantitative" adjective sequence suggested by Bartleson (1984) for a nine-point category scale of increasing amounts of "ness," is as follows:

1. Least imaginable "ness"
2. Very little "ness"
3. Mildly "ness"
4. Moderately "ness"
5. "Ness"
6. Moderately highly "ness"

7. Highly "ness"
8. Very highly "ness"
9. Highest imaginable "ness"

Note the symmetry of the adjectives around the midpoint. This helps to keep the category intervals approximately the same.

Sometimes a scale that has a center point of indifference is required. Jones (1960) and Meilgaard, *et. al.* (1991) offer a nine-point "liking" scale, which in some respects is similar to Bartleson's scale above, and is symmetrical about the neutral point of "Neither like nor dislike."

1. Like extremely
2. Like very much
3. Like moderately
4. Like slightly
5. Neither like nor dislike
6. Dislike slightly
7. Dislike moderately
8. Dislike very much
9. Dislike extremely

Again there is the symmetry in the adjectives used, which helps to keep the scale symmetric about the neutral or indifference point.

An adaptation of this approach can be a sequence of categories with only the extremes labeled, or the extremes plus a neutral center point labeled (Meilgaard, *et. al.*, 1991). Labeling the extremes and the center point should be done with care. Bartleson and Woodbury (1965) showed, in an image quality study, that three points break the scale into two regions, generating an overall distorted scale.

An interesting variant of the quantitative category scales described above is that recommended by the ITU (Recommendation ITU-R BT.500-7, 1995) which has been widely applied in the imaging field. The specific focus of this qualitative adjectival scale is the evaluation of the quality of television pictures, and it comprises two recommendations. One recommendation is a five-category qualitative scale of image quality, with categories going from:

5. Excellent
4. Good
3. Fair
2. Poor
1. Bad

For scale generation purposes, the adjectives are assigned the point values preceding the adjective; e.g., an "excellent" quality picture gets five points, and a "bad" quality picture gets 1 point.

The second recommended scale is an impairment category scale. Here the assumption is that the scale starts from some high or reference-quality level and, because of various television system impairment factors, the quality is degraded. The levels of impairment comprise a five-category qualitative scale with the following categories of impairment descriptors:

5. Imperceptible
4. Perceptible, but not annoying
3. Slightly annoying
2. Annoying
1. Very annoying

The recommended analysis of the category scaled data assumes that the categories of the quality and impairment scales have equal intervals. This implies that the psychological, or "ness," distance between the impairment categories of "Very annoying" and "Annoying" is the same as the distance between "Imperceptible" and "Perceptible, but not annoying." However, adjectives used in ITU-R BT500.7 have received criticism from several sources for not having equal intervals. Zwick (1984), and Jones and McManus (1986) used a graphical rating scale method to assess the equal-interval properties of the five-category quality scale. The observers in the Jones *et. al.* study were from several geographic areas of the U.S. and Italy. The results from both studies show that the intervals described by the five image quality adjectives are not at all uniform. Further, the "poor" and "bad" categories are almost the same, according to Jones, *et al* (1986). In a similar study of the impairment categories, Zwick (1984) found that they are not of uniform category width. Inexperienced observers, in particular, had difficulty in using them.

If one assumes an underlying interval scale, it is important that the choice of adjectives reflects equal intervals in the minds of observers. In a study of text print quality where the observers used a four-category scale of print quality–draft quality, near-letter quality, letter quality, and typeset quality–Engeldrum (1991) showed that the width of these quality categories is not equal; with near-letter quality being wider than letter quality.

Caution is strongly advised when using arbitrary category names combined with an analysis technique that implies or assumes an equal width between the category labels. For equal-appearing intervals, one should be cautious about straying from the recommended categories described earlier.

Adjectives to be used as labels for categories can, in fact, be tested using Torgerson's Law of Categorical Judgment. The procedure yields both the sample scale values and category boundaries on the same scale. The method can also be used to compute the widths or equal-interval properties of categories, and a statistical test of the Law, described later, can be performed following the data analysis.

10.1.2 Observer Instructions

Category scaling requires the observer to place each sample into a category or pile. Usually, the categories have adjectives or numbers as labels. An instruction prototype for scaling a series of colored papers for colorfulness (Bartleson, 1984) appears below. It should be adapted by changing the word "papers" to the appropriate description of the samples.

> "You will be shown [presented] each sample of a series of colored papers. We would like to know how ('...ness') you think each paper is. Please express your opinion on a scale of numbers from 1 to 9 where 1 represents a complete lack of ('...ness') and 9 represents the most ('...ness') you can imagine. Use numbers between 1 and 9 to represent equal intervals of ('...ness'). [OPTION: For example, you might think of the scale in the following way-(categories are enumerated here).] The difference in the ('...ness') between the numbers 3 and 4 is the same as the difference between categories 7 and 8. You may not use fractions or decimals; you must use integers. The integers should be from 1 to 9. No larger or smaller integers may be used."

Note the definition of equal intervals for the difference between the numbers or adjectival categories. The samples are, by implication, presented one by one, but this is not a requirement. See Chapter 3 for a complete discussion on presentation modes.

The instructions can be altered to ask the observer to sort a set of samples into a series of categories, designated either by numbers or adjectives. For example:

> "You will be shown [presented] each of a series of colored papers. We would like to know how ('...ness') you think each paper is. Please express your opinion by placing the colored paper under the number [on a table or work space]. The numbers range from 1 to 9 where 1 represents a complete lack of ('...ness') and 9 represents the most ('...ness') you can imagine. Use numbers between 1 and 9 to represent equal intervals of ('...ness'). [OPTION: For example, you might think of the scale in the following way-(categories are enumerated here).] The difference in the ('...ness') between the numbers 3 and 4 is the same as the difference between categories 7 and 8. You may not place the sample between the number, and you must use the designated numbers. No larger or smaller integers may be used."

A recommended option is to use one of the nine-level quantitative adjectival category scales described above. This will reduce the scaling difficulty for inexperienced observers, and it will go a long way to ensure that the intervals are approximately equal.

10.1.3 Equal-Appearing Intervals Scale Generation

When observers can construct equal intervals, the computed scale can be assumed to be an interval scale. Data analysis requires the assignment of arbitrary values, or weights, to the categories to compute an average category value for each sample. Usually the first category is given the value *1*, the second *2*, and so forth, up to $m+1$ categories. The scale value consists of the average category of each sample and can be calculated by equation (10.1).

$$AvgCat = \frac{1}{J}\boldsymbol{K}\left[1\,2\,3 \ldots m+1\right]^T \qquad (10.1)$$

The elements of the row vector in equation (10.1) are the weights assigned to each category. Equation (10.1) computes the weighted row sum and divides the result by the number of observers, J, yielding the average category for each stimulus or sample. If all observers do not judge all samples then the division by J must be altered. In general the divisor is the row sum of each sample. The vector $AvgCat$ has length n, the number of image samples.

Using the equal-appearing intervals category scaling method is not highly recommended. It survives because it is extremely simple, but the scale is only ordinal at best, and is influenced by all sorts of factors that have a tendency to lead to unequal intervals. Equal-appearing intervals may be used as a fall-back method when statistical tests reveal that the category scaling data, described in the next sections, do not fit the underlying models.

10.2 Torgerson's Law of Categorical Judgment

A data analysis procedure that addresses the issues raised by the equal-appearing intervals method is Torgerson's Law of Categorical Judgment, more widely known as successive intervals scaling (Adams and Messick, 1958). Torgerson unified many of the then-existing methods of category judgment with his Law of Categorical Judgment (Torgerson, 1958). Its development parallels Thurstone's Law of Comparative Judgment. The Law of Categorical Judgment has a similar formulation, but the data reduction is somewhat more complex. We quote Torgerson's (1958) description of the underlying framework regarding the Law of Categorical Judgment:

> "A psychological continuum of the attribute of interest is postulated. Each time a stimulus is presented to an observer, it brings about some sort of a discriminal process that has a value on this continuum ['ness' dimension]. Owing to various and sundry factors, upon repeated presentation, the stimulus is not always associated with a particular value, but may be associated with one higher or lower on the continuum. It is postulated that the values associated with any given stimulus project a normal [Gaussian] distribution on the continuum. Different stimuli have different means [scale values] and different standard deviations [discriminal dispersions]."

This is essentially the framework for Thurstone's Law of Comparative Judgment, to which Torgerson added the following assumptions for his Law of Categorical Judgment:

1) The psychological continuum (the "ness" dimension) of the observer can be divided into a specified number of ordered categories or steps.
2) Owing to various factors, a given *category boundary* may not necessarily always be found at a particular point on the continuum. Rather, it is assumed that the category boundary follows a normal distribution of positions on the continuum. Each category boundary may have a different location (mean) and different dispersion (standard deviation).
3) The observer judges a given stimulus to be below a given category boundary whenever the value of the stimulus on the continuum is less than that of the category boundary.

Thurstone's Law of Comparative Judgment is formulated in terms of the scale difference between the samples. With Torgerson's Law of Categorical Judgment, the difference is between the sample scale value and the category boundary. The formal model of Torgerson's Law of Categorical Judgment is given by equation (10.2), where t_g = mean location of the upper *gth* category boundary, S_j = scale value of the *jth* sample, z_{jg} = unit normal deviate corresponding to the proportion of times stimulus *j* is sorted below category boundary *g*, σ_g = the dispersion (standard deviation) of the *gth* category boundary, σ_j = the dispersion (standard deviation) of the *jth* sample, ρ_{jg} = the correlation between the momentary positions of the category boundary *g* and stimulus *j*, *m+1* = number of categories, and *n* = number of samples.

(10.2) $$t_g - S_j = z_{jg}\sqrt{\sigma^2{}_j + \sigma^2{}_g - 2\rho_{jg}\sigma_j\sigma_g}$$
$$g = 1, 2, \ldots m+1;\ j = 1, 2, \ldots n$$

An axiomatic formulation and generalization of successive intervals scaling can be found in Adams and Messick (1958).

Again we have a situation where the number of unknowns exceeds the number of knowns and some assumptions must be made to simplify the application of the law. The sets of assumptions leading to viable solutions are what Torgerson called Classes and Conditions.

10.2.1 Classes and Conditions

Torgerson (1958) provided an array of experimental situations that he called *Classes and Conditions*. His three Classes refer to replications of the category scaling process over trials, over individuals, or over a combination of individuals and trials. The formal models for the various Classes are identical, so we will only consider the Conditions A, B, C and D. The set of simplifying assumptions (Conditions) is made with respect to the variance (standard deviation) and correlation terms in equation (10.2).

Table 10.1 summarizes the assumptions and applicable model for the four conditions. In this table, *C1, C2, C3, k1, k2,* and *r* are all constants.

Table 10.1 Torgerson's Four Conditions of the Law of Categorical Judgement

Condition	Correlation Coefficient	Variances	Model Equation
A	$\rho_{jg}\sigma_j\sigma_g = C1$	$\sigma^2{}_g \neq \sigma^2{}_j$	$t_g - S_j = z_{jg}\sqrt{\sigma^2{}_j + \sigma^2{}_g - 2\rho_{jg}\sigma_j\sigma_g}$
B	$\rho_{jg} = 0$	$\sigma^2{}_g = C2$ $\sigma^2{}_g = 0$	$t_g - S_j = z_{jg}\sqrt{\sigma^2{}_j + C2}$ $t_g - S_j = z_{jg}a_j$
C	$\rho_{jg} = 0$	$\sigma^2{}_g = C3$ $\sigma^2{}_g = 0$	$t_g - S_j = z_{jg}\sqrt{\sigma^2{}_g + C3}$ $t_g - S_j = z_{jg}b_g$
D	$\rho_{jg} = r$	$\sigma_j = k1, \sigma_g = k2$ $\sigma_j = \sigma_g = 0$	$t_g - S_j = z_{jg}\sqrt{k1^2 + k2^2 - 2rk1k2}$ $t_g - S_j = z_{jg}$

Of the four Conditions in Table 10.1, only Conditions B, C and D have wide practical application. Both Condition B and C are formally equivalent, the difference being the interchange of the stimuli and category dispersion. Condition B assumes that each category boundary has a constant discriminal dispersion and that the correlation is zero. In the general case, a_j (in Table 10.1) is only proportional to the sample discriminal dispersion because of the additive constant-category-boundary standard deviation, *C2*. All the solutions described in this chapter make the implicit assumption that the category boundaries are fixed and therefore *C2* = *0*. Then the solution for a_j is equated to σ_j, the sample discriminal dispersion.

Condition C assumes that the sample dispersions are fixed, and that the category boundaries vary. The constant b_g of Condition C is now proportional to the category standard deviation. Generally, the sample standard deviations are assumed constant = *C3*, but practical solutions only estimate a value that is proportional to the category standard deviation. Thus, estimating the category standard deviation independently is not practically possible. This would require the assumption of zero discriminal dispersion for the samples, an assumption that is unrealistic.

Condition D makes the minimum assumptions regarding the category and sample variances, and in this sense it is the equivalent of Thurstone's Case V of the Law of Comparative Judgment. The assumption for Condition D is that all the terms under the square root sign are constant and equal to 1.0. This is equivalent to assuming all the discriminal dispersions and correlations are constant, independent of category or sample. These assumptions make Condition D amenable to simple techniques for determining the scale values, but at the cost of not being able to estimate the sample dispersion or standard deviation.

Before going into the methods of data analysis, a remark is in order about using the Law of Categorical Judgment. This law, like Thurstone's Law of Comparative Judgment, hinges on the confusion by observers in placing a sample in a category. If there is no confusion about a sample, all the judges place the sample in the same category. When this happens, some of these methods will not yield a solution. Therefore, to compute the widths of adjectival categories, there must be sufficient confusion among the categories. Confusion is assured if a given sample finds itself in all of the categories at least once, but achieving this goal depends on the range of the "ness" in the samples and the nature of the specific categories. If this ideal is not reached (the usual case), then an incomplete matrix results, and more sophisticated analysis methods must be used. Many remarks on incomplete proportion matrices discussed in Chapter 9 apply here.

Jones (1960) provides some evidence that, when using the Law of Categorical Judgment, the scale is stable over the changes in the number of categories, over changes in observers, and over the "ness" distribution in the sample. A substantial body of literature seems to cast doubt on this conclusion, but almost all of the reports used the assumption of equal appearing intervals–an untested assumption. Parducci and Wedell (1986) proposed a model that accounts for the average category rating as a function of thc number of categories, samples, and other factors.

10.2.2 Data Analysis

The four Conditions, or simplifying assumptions, of Torgerson's Law of Categorical Judgment allow for varying degrees of analysis from the simplest Condition D to the more complex Conditions B and C.

Observer data for analysis via the Law of Categorical Judgment starts with an n by $m+1$ data matrix. This data matrix is a frequency matrix $\boldsymbol{K}$, where the data elements, k_{jg}, are the number of times stimulus j (row) was put in category g (column).

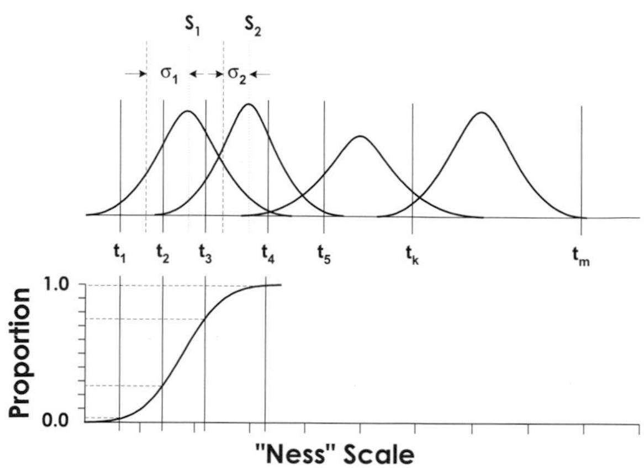

Figure 10.1 The top half of the figure illustrates the discriminal dispersion of the samples, the sample mean values, S's, the discriminal dispersions and the category boundaries, t's. The lower half shows the proportion of times the first sample appeared, below each category boundary. After Gulliksen (1954).

Figure 10.1 illustrates the model parameter relationships. The top part of the figure shows the distributions of the sample judgments along the "ness" axis or dimension. The means of the distributions shown by the S's denote the sample scale value with the σ's denoting the discriminal dispersions for each sample. Vertical solid lines in the figure represent the category boundaries, denoted by the t's. There are only m boundaries, but $m+1$ categories. The lower half of the figure shows the cumulated proportions of the first sample that depicts the proportion of time the sample was placed in a category below each category boundary, t_1, $t_2 ... t_m$. In this example, the sample appeared in four categories whose boundaries are t_1 to t_4.

The next analysis step forms the cumulative frequency matrix, Φ, which is a matrix of cumulative row sums of the frequencies of the $\boldsymbol{K}$ matrix. This operation computes the number of times each sample appears below each category boundary, and is analogous to computing the definite integral of an empirical probability density function.

This operation is represented by a matrix multiplication of $\boldsymbol{K}$ with a special matrix, $\boldsymbol{C}$. The $(m+1)$ by $(m+1)$ matrix $\boldsymbol{C}$ has 1's on its diagonal and 1's in all elements above the diagonal and 0's below the diagonal. This is shown in equation (10.3).

$$\Phi = \boldsymbol{KC} \tag{10.3}$$

In summation notation we can also perform the cumulation (definite integral) using equation (10.4).

$$\phi_{jg} = \sum_{k=1}^{g} K_{jk} \quad g = 1, 2, \ldots m+1 \tag{10.4}$$

The next step is to calculate the n by m proportion matrix, $\boldsymbol{P}$. We do this by dividing each row element of the Φ matrix by the value of the last column of Φ according to equation (10.5).

$$\boldsymbol{P} = p_{jg} = \frac{\phi_{jg}}{\phi_{j,m+1}} \tag{10.5}$$

After this calculation, the last column of $\boldsymbol{P}$ will have values of 1.0 for every row, and is dropped from the matrix. The resulting matrix $\boldsymbol{P}$ is n by m in size. A consequence of dropping the last column is that the first and last category are open-ended intervals; we can determine neither the lower boundary of the initial category nor the upper boundary of the final category.

The final preparatory step before the calculations for scale values is the conversion of the proportions in the $\boldsymbol{P}$ matrix into a $\boldsymbol{Z}$ matrix whose elements are the unit standard normal deviates of the proportions. This is the same procedure we used in the paired comparison example. It is the common matrix used in the solution of Conditions D, C, and B. To obtain the z-values, z_{jg}, the inverse of equation (10.6), the definition of the standard unit normal, is needed for each p_{jg} of equation (10.5).

$$p_{jg} = \int_{-\infty}^{z_{jg}} e^{-\frac{w^2}{2}} dw \tag{10.6}$$

Although the usual transformation function from proportion to z-value is the Gaussian, or normal, the same set of transformations that can be used in the Law of Comparative Judgment is applicable here. The solutions described here are valid for any of the transformations described in Chapter 9, Table 9.1 (Adams and Messick, 1958).

10.2.2.1 Condition D Solution–Complete Matrix

Condition D, the simplest case, assumes that the correlation coefficients and the discriminal dispersions of both the samples and the categories are constant. This assumption means that all the elements under the square root sign in equation (10.2) are constant and sum to one (See Table 10.1). If there are no zeros and ones in the proportion matrix, $\boldsymbol{P}$, it is a complete matrix, and the following least squares solution applies (Torgerson, 1958). The vector of m category boundaries, $\boldsymbol{t}$, is simply the column averages of the $\boldsymbol{Z}$ matrix. In matrix notation, we have the column averages given by equation (10.7) or in summation notation given by equation (10.8).

$$\boldsymbol{t} = \frac{1}{n}[1 \ \ 1 \ \ 1 \ \ \ldots \ \ 1_n]\boldsymbol{Z} \tag{10.7}$$

$$t_g = \frac{1}{n}\sum_{j=1}^{n} z_{jg} \tag{10.8}$$

A vector of scale values, $\boldsymbol{S}$, can be determined by subtracting the row averages from the overall mean of the n by m $\boldsymbol{Z}$ matrix. In matrix formalism we have equation (10.9) for the vector $\boldsymbol{S}$ of n scale values.

$$\frac{1}{mn}\left\{\left(\begin{bmatrix}1 & 1 & 1 & \ldots & 1_n\end{bmatrix} \boldsymbol{Z} \begin{bmatrix}1\\1\\1\\\vdots\\1_m\end{bmatrix} \begin{bmatrix}1 & 1 & 1 & \ldots & 1_n\end{bmatrix}\right)^T - n\boldsymbol{Z}\begin{bmatrix}1\\1\\1\\\vdots\\1_m\end{bmatrix}\right\} \tag{10.9}$$

$$S_j = \frac{1}{mn}\sum_j\sum_g z_{jg} - \sum_g z_{jg} \tag{10.10}$$

A clearer formulation of the scale values is in summation notation given by equation (10.10).

MathCad® sheet `lcajd1.mcd` provides an example of calculating scale values and category boundaries for Condition D of Torgerson's Law of Categorical Judgment.

10.2.1.2 Condition D Solution–Incomplete Matrix

$$t_g - S_j = z_{jg} \tag{10.11}$$

In the more usual category scaling situation, the $\boldsymbol{P}$ matrix will have 1's and 0's as some of its elements, due to a lack of confusion (or presence of a consensus) among observers. This method is modeled after the least squares technique outlined by Morrisey (1955) and Gulliksen (1956) for paired comparisons data analysis, and is a solution to equation (10.11).

$$\begin{bmatrix} t_1 - S_1 \\ t_1 - S_2 \\ t_1 - S_3 \\ t_1 - S_4 \\ t_2 - S_1 \\ t_2 - S_2 \\ \vdots \\ 0 \end{bmatrix} = \begin{bmatrix} 1 & 0 & 0 & -1 & 0 & 0 & 0 \\ 1 & 0 & 0 & 0 & -1 & 0 & 0 \\ 1 & 0 & 0 & 0 & 0 & -1 & 0 \\ 1 & 0 & 0 & 0 & 0 & 0 & -1 \\ 0 & 1 & 0 & -1 & 0 & 0 & 0 \\ 0 & 1 & 0 & 0 & -1 & 0 & 0 \\ \vdots & \vdots & \vdots & \vdots & \vdots & \vdots & \vdots \\ 0 & 0 & 0 & 1 & 1 & 1 & 1 \end{bmatrix} \begin{bmatrix} t_1 \\ t_2 \\ t_3 \\ S_1 \\ S_2 \\ S_3 \\ S_4 \end{bmatrix} \tag{10.12}$$

The solution is motivated by the observation that equation (10.11) is a linear equation with two unknowns (the category boundary and sample scale value) and one known (the corresponding z-value). As an example: for three categories and four samples, equation (10.11) can be written in matrix form as shown in equation (10.12).

The last row in the matrix forces the sum of the scale values to be equal to zero, which is acceptable for an interval scale. Equation (10.12) can be written in a more compact form using matrix notation as equation (10.13) by substituting the z-values according to (10.11) for the column vector of boundary-scale value differences in equation (10.12).

$$\boldsymbol{z*} = \boldsymbol{Xy} \tag{10.13}$$

For a full or complete proportion matrix, $\boldsymbol{z*}$ is a *(mn+1)* by *1* vector, $\boldsymbol{X}$ is *(mn+1)* by *(m+n)*, and $\boldsymbol{y}$ is a *(mn+1)* by *1* vector. When the proportion matrix $\boldsymbol{P}$ is incomplete, the procedure is to eliminate the rows in $\boldsymbol{X}$ that correspond to these 0 or 1 proportions. This reduces the number of rows in the $\boldsymbol{X}$ matrix by the number of 0 or 1 elements in the $\boldsymbol{P}$ matrix. Solution of equation (10.13) is via least squares according to equation (10.14).

$$\boldsymbol{y} = \left(\boldsymbol{X}^T\boldsymbol{X}\right)^{-1}\boldsymbol{X}^T\boldsymbol{z*} \tag{10.14}$$

The first m elements of the solution vector $\boldsymbol{Y}$ are the category boundaries, and the remaining n elements are the scale values.

A few remarks about the solution given by equation (10.14) are in order. First, this is a general solution for Condition D, and can be used instead of equations (10.7-10.10). Secondly, a limit exists for the number of missing or 0 and 1 elements allowed before there is no solution, according to equation (10.14). Specifically, the number of rows in X must be at least $(m+n+1)$.

The details of this Condition D incomplete matrix method can be found in MathCad® sheet `lcajdi1.mcd`.

10.2.2.3 Condition B and C Solutions–Complete Matrix

Conditions B and C are similar in terms of solution. Condition B assumes that the category boundary discriminal dispersions are constant, while Condition C assumes the sample dispersions are fixed. A solution for one is formally the same as the other, providing the discriminal dispersions of the samples are interchanged with the categories. The solution of Condition C would yield the scale values, the category boundaries, and the category dispersions. However, the use of Condition C is not common, so we will focus only on Condition B. Also, the usual assumption of fixed category boundaries requires the category discriminal dispersion to be zero. Then the estimate of a_j in Table 10.1 is identical to the standard deviation of the sample standard deviation or discriminal dispersions.

Two solutions for Condition B, with a complete matrix, are presented here. The first is a straightforward algebraic solution, and the second is a more sophisticated approach that requires the singular value decomposition of the proportion matrix.

The simplest solution to Condition B for computing the scale values, the discriminal dispersions, and the category boundaries follows Torgerson (1958). It is an approximation that does not have any least squares properties. The formal model is Condition B, where the sample discriminal dispersion and the assumed constants are incorporated into a new constant, a_j, in equation (10.15).

$$t_g - S_j = z_{jg} a_j \tag{10.15}$$

Starting with the Z matrix of the transformed cumulative proportions, the first step is computing the row means and row standard deviations according to the equations 10.16-10.18. Row means are given in matrix notation by equation (10.16). In summation notation the row averages, avg_j, are computed by equation (10.17).

$$\boldsymbol{avg} = \frac{1}{m}[1 \quad 1 \quad 1 \quad \dots \quad 1_n]\boldsymbol{Z}^T \tag{10.16}$$

$$avg_j = \frac{1}{m}\sum_{g=1}^{m} z_{jg} \tag{10.17}$$

For the estimate of the discriminal dispersions a_j, use the reciprocal of the row standard deviation. The standard deviation of each row, sd_j, can be computed using equation (10.18).

$$sd_j = \sqrt{\frac{1}{m}\sum_g \left(z_{jg} - avg_j\right)^2} \tag{10.18}$$

The sample discriminal dispersions are just the reciprocals of the row standard deviations, $a_j = 1/sd_j$. Category upper boundaries, t_g, are computed by calculating the weighted column (category) average of the Z matrix. The weights are the row (or sample) standard deviations, as shown in equation (10.19).

$$t_g = \frac{1}{n}\sum_{j=1}^{n}\left(\frac{z_{jg}}{sd_j}\right) \tag{10.19}$$

Finally, the scale values can be computed as the difference of the row (sample) means divided by the row standard deviations, from the average category values (equation 10.20). With this method the

$$S_j = \frac{1}{m}\sum_{g=1}^{m} t_g - \left(\frac{avg_j}{sd_j}\right) \tag{10.20}$$

average of the scale values assumes the customary value of zero, and the discriminal dispersions sum to n.

An example of this Condition B solution with a complete matrix is illustrated in the `lcajc1.mcd` MathCad® sheet.

The second least squares solution is for Condition B with a complete matrix (Gulliksen 1954). This method essentially determines the eigenvalues and vectors of the row-normalized covariance matrix of the $\boldsymbol{Z}$ matrix, and uses the first eigenvector to compute the discriminal dispersions and the scale values. Since the data analysis is complicated, it will be described in steps.

1) Compute the row means, avg_j, and row standard deviations, sd_j, of the $\boldsymbol{Z}$ matrix.
2) Standardize the $\boldsymbol{Z}$ matrix by subtracting the row mean, avg_j, from each element in the row and divide this difference by the standard deviation, sd_j and call this matrix $\boldsymbol{Z'}$. This puts the rows, or samples, on the same scale units; zero mean and unit standard deviation.
3) Form the correlation matrix, $\boldsymbol{C}$, by $(\boldsymbol{Z'Z'}^T)/(number\ of\ samples)$.
4) Decompose matrix $\boldsymbol{C}$ using singular value decomposition (SVD). (See, for example, Strang, 1980.) SVD decomposes the $\boldsymbol{C}$ matrix into its underlying structure according to equation (10.21).

   $$\boldsymbol{C} = \boldsymbol{UDV}^T \qquad (10.21)$$

   Both $\boldsymbol{U}$ and $\boldsymbol{V}$ of equation (10.21) are orthogonal and $\boldsymbol{D}$ is a diagonal matrix with the singular values on the diagonal. This is not unlike finding the eigenvectors and eigenvalues of a matrix. In fact, for some matrices, SVD gives the eigenvectors and eigenvalues directly (Weller and Romney, 1990).
5) Compute the discriminal dispersions of the samples, a column vector $\boldsymbol{d_j}$, from the SVD matrix $\boldsymbol{U}$ and the singular values, $\boldsymbol{D}$, according to equation (10.22).

   $$d_j = \frac{-D_{1,1}U_{j,1}}{sd_j\sqrt{n}} \qquad (10.22)$$

   In other words, the first column of the matrix $\boldsymbol{U}$ is multiplied by the negative of the first singular value, $-D_{1,1}$, and divided by the row standard deviation times the square root of the number of samples, or the number of rows in $\boldsymbol{Z}$.
6) The scale value vector, $\boldsymbol{S}$, can be recovered by using equation (10.23). Each scale value is calculated by taking the element-by-element product of the discriminal dispersion vector, $\boldsymbol{d}$, and the row means of the $\boldsymbol{Z}$ matrix.

   $$S_j = -d_j avg_j \qquad (10.23)$$

7) Finally, the vector of category boundaries, $\boldsymbol{t}$, can be determined from the following equation (10.24).

   $$t_g = -V_{g,1}\sqrt{n} \qquad (10.24)$$

The category boundary vector is just the negative of the first column of $\boldsymbol{V}$, multiplied by the square root of the number of samples or stimuli. This completes the method. An example is illustrated in the MathCad® sheet `lcajc2.mcd`.

10.2.2.4 Condition B and C Solutions–Incomplete Matrix

The most prevalent category scaling data analysis situation is Condition B or C, with an incomplete frequency data matrix. The literature offers some solution options, but most of the widely used methods are approximations. However, two least squares methods have been described–one by Diederich, Messick and Tucker (1957), which we call the DMT method, and another by Bock (1957). There is a small difference between the two methods. The *DMT method* estimates the conventional category boundaries, while *Bock's method* estimates the median, or the middle category position. A discussion of the DMT method follows.

The DMT solution, which provides the category boundaries by minimizing the mean-squared-error, ε, is given by equation (10.25); here w_{jg} is an arbitrary weight chosen so that $w_{jg} = 0$ when the proportion matrix value equals 1 or 0, and a_j is the standard deviation or discriminal dispersion of the scale value, S_j. This is an iterative method that yields a weighted least squares solution to the category boundaries, the sample scale values, and the discriminal dispersions for each sample.

(10.25) $$\varepsilon = \sum_{j=1}^{n} \sum_{g=1}^{m} w_{jg} \left(S_j + a_j z_{jg} - t_g \right)^2$$

The DMT method contends with the incomplete matrix by using a weighting function for the unity and zero values in the proportion matrix that is identically zero. No specific weighting procedures for the non-zero proportion values are suggested by DMT. The MathCad® implementation uses a weighting related to the variance of the proportion, the so-called Müller-Urban weights (Bock and Jones, 1968). A complete description of the DMT iterative method of solution will not be given here. A note of caution is in order, though. The Law of Categorical Judgment, like Thurstone's Law of Comparative Judgment, is a "confusion" scaling method. It needs confusion among the observers for the model to be useful. As a minimum, there must be non-zero frequencies of each sample in at least three categories. If only two categories contain frequency data, the method will produce a fatal error.

This general solution is given in the MathCad® sheet `lcajg.mcd` as a program, or subroutine, called DMT. Raw data is a frequency matrix with columns equal to the number of categories and the rows equal to the number of samples. Matrix elements are the number of times the sample, in the row, is put in the category associated with the column.

10.3 Test of the Law of Categorical Judgment

There are basically two Conditions, B and D, that generally apply to category scaling. A useful question to answer is which condition "better" fits the experimental proportions. This suggests a statistical test of the difference in proportions like Mosteller's (1951c) test for the Law of Comparative Judgment in Chapter 9.

Torgerson (1958) suggested that the average absolute difference in the proportions be used as an "index of agreement." Yet a statistical test of the average absolute difference was not provided. Guilford (1954) proposed the use of Mosteller's (1951c) chi-square test, but Torgerson objected to this application of the test because, while cumulating the proportions across the categories, the proportions lose their assumed statistical independence. Bock (1968) proposed the chi-square goodness-of-fit test with a modification that addressed Torgerson's main objection. The modification is to compute the differences in the cumulative proportions for adjacent categories, which yields the individual proportions for each sample category. This differencing is equivalent to differentiating the cumulative probability function. It "undoes" the proportion cumulation of equations (10.4) and (10.5).

Bock's chi-square test statistic, which is in the tradition of a goodness-of-fit test on the number of responses, is given in equation (10.26), where $p_{j,g}$ = the empirical cumulative proportion of the jth sample in the gth category, $P'_{j,g}$ = the cumulative proportions from either Condition B or D, and J_j = the number of observers scaling the jth sample. Note that this chi-square test statistic is the classical goodness-of-fit test on the frequencies, and is subject to the usual limitations if $J_j < 5$ (Sachs,1984).

(10.26)

$$\chi^2 = \sum_{j=1}^{n} \left\{ \sum_{g=2}^{m} \frac{\{[(p_{j,g} - p_{j,g-1}) - (P'_{j,g} - P'_{j,g-1})]J_j\}^2}{(P'_{j,g} - P'_{j,g-1})J_j} + \frac{[(p_{j,1} - P'_{j,1})J_j]^2}{P'_{j,1}J_j} + \frac{\{[(1-p_{j,m}) - (1-P'_{j,m})]J_j\}^2}{(1-P'_{j,m})J_j} \right\}$$

The model proportions to be used in equation (10.26) are calculated from the estimates of the scale value, the discriminal dispersions, and the category boundaries, depending on the Condition. For the Condition D model, the theoretical proportions are calculated from equation (10.27), where the primes indicate model estimates.

(10.27)

$$P'_{jg} = \frac{1}{\sqrt{2\pi}} \int_{-\infty}^{(t'_g - S'_j)} e^{-\frac{w^2}{2}} dw$$

When testing Condition D using equation (10.26), the degrees of freedom for determining the critical chi-square value are $df = n(m-2)+1$.

(10.28)

$$P'_{jg} = \frac{1}{\sqrt{2\pi}} \int_{-\infty}^{\left(\frac{t'_g - S_j}{\sigma_j}\right)} e^{-\frac{w^2}{2}} dw$$

For Condition B, model equation (10.28) is used for calculating the theoretical proportions.

The degrees of freedom for this chi-square test, according to Bock and Jones (1968), are $df = (n-1)(m-3)$. This implies that at least two samples and four categories are needed for application of the test.

Using Mosteller's test is also possible (Chapter 9) with the differencing modification given by equation (10.26). The angular transformation is used to convert proportions, which are binomially distributed, to normally distributed random variables that more closely approximate the underlying assumptions of the chi-square test. The transformation of the proportions is now performed on the difference of the cumulated proportions, and is given in equation (10.29).

(10.29)

$$\theta_{jg} = \sin^{-1}[2(p_{j,g} - p_{j,g-1}) - 1]$$

$$(10.30)\quad \chi^2 = \sum_{j=1}^{n} J_j \sum_{g=2}^{m} \left(\theta_{j,g} - \theta'_{j,g}\right)^2 + J_j\left(\theta_{j,1} - \theta'_{j,1}\right)^2 + J_j\left(\theta_{j,m+1} - \theta'_{j,m+1}\right)^2$$

Equation (10.30) gives the formula for computing the chi-square test statistic. The degrees of freedom are the same as for equation (10.26) and depend on whether the model of equation (10.27) or (10.28) is used.

These two chi-square tests will give different numerical values for the same data. They are two different estimators of the chi-square test statistic. In both cases the test statistic will increase in accuracy as the number of observers increases. Preference should be given to the computation of chi-square based on equation (10.30). It should be less affected by small numbers of frequencies in the ***K*** matrix and more sensitive to deviations in small proportions. This test is included in the MathCad® worksheet in file `lcajg.mcd`.

10.3.1 Diagnostics

The chi-square values, computed via either equation (10.26) or (10.30) for each proportion, can be used for diagnostics in the case where the model fails. The model fails if the computed chi-square value exceeds the critical value. If the chi-square values for each sample are summed across the categories (the row sums), they can be compared to the approximate expected value. Ignoring the degrees of freedom lost to the categories, the expected chi-square value is approximately the number of categories minus one—m+1-2 = m-1 (Bock and Jones, 1968). Samples with larger-than-expected values are the samples that do not fit the appropriate model of the Law of Categorical Judgment. One cause is they do not fit the underlying distribution describing the discriminal dispersion, for some reason.

To confirm whether the judgments fit the assumed underlying distribution, particularly for the samples with chi-square values that exceed the expected value, the actual z-values of the sample can be plotted against the model z-values. If all is well, the line should be straight. Lack of straightness suggests a different observer distribution, and reviewing the sample(s) would be prudent to see if there are unanticipated "nesses" affecting the observers' judgments.

This chapter concludes interval scale methods. In Stevens' scale classification system there is still another scale type to consider: the ratio scale. This is the topic of the next chapter.

Chapter 11

Ratio Scaling

Previous chapters have described methods of ordinal and interval scale generation using various data collection and analysis methods. In this chapter we cover the last of Stevens' scaling categories, ratio scales. Scale values of ratio scales are a linear function of the "nesses," modified only by an undetermined multiplier. The arbitrary additive constant that is part of an interval scale is zero with a ratio scale.

Stanley Smith Stevens, a pioneer in the development and use of ratio scaling methods in psychophysics, also proposed a power function as a description of human sensory processes. For example, brightness is a power function of luminance, with an exponent of about one third. Over many years, Stevens determined the power functions for quite a diverse array of sensory attributes or "nesses," ranging from loudness and brightness to vibration, visual length, and thermal pain (Stevens, 1975). Both the ratio scaling method and the sensory power law model initially stirred controversy. However, ratio scaling methods are now accepted and widely used.

Although Stevens was a notable proponent of ratio scales, he was not the first to use them. One of the earliest applications of the ratio scaling method was the respacing of the Munsell colors by Newhall (1939). Newhall credits Richardson (1929) with originating the ratio scaling method. Panek and Stevens (1966), Indow and Stevens (1966), Bartleson (1984, 1979), Tyrell *et. al.* (1990, 1993), Luo *et. al.* (1991) describe some imaging and color applications of ratio scaling. A recent summary of the status of ratio scaling is given in Bolanowski and Gescheider (1991). Lodge (1981) provides a summary of ratio scaling applications for such diverse "nesses" as the prestige of occupations, social status, strength of religious attitudes, moral judgments, importance of political office, and other areas of social opinion research. (See also Wegener, 1982.)

11.1 Ratio Scaling Methods

Ratio scale generation has evolved along two paths: *magnitude estimation* and *magnitude production* (Stevens, 1957).

Magnitude estimation requires the observers to give a numerical response in proportion to how they perceive the strength of the "ness." Observers respond with a number for a stimulus expressed as a ratio compared to a reference stimulus. For example, if the observer chooses a number, say 10, for a darkness reference sample, the observer is instructed to give a number that is twice as much as the reference for a sample that has twice as much darkness. The key notion underlying ratio scaling is that the numeric responses by the observers should represent the *ratio* of the strength of the "ness" in the sample to the strength of the "ness" in the reference.

The technique traditionally used a "ness" or image quality reference assigned a value by the scaling administrator. This number assigned to the reference is called the modulus, and is related to the multiplier of the scale. The current practice in psychophysics, though, is to let the observer assign the modulus to the reference (Gescheider, 1997; Bolanowski and Gescheider, 1991).

Magnitude production is the inverse of magnitude estimation. Here the observer is given a number and is asked to adjust a "ness" to correspond to the number. Right now this technique has limited applicability in imaging because of the difficulty of adjusting "nesses" within images. With greater understanding of image quality and its components, and inevitable increases in computational power, magnitude production will assume a greater role in the future.

Several variations of the magnitude estimation method exist. An interesting and controversial variant proposed by Zwislocki and Goodman (1980) is a method called *absolute scaling*. Absolute scaling is essentially conventional ratio scaling without a reference or modulus–observers are free to choose their own numbers. The concept of absolute scaling is to accept that observers will respond with numbers on some absolute basis. To an extent, the Image Quality Circle also accepts the idea that observers can judge image quality on some absolute basis. Since the only operational difference between absolute scaling and magnitude estimation is modulus assignment, we will not distinguish this variation from the well-established magnitude estimation in the following descriptions. The focus of this chapter is on the magnitude estimation method of ratio scaling.

11.2 Ratio Scaling Considerations

Ratio scaling, like interval scaling methods, has several inherent sources of variability (Stevens, 1961). Four important sources are: 1) observer training, 2) observer calibration, 3) reference standard and modulus setting, and 4) observers' use of numbers. These sources of data variability are amenable to various forms of correction that can be employed to improve the quality of the ratio scale. This section provides useful techniques for coping with these sources of variability.

11.2.1 Observer Training

The idea of ratio scaling is straightforward, and can be performed by children as young as six years old (Zwislocki and Goodman, 1980). Without some observer training however, the scales generated have substantial variance (e.g., Zwislocki and Goodman, 1980, 1983; Lodge, 1981; Bartleson, 1979, 1984).

One contributing factor to this scale variance is the observers' experience with judging ratios. Training, which in some situations provides the only observer experience, is essential if low-variance "ness" scales are to be determined.

Training can be extensive if the judgment task, or "ness," is complex. If observers have experience or are familiar with the "ness" to be scaled, then basic training should suffice. A common form of "training" in simple ratio judgment tasks is simply to discard the responses of the initial trials. Conceptually, the observer is being trained by performing the actual judgment task. Pilot studies, discussed in Chapter 3, are helpful in determining the necessary amount of observer training. Of course, if there is high confidence in an observer's ability to make consistent ratio judgments, then training may not be necessary at all.

11.2.2 Observer Calibration

In ratio scaling the usual scale "currency" is the number scale, but Stevens (1975) put forth the possibility that something other than numbers could serve as a scale reference. This idea suggests the possibility that observers can be calibrated. A strong motivation for observer calibration is the empirical observation that observers do not use number responses as expected (Baird, Lewis and Romer, 1970). Baird's Number Preference Model (1997) will be explored in detail later in this chapter.

One effective calibration and training technique is ratio scaling of line lengths (Stevens, 1975). The idea is to first determine the "ness" scale in terms of numerical responses by the observers, and then to transform all the "ness" numbers to line "lengthness." Numerous experiments have shown that, averaged over a population, observers' perceptions of "lengthness," over short distances, bears a one-to-one relationship to the physical length (e.g., Stevens and Guirao, 1963; Zwislocki, 1983). This calibration process references the observer's numerical responses to the scale of line length, thus "calibrating out" the observer's use of numbers. This calibration idea is quite similar to the response transformation (sensory-response law) of Shepard (1981) and Berglund's (1991) master scaling.

Two useful results come from this line-length scaling exercise. First, it gives the observer experience in generating ratios, and secondly, the test administrator has a calibration of the observer's use of numbers (Zwislocki, 1983) or his sensory-response function.

A typical line-length calibration procedure is to have each observer estimate the ratios of a series of lines printed on a card (Lodge, 1981; Stevens, 1975). A total of about 10 lines with a maximum length ratio of about 100:1 is usually adequate (Stevens, 1966). In the training exercise, the first line on the card (the reference) is assigned a numbe (the modulus) by the observer. Next, the observer is asked to assign numbers to the other line lengths in proportion to the ratio of these line lengths to the reference line length. Each observer will then generate pairs of x-y data, consisting of line-length ratio estimates and actual physical line lengths.

The observers' calibration curve can be determined by plotting the magnitude estimate of line length versus the physical line length. Underlying the calibration of line length is Stevens' Power Law. Simply stated, *Stevens' Power Law*, in this context, states that the number response scale, *S*, is related to the line length, *L*, raised to some power, β. Equation (11.1) is a formal statement of what is widely known as Stevens' Law.

$$S = \alpha L^{\beta} \tag{11.1}$$

In equation (11.1) the constant α is the observer's modulus, or overall multiplying factor, that varies among observers and scaling situations. The exponent, β, is a parameter that characterizes the observer's use of numbers. If an observer used numbers "correctly," and the empirical observation that the perceived line length is equal to the physical line length is true, then β = 1 (Baird, 1970). Since it is assumed that the observer's perception of length is proportional to the physical length, then the exponent, β, must be associated with the observer's use of numbers.

The simplest method to estimate the two parameters in equation (11.1) is by a least squares fit. Taking the logarithms of equation (11.1) transforms it to a linear equation in the logarithms of the numerical line-length estimates and the logarithm of the physical line length (Gescheider, 1997). At this point an ordinary least squares fit routine can be used. This empirical "calibration" curve for each observer provides a means of referencing the observer's number response to line length or distance.

This "calibration" function is an example of a scaling method Stevens (1975) pioneered, called *cross-modality matching*. In cross-modality matching, the observer uses one response modality, say the intensity of sound, to match the intensity of light. In this calibration example, the modalities are numbers and physical line length.

Using the line-length calibration data for each observer, the number responses to a "ness" can be referenced to line length, *L*. The calibration equation is given by equation (11.2). Here α_i and β_i are the parameters for the number-line length power function, equation (11.1), for the ith observer, and *ness* is the number response of the observer when judging a "ness."

$$L = \left(\frac{ness}{\alpha_i} \right)^{\frac{1}{\beta_i}} \tag{11.2}$$

The major purpose of this calibration strategy is to reduce the variance in the ratio scale estimates of any "ness" by accommodating each observer's different use of numbers. Equation (11.2) puts each "ness" scale on a common reference, literally line length or distance.

Individual observers exhibit a tendency to use numbers in the same way in similar scaling studies (Bartleson, 1978). If an individual's calibration curve is available, then it can be applied to subsequent scaling studies.

Another method for reducing the variance of the scale value normalizes the variance on an observer-by-observer basis. It is not a calibration method in the sense described here, but it accomplishes a similar objective. A detailed description will be provided later in section 11.5.2.

11.2.3 Reference Standard and Modulus Setting

The magnitude of each observer's response scale is a consequence of the choice of reference number or modulus selected for the reference sample.

Typically there are two choices for the selection of a number for the reference stimuli. The first choice is the selection by the scaling study administrator, and the second is to let the observer select it. Letting the study administrator select the modulus and the reference has been shown to affect both parameters of Stevens' power law in classical psychophysical experiments (Gescheider, 1985). The present recommended practice for assigning a number, the modulus, to the reference sample is to let the observers select their own number. Yet this is no panacea. Suppose, for example, that the true response scale, R_t, is related to the ith observer's response scale, R_i, by a constant, α_i, thus, $R_i = \alpha_i R_t$. If α_i varies randomly from observer to observer, its effect will be to increase the range of responses and therefore increase the variance of the calculated sample scale values.

An important rule for reference stimuli selection is to avoid samples that may be at the ends of the "ness" scale–samples with the smallest or largest amount of the "ness." Some mid to low value is suggested. However, there is a bit of circularity in this suggestion because the study administrator generally does not know the scale values. A simple procedure is to rank-order the samples and select one for a reference based on its position in the middle of the ranking. Stevens (1975) has suggested that only in the initial stages of the scaling do the observers pay attention to a reference. As the scaling study proceeds the reference has little influence on the observer's response.

11.2.4 Observers' Use of Numbers

Two significant issues arise with observers' use of numbers in ratio scaling. The first is the *specific number set*, and the second is the *range of numbers used* by observers.

Specific Number Set. It has been recognized (Baird, 1975, 1997) that observers do not use the complete continuum of numbers when responding. Their responses are often limited to single digits from a base of 5 or 10 (Baird, 1997). If a scale of 1 to 100 is to be used, one can rely on certain numbers being mentioned frequently: 1, 2, 3, 4, 5, 6, 7, 8, 9, 10, 15, 20, 25, 30, 40, 50, 60, 70, 75, 80, 90, 100. According to Baird's Number Preference Model (Baird, 1997), the preferred number, *PN*, is given by equation (11.3), where k is an integer from 1 to $B\text{-}1$, B is the base of the number, 5 or 10, and n is an integer, 0, 1, 2, ..etc. Some numbers appear in both base systems, e.g., $10 = 2 \times 5^1$ and 1×10^1, so the above equation does not define a unique set.

$$PN = kB^n \tag{11.3}$$

The Number Preference Model as applied to ratio scaling has a significant implication regarding data analysis. The continuum of scale values is clustered, or quantized, around the set of preferred numbers. Responses used by observers are not, as is widely assumed, a continuum of numbers, but rather a set of discrete values. Please refer to Baird (1975) to review the wider theoretical implications of the Number Preference Model.

We must understand the implications of working with quantized data to avoid unintended consequences. Using discrete numbers as a representation of the number continuum is similar to the representation of numbers in a digital computer. The conversion from continuous or analog data to finite-bit digital data is performed by a quantizer or digitizer. Quantizing is a many-to-one mapping. A range of numbers around the quantized value is assigned one number. For example, an integer-rounding quantizer "maps" the continuous number interval from 1.50 to 2.50 into the integer 2. Note that we observed the quantization of the proportions in all the previous (interval) scaling methods, for a completely different reason, so it is not a phenomenon associated only with ratio scaling.

A linear quantizer will produce constant differences in the output for constant differences in the input. However, linear quantizers are not the only type, particularly in imaging and audio applications. In such applications, there are *unequal* differences between input and output. Very often the relationship between an input of continuous data and the quantized output numbers is logarithmic.

Under the Number Preference Model, the spacing between the response numbers, the quantization, is not uniform. In other words, the differences between the quantized values are not constant. One way to visualize this is to think of quantization in terms of a mapping, or transformation, from the "ness" or stimulus dimension to the response (number) dimension. When the mapping is a straight line, the output is the number continuum. The map for quantized data looks like a flight of stairs, and a nonuniform quantizer looks like a set of stairs where the tread height varies as the horizontal distance increases.

The nonlinear quantization implied by the Number Preference Model becomes a practical consideration when any statistical analysis is performed on the observers' responses. If the Number Preference Model holds, then the assumption of normally distributed random variables as the underlying probability density of the ratio scale responses is not justified. Any tests using statistics that have normality as the underlying assumptions are likely to be suspect. Specifically, this means that conclusions from the usual t-tests, F-tests and Analysis of Variance may be in error.

Baird, Lewis and Romer (1970) give a brief analysis of the ratio scale mean and standard deviation using discrete number response with an underlying normal distribution. They conclude that if the standard deviation is at least half the quantization interval, then the errors in computing these parameters are tolerably small.

Range of Numbers Used. Another concern is the range of numbers used as a response by observers. With the assumption that Stevens' Power Law describes the relationship between the sample "ness" value and the observer response, equation (11.1), the choice of the number range that any given observer will use in a scaling study strongly influences the exponent, β. For a fixed "ness" range, the exponent varies directly with the range of numbers the observer uses for ratio responses. For example, if one observer uses the numbers one to ten to describe a fixed "ness" range and another observer uses the range one to one thousand, then the computed exponents will differ by a ratio of two–the difference in the logarithms of the number response range.

Each observer's data can be adjusted for the observer's use of numbers. The line calibration procedure described in section 11.2.2 is one adjustment method. Another method will be described in section 11.5.

11.2.5 Observer Instructions

Stanley Smith Stevens (1975), the developer of the ratio scaling method, proposed a simple set of observer instructions widely used in many ratio scaling studies. Upon presentation of a sample, the observer's task is to respond with a number that is in proportion to the "ness" relative to the first sample. "In proportion" means the observer is to reply with a ratio. The prototype below is similar to that used by Tyrell, *et. al.* (1990).

> "You will be presented with a series of stimuli (samples) in irregular order. Your task is to tell how much of the ('...ness') they seem to have by assigning numbers to them. Call the first sample (stimulus) any number that seems appropriate to you. Then assign successive numbers so they reflect your subjective impression of ('...ness') relative to the first sample. If the sample appears to have twice the ('...ness') as the first sample, assign a number twice as large. Similarly, if the sample has a ('...ness') only half of the first sample, assign a number one-half the first sample. There is no limit to the range of numbers that you may use. You may use whole numbers, decimals, or fractions. Try to make each number match the amount of the ('...ness') as you perceive it"

When using this prototype, replace the parenthetical word "...ness" with the actual "ness" of interest. The words used in the observer instructions are usually presented in the study report methodology sections as the word definition of the scale.

11.3 Ratio Scaling Data Collection

The usual ratio scaling procedure is first to present a sample to an observer, and ask that the observer to respond with a number to represent the strength or amount of the "ness" in the sample. This sample will serve as the observer's reference. The number he or she responds with is that observer's modulus.

Further samples are presented to the observer, usually one at a time, and the observer is asked to respond with a number that represents the ratio of the "ness" in the present sample to the reference "ness." The numerical response of the observer is recorded for each sample.

Data is recorded in a matrix where each column represents a sample and each row represents an observer. This results in a J by N matrix, $\boldsymbol{RN}$, with the rows $i = 1$ to J, and the columns, $j = 1$ to N. This is the basic ratio scale data matrix from which the scale values are generated.

11.4 Scale Generation

The standard procedure for computing the scale values, $\boldsymbol{S}_j$, is to take the geometric mean of the columns of $\boldsymbol{RN}$, assuming there are no response values of zero (Stevens, 1975; Bartleson, 1984). The rationale for using the geometric mean is to make an estimate of the scale value that is not excessively influenced by large values. The traditional arithmetic mean would be biased by large values that occur because each observer uses his or her own response constant, α in equation (11.1).

If one assumes that the responses are statistically distributed according to a log-normal probability density, then the geometric mean is an unbiased estimate of the expected scale value. The geometric mean is the Jth root of the product of all J responses and is calculated according to equation (11.4).

$$S_j = \left(\prod_{i=1}^{J} RN_{ij} \right)^{\frac{1}{J}} \quad (11.4)$$

A more convenient computational method is to take the logarithms of the elements of $\boldsymbol{RN}$ and compute the average of the column sum and then exponentiate the result. The following equations (11.5 and 11.6) in summation form give results identical to using equation (11.4).

$$\ln(S_j) = \mu_j = \frac{1}{J} \sum_{i=1}^{J} \ln(RN_{ij}) \quad (11.5)$$

$$S_j = e^{\ln(S_j)} = e^{\mu_j} \quad (11.6)$$

In keeping with our matrix vector notation, we can rewrite equations (11.5 and11.6) as equation (11.7). Note that in equation (11.7) $\boldsymbol{LRN}$ is the logarithm of $\boldsymbol{RN}$, element-by-element, $\boldsymbol{S}$ is a vector of scale values, and the exponentiation is taken element-by-element. This equation may be more convenient for scale value calculation in some circumstances.

$$\boldsymbol{S} = \exp\left(\frac{1}{J} [1 \quad 1 \quad 1 \quad \dots \quad 1] \boldsymbol{LNR} \right) \quad (11.7)$$

11.4.1 Zero Responses

A fundamental property of a ratio scale is that it has an absolute zero. In practical scaling situations, one does not expect to encounter an attribute with zero value, but there are exceptions. One noteworthy exception is the scaling of colorfulness of colored patches (Bartleson, 1985). If an observer is presented with a gray patch, the response will probably be zero as the ratio. Of course, the instructions to the observer could prohibit a zero response, but that may place an artificial constraint and a potential source of scale bias.

If there is a zero response in any column of the data matrix, ***RN***, the geometric mean is necessarily zero. This, in effect, throws away all the data for that sample. Solutions to this problem include using the median or the mode of each column of ***RN*** as the estimate of the scale value. Of the two, the median is more widely used (Marks, 1974).

An alternative method of computing the geometric mean of data with zero number response is based on the geometric mean inequality of Hoehn and Niven (1985). The procedure is to first add a small constant, c, to each observer's response. Next, compute the geometric mean using any of the equations (11.4-11.6) and subtract the constant from this result. The computation is given by equation (11.8).

$$S_j \approx \left[\prod_{i=1}^{J}(RN_{ij}+c)\right]^{\frac{1}{J}} - c \tag{11.8}$$

An appropriate value of c should be small, say 0.001, otherwise it can seriously affect the computed value if there are several zero responses. Equation (11.8) gives a positively biased estimate of the "true" geometric mean that depends on the selection of c. No studies seem available that give any guidance for its selection.

11.4.2 Scale Standard Deviation

In practical applications, knowledge of the scale variance is a prerequisite for statistical testing. The geometric mean is used as the estimate of the scale value. To find the scale variance, an estimator of the geometric mean variance is needed.

Alf and Grossberg (1979) provide a general approximation for estimating the variance of the scale value. This variance approximation, which makes no assumption about the statistical distribution of the observers' responses, is given by equation (11.9).

$$\mathrm{var}(S_j) \approx S^2{}_j\ \mathrm{var}\left[\ln(S_j)\right] \tag{11.9}$$

A simple procedure for calculating the variance of the logarithm, *var[ln(*S_j*)]*, is to use the standard formulas except that the numerical responses are first converted to logarithms. Equation (11.10) gives the details of the computation.

$$\mathrm{var}\left[\ln(S_j)\right] = \frac{1}{J-1}\sum_{i=1}^{J}\left[\ln(RN_{ij}) - \ln(S_j)\right]^2 \tag{11.10}$$

Again, we have computational difficulty with zero responses since the logarithm of zero is infinite. One solution is to substitute the average scale value for a zero response value in the ***RN*** matrix. Although quite usable, this solution tends to underestimate the variance of the scale value, particularly if there are many zero responses. An alternative possibility is to ignore the zero responses and reduce the *J-1* factor in equation (11.10) by the number of zero responses: that is make *J-1* equal to the number of non-zero values.

MathCad® sheet `ratio1.mcd` is an example of scale value and scale variance calculations.

11.5 Correcting for Observer Modulus and Exponent

Adjustment for the observer's choice of modulus in ratio scaling is not particularly common in the field of psychophysics. The most likely reason is that most psychophysicists are interested in the exponent of Stevens' Power Law, equation (11.1), which describes the sensory transducer characteristics. However, for the reasons put forth in previous sections of this chapter, the next sections describe methods for correcting the scaling responses for the individual observer's modulus and scale range.

11.5.1 Observer Modulus Correction

Lane *et. al.* (1961) used the following modulus adjustment technique, which estimates each observer's modulus, either as a multiplicative factor or as an addition of a logarithm.

1) First calculate the grand geometric mean, *GM*, for *all* samples and observers' responses according to equation (11.11).
2) Calculate the geometric mean for *each* observer's responses using equation (11.12). This is the geometric mean over all samples for each observer.
3) Compute the scale values from the response matrix by correcting each observer's response according to equation (11.13).

(11.11)
$$\overline{\boldsymbol{GM}} = \left(\prod_{i=1}^{J} \prod_{j=1}^{N} RN_{ij} \right)^{\frac{1}{J+N}}$$

(11.12)
$$GM_i = \left(\prod_{j=1}^{N} RN_{ij} \right)^{\frac{1}{N}}$$

(11.13)
$$S_j = \left(\prod_{i=1}^{J} RN_{ij} \frac{GM_i}{\overline{GM}} \right)^{\frac{1}{J}}$$

This procedure will only correct for the observer's choice of modulus, and will not change their individual exponents.

11.5.2 Group Means Scale Normalization

If each observer has been "calibrated" using the line length estimation procedure described in section 11.2.2, then equation (11.2) can be used to put each observer's number response on the scale of line length.

In those situations where no calibration is available and adjustment for the observer's number-use rule is desired, a common practice in the imaging field is to adjust each observer's response to the geometric mean of the group response (e.g., Bartleson, 1979; Tyrell *et. al.*, 1990; Luo *et. al.*, 1991; Tyrell *et. al.* 1993). This is not a calibration procedure. Rather, it is more accurately termed a scale normalization, since each observer's scale is normalized to the geometric mean of the group.

The adjustment process begins by determining the *a0* and *a1* coefficients for each observer, using least squares linear fitting procedures on the logarithms of the numerical responses. The independent variable is the geometric mean of all observers' responses for the jth sample, S_j from equation (11.4). Equation (11.14) defines the linear relationship for adjusting the response from observer, *i*, and sample, *j*.

(11.14) $$\ln(RN'_{ij}) = a0_i + a1_i \ln(S_j)$$

Once the $a0_i$ and $a1_i$ coefficients are determined for each observer, by linear least squares fits, equation (11.14) can be inverted to calculate an adjusted observer response matrix, ***LRN′*** according to equation (11.15).

(11.15) $$\boldsymbol{LRN'} = [\boldsymbol{a1}]^{-1}[\boldsymbol{LRN} - \boldsymbol{a0}]$$

In equation (11.15) ***a1*** is a *J* by *J* diagonal matrix of each observer's *a1* coefficient, and ***a0*** is a *J* by *1* column vector of *a0* coefficients determined from the least squares fits to equation (11.14). These coefficients are subtracted from each column of the matrix ***LRN***. Once the matrix ***LRN′*** is computed, the scale values can be computed using equations (11.5-11.7).

After applying this normalization, variability due to the observer's choice of modulus, α, and number response range, β, has been removed. The principal benefit is the reduction of the response variance for each sample.

This method of scale computation is illustrated in MathCad® sheet `ratio.mcd`.

11.6 Confidence Intervals and Number of Observers

The distribution, or histogram, of the uncorrected observers' numerical responses does not have a widely accepted underlying theoretical probability density function. The usual assumption is that the numeric responses follow a lognormal probability density function (Marks, 1974; Stevens, 1966). However, some data do not support this assumption (Luce and Mo, 1965). Green and Luce (1974) explored the possibility of using a gamma function, but this probability density function did not fit all observers' data equally well. The probability density function describing observers' responses in ratio scaling is still an open theoretical issue.

Assuming the numerical responses follow lognormal probability density function given by equation (11.16), the mean and variance of the sample scale values are given by equations (11.17 and 11.18). In these equations μ = mean of the logarithms of the observers' responses, equation (11.5), and σ^2 = the variance of logs, equation (11.9 and 11.10).

(11.16) $$p(y) = \frac{1}{y\sigma\sqrt{2\pi}} e^{-\left[\frac{\ln(y)-\mu}{\sigma}\right]^2}$$
$$y > 0, \sigma > 0, -\infty < \mu < \infty$$

Compare equations (11.6) and (11.17), and note that the geometric mean is a biased estimate of the scale value if the observer response distribution is lognormal. This bias occurs because the geometric mean estimated by equation (11.5) does not include the variance factor that appears in the exponent of (11.17). The

(11.17) $$\overline{S}_j = e^{\left(\mu_j + \frac{\sigma^2_j}{2}\right)}$$

conclusion to be drawn is that the usual formula for the geometric mean, equation (11.5), may underestimate the scale value if the variance, σ_j^2, is not small.

(11.18)
$$\mathrm{var}(S_j) = e^{(2\mu + \sigma^2_j)}\left(e^{\sigma^2_j} - 1\right) = \bar{S}^2_j\left(e^{\sigma^2_j} - 1\right)$$

Also, from equation (11.18), note that the variance in the scale value varies with the square of the geometric mean and the variance of the response logarithms. If the variance of the logs is small, $\sigma_j^2 < 1$, a series expansion of the exponent in equation (11.18) reveals that the variance of the scale value is equal to equation (11.9).

(11.19)
$$e^{\left[\ln(\bar{S}_j) - \frac{\sigma_j t_{\left(\frac{\alpha}{2},\nu\right)}}{\sqrt{J}}\right]} < \bar{S}_j < e^{\left[\ln(\bar{S}_j) + \frac{\sigma_j t_{\left(\frac{\alpha}{2},\nu\right)}}{\sqrt{J}}\right]} = \bar{S}_j e^{\mp\left[\frac{\sigma_j t_{\left(\frac{\alpha}{2},\nu\right)}}{\sqrt{J}}\right]}$$

With the assumption that the logarithms of the response values are normally distributed (lognormal), we can use all of the statistics appropriate for normal Gaussian distributions. Specifically, we can compute the (1-α) confidence interval of the mean scale value, S_j (Alf and Grossberg, 1979). Straightforwardly we have equation (11.19), where $t_{(\alpha/2,\nu)}$ = the critical t-value for $\alpha/2$ and ν degrees of freedom = $J-1$, and σ_j^2 = the estimate of the variance of logs and J = the number of observers comprising the geometric mean. Note that the factor in the exponent in the second equation of (11.19) *multiplies* the scale value estimate.

Using the right-hand equality of equation (11.19), one can determine the number of observers, J, needed to achieve some fractional precision, F, in the scale estimate. For example, if there is a requirement for a +0.10 (+10%) precision in the scale value, then $F = 1.10$. Setting the factor equal to the right-hand-side of (11.19) and solving for the number of observers, J, yields equation (11.20). In this equation, σ_j = the estimate of the standard deviation of logs, and t = the critical t-value. Strictly speaking t depends on J, but a t-value of about two can be used for practical applications. The largest estimated value of the standard deviation should be used when applying equation (11.20).

(11.20)
$$J \approx \left[\frac{\sigma_j t_{\left(\frac{\alpha}{2},\nu\right)}}{\ln(F)}\right]$$

Although equation (11.20) is based on the lognormal assumption of observer response, lacking another theoretical alternative, one cannot go too far wrong by using it in practical situations. When there are doubts, the safest course is to err on the side of increasing the number of observers.

11.7 Relationship to Other Interval Scales

The interval scaling methods described in the previous chapters can be expected to give equivalent results under comparable scaling conditions. For a specific set of samples, an interval scale generated using category methods will be linearly related to a scale using the graphical rating scale method (Engeldrum, 1991), or to a paired comparison with Thurstone's Case V (Woodbury and Bartleson, 1962). Extensive experience by many workers using the interval scaling methods described in this book supports this expectation.

Mathematically, ratio scales do not have the additive constant of an interval, so one might reasonably assume that interval category scales are linearly related to ratio scales. Unfortunately, there is a large body of experimental evidence that shows this is generally not true (Stevens, 1975). Typically, a power function describes the relationship between the ratio scale, as the independent variable, and the equal-appearing intervals category scale, as the dependent variable. Empirically, the exponent is 1.00 or less, often around 0.50, but the theoretical issue is not so clear. Baird (1997) has shown that the exponent based on the Preferred Number Model is about 0.44. Tyrell, *et. al.* (1990), using successive interval category scaling and ratio scaling of graininess, found that the power was 0.66. Bartleson (1984) advocated the square root, power of 0.50, as an approximation when lacking specific knowledge of the two scales. Baird (1975) offers a theoretical explanation for these discrepancies that is based on observers' use of numbers.

Overwhelmingly, the comparisons between ratio and category scales reported in the literature assume equal difference between categories and use the mean category as the scale value. Sufficient experimental results exist to cast doubt on this equal-intervals assumption. Giving useful generalizations about similarities between the two scaling methods is therefore difficult.

Always, the safest method of analysis would be to use the appropriate solution to the Law of Categorical Judgment described in Chapter 10 to find the category widths and see if, in fact, they are equal.

The key point is not to expect a linear relationship between ratio scales and interval scales for the same set of samples. The general rule states that it will be a nonlinear relationship.

Chapter 12

Selecting the Best Method

No single best scaling method exists, although some methods are more popular than others. This chapter describes a logical procedure to select an appropriate scaling method based on three factors:

1) Confusion in the sample set.
2) The number of samples to be scaled.
3) Observer effort.

In establishing these factors, the emphasis is on the observers' judgment and on the data collection parts of the scaling process, not the effort for data analysis, which is small in contrast.

12.1 Sample Set Confusion

One major distinguishing feature of the scaling methods covered in this book is whether or not the method requires confusion among the samples. The presence of confusion in a sample set is not necessarily easy to decide, especially without a pilot study or some scaling experience with the "ness" or image quality level in question. Confusion in a set of samples is clearly a matter of degree.

All of the confusion methods described in this book are tolerant to various levels of agreement among observers, as typically evidenced by zeros or ones on a proportion matrix. (The zero-one proportion or incomplete-matrix problem is discussed in Chapter 9.) Typically, extreme samples have no confusion, and there is complete agreement among observers. Adjacent samples have *some* confusion. The number of filled elements required in the proportion matrix depends on the data analysis method. An absolute minimum number of filled matrix elements should equal the number of parameters to be estimated. This criterion is what practically establishes the successful application of a confusion method.

Still, how does one go about getting an idea of the confusion in a set of samples? One general method would be to perform a pilot scaling study with a few observers, using the graphical rating scale method from Chapter 7. One could determine, from the scale values and the standard deviations, if there is any overlap in the observers' judgments for adjacent samples on the "ness" scale. Some form of statistical multiple-comparison procedure could be applied to the scale values and standard deviation data. Good sources of multiple-comparison procedures are Klockars and Sax (1986) and Toothaker (1993). The obvious criticism to this pilot-study approach is the fact that after the graphical rating scale study, one already has the scale values! However, this is only a macro-view. If the goal is to determine just-noticable-differences, then the results of the graphical rating scale study are only a starting point.

A simpler and probably quicker approach is a simple ranking of the samples. Samples that consistently receive the same rank are not confused with other samples, either adjacent or surrounding. Samples ranked in at least three different rank orders are probably sufficiently confused.

Confusion can be reasonably assumed if the "ness" range is small, but this is not foolproof. Determining the confusion of a set of samples can be difficult without subjecting the samples to observer judgments, or invoking experience.

12.2 Numbers of Samples

The number of samples is directly proportional to the amount of time the observers' judgments will consume, and therefore to the length of the scaling study. A constant tradeoff exists between the desire to have large sample numbers (to address the concerns outlined in Chapter 3) and acceptable resources (time, money, and access to observers) for the scaling study. For selecting a scaling method, ten samples have been adopted as the criterion. Although this value is arbitrary, it is a reasonable midpoint in the typical range of sample numbers.

In practice, the time for an observer to scale a set of n samples is limited. Fatigue–both physical and psychological–boredom, and a host of other factors start to be of concern if the scaling takes too much time. The governing rule concerning time is this: the shorter the better. Again, there are no standards in this area, but an hour is the recommended maximum amount of time one can ask of an observer. Of course, one hour is not an ironclad rule. It depends on the task.

If the scaling task must take more than an hour, consider offering some form of incentive or reward to maintain observer interest and motivation. Better yet, divide the scaling study into segments conducted on sequential days or add rest periods.

12.3 Observer Effort

Observer effort is defined to be the number of judgments required of an observer when scaling n image samples. Generally, observers provide one judgment for each sample, except paired comparisons and the sorting steps used in ranking. The minimum effort is n, assuming each observer judges all samples.

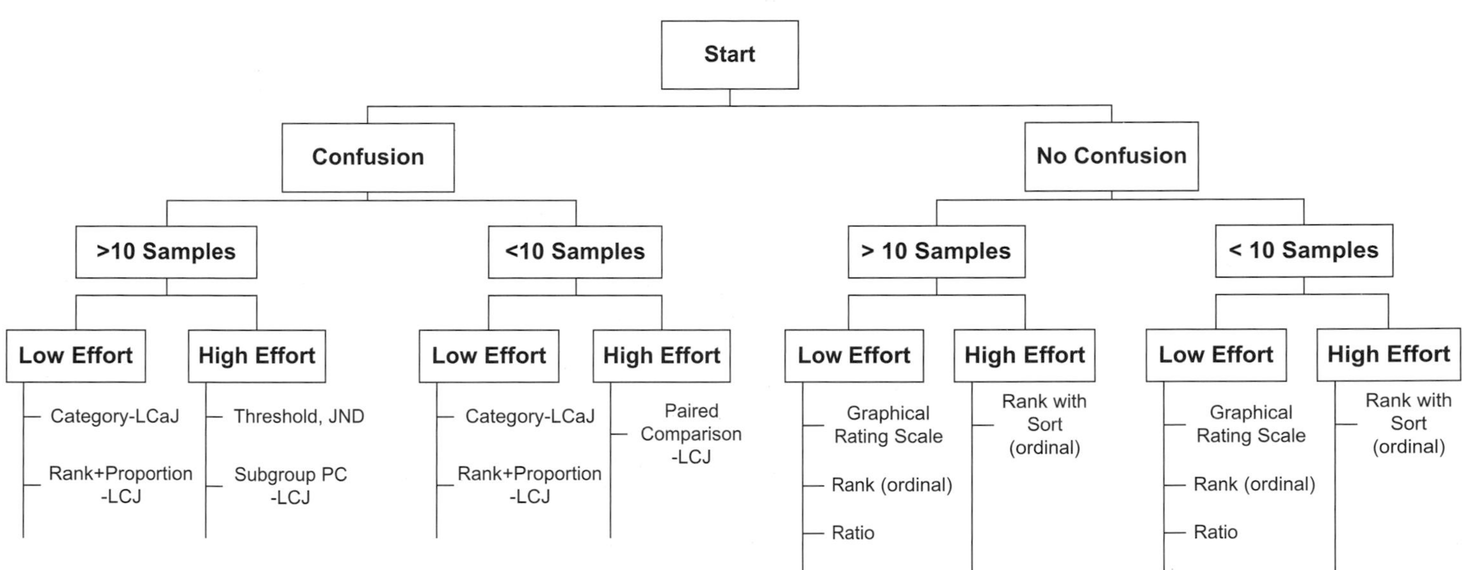

Figure 12.1 Flow chart for selecting the appropriate scaling method. Knowledge of the sample set confusion, sample numbers and the amount of effort to impose on the observers is required. In this figure LCaJ = Law of Categorical Judment, PC = paired comparison, and LCJ = Law of Comparative Judgment. See text for details.

The number of observer judgments required for n samples for paired-comparison methods is $n(n\text{-}1)/2$. For ten samples, the number of comparisons is forty-five, which is a reasonable maximum. Using overlapping sample subgroups can reduce the overall number of judgments required, but it increases scaling study complexity both in terms of administration and data analysis. If k subgroups of m samples each are used, then a total of $km(m\text{-}1)/2$ judgments are needed. This compares with a total of $km(km\text{-}1)/2$ for a complete paired-comparison experiment, a significant reduction. However, using subgroups usually means that each of the subgroup scales will be combined into one complete scale, so at least two samples must appear in adjacent subgroups causing a slight reduction in efficiency.

Some ordinal ranking techniques described in Chapter 6 are equivalent to computer sorting methods. One of these methods is the bubble sort requiring, on average, a total of n^2 judgments, far more than the $n(n\text{-}1)/2$ required for paired comparison. Observers have far more intelligence than computers, so enforcing any particular sorting algorithm can substantially increase observer effort. If the most efficient sorting algorithms are used, the observers' effort can be reduced to a minimum of $nlog_2(n)$, but this advantage can only be realized for more than six samples.

12.4 Scaling Method Selection

A process for selecting an appropriate scaling method is illustrated in Figure 12.1. To use the method one needs to know if the sample set is sufficiently confused, what the number of samples is in the set, and the amount of observer effort you are willing to impose.

To use the flow diagram (or binary tree) in Figure 12.1, the first decision regards the confusion level of the sample set. If there is sufficient confusion then go to the box labeled "Confusion." Otherwise go to the "No Confusion" box. The sample size next determines the selection: greater than or fewer than 10 samples. Finally, a decision on observer effort ("Low" or "High") is needed. This is a qualitative judgment that directly relates to the time allotted for the scaling study.

Below each box labeled "Low Effort" or "High Effort" are the recommended methods. Frequently they are a combination of the data collection plus the data analysis method. Following the *Confusion* branch in Figure 12.1, for example, one can see that with more than ten samples in the sample set and a low-effort observer activity, one recommendation is to use the *Category* data collection method combined with the *Law of Categorical Judgment* to generate the scale values. An alternative in these conditions is to use a *Ranking plus Proportion* study, with *Thurstone's Law of Comparative Judgment.*

The categorizations in this scaling selection method are hardly universal. Applying good judgment by the scaling study planner is also essential in selecting the best method.

Two of the most popular confusion methods are paired comparisons with the Law of Comparative Judgment, and category scaling with the Law of Categorical Judgment. Both methods can be used when confusion is not complete across all samples. Having samples widely spaced on the "ness" dimension does not prohibit the use of these methods, but this is generally less than optimum. The distinctive difference in these methods is the number of samples to be scaled.

For a large confused sample set, a good choice is ordinal ranking with the conversion of the rank data into a proportion matrix. Thurstone's Law of Comparative Judgment can then be applied to the proportion matrix to compute the scale values.

Threshold and just-noticeable-difference scaling studies inherently require high effort because of the number of judgments typically required by each observer. The actual sample number may or may not be large, depending on the complexity of the study.

When sample sets are large, straightforward paired comparison is prohibitive in practice. Paired comparison is a small-sample-number method. The maximum number of samples that can be scaled using paired-comparison methods is largely a local decision. In practice, it seems that paired comparison is more widely used than it probably should be.

Paired comparisons with overlapping subgroups can also be used effectively, but this is usually more time consuming than the graphical rating scale method. The use of subgroups accomplishes two objectives: reducing the overall effort and assuring confusion by using only groups of close samples.

No-confusion methods are not particularly sensitive to sample counts. These methods can handle 30 or more samples depending on the mechanical details of sample presentation, viewing and data collection. Presenting them to the observer one at a time may be more appropriate for very large-size samples, because physical handling can become bewildering for both the observer and study administrator.

If the range of "nesses" in the sample set is large, then the graphical rating scale method is a good choice. It is a highly recommended method for initial scaling studies, because it is an easy task for observers and the data analysis is simple. It gives a "picture" of the sample set with a minimum of scaling effort.

Two remaining low-effort scaling methods in the no-confusion category are ratio and rank order. Their distinction lies in the fact that neither method yields interval scales. Rank order is strictly an ordinal method, and has limited utility within the Image Quality Circle. However it can be very useful for answering "greater-than" questions, selecting anchors, and for pre-pilot studies, among others.

Ratio scaling is not widely used in imaging applications, but it does have the useful property of a true zero. This can raise a philosophical issue of the interpretation of zero image quality, and perhaps this has contributed to its disuse.

12.5 A Cautionary Note

A question closely related to "best methods" is the question of "what to scale." No attempt has been made in this book to address this question, but expressing a view regarding "nesses," and image quality scaling seems appropriate at this point.

A propensity exists in product development environments to go directly for image quality judgments, when asking for a judgment about one or several "nesses" would be more appropriate. This is driven by a desire to obtain a single number for image quality that can be widely communicated. Scaling merely for image quality and not the component "nesses" robs the development team of valuable information about needed changes in these components. Although this is not disastrous, it is not resource-efficient either. Largely for this reason, scaling for image quality alone at the expense of the "nesses" is not recommended.

Bibliography

Adams, E. & Samuel Messick, *An axiomatic formulation and generalization of successive intervals scaling*, Psychometrika 23:355(1958)

Adams, Elliot Q., *X-Z Planes in the 1931 ICI system of colorimetry*, Jour. Opt Soc Amer. 32:168(1942)

Aldrich, John H. & Forrest D. Nelson (1985) ***Linear Probability, Logit, and Probit Models***, Sage University Paper series on Quantitative Applications in the Social Sciences, 07-45. Beverly Hills & London: Sage Publications. ISBN 0-8039-2133-0

Anscombe, F. J., *The transformation of Poisson, Binomial and Negative-Binomial data*, Biometrika 35:246(1948)

Anscombe, F. J., *On estimating binomial response relations*, Biometrika 42:461(1956)

ASTM E 1808-96, ***Standard Guide for Designing and Conducting Visual Experiments***, Amer. Soc. Testing & Materials, 100 Bar Harbor Dr., Conshohocken, PA 19425, www.astm.org

ASTM E 1499-97, ***Standard Guide for Selection, Evaluation, and Training of Observers***, Amer. Soc. Testing & Materials, 100 Bar Harbor Dr., Conshohocken, PA 19425, www.astm.org

Baird, John C., ***Psychophysical Analysis of Visual Space***, Pergamon, London, 1970.

Baird, John C., Charles Lewis, & Daniel Romer, *Relative frequencies of numerical responses in ratio estimation*, Perception & Psychophysics 8:358-362(1970)

Baird, John C., *Psychophysical study of numbers*, Psychol. Res. 38:189-207(1975)

Baird, John C. & Elliot Noma, ***Fundamentals of Scaling and Psychophysics***, John Wiley & Sons, New York, NY, 1978, ISBN 0-471-04169-6

Baird, John C., ***Sensation and Judgment—Complementarity Theory of Psychophysics***, Lawrence Erlbaum Associates, Mahwah, NJ, 1997, ISBN 0-8058-1830-8

Bakshi, M., D. R. Fuhrmann, *Improving the visual quality of JPEG-encoded images via companding*, Jour. Elect. Imag. 6:189(1997)

Bartleson, C. J., & W. W. Woodbury, *Psychophysical methods for evaluating the quality of color transparencies: II. Control of observer adaptation in categorical judgments*, Photo. Sci. & Eng. 6:15(1962)

Bartleson, C. J. & C. P. Bray, *On the preferred reproduction of flesh, blue-sky and green-grass colors*, Photo. Sci. & Eng. 6:19(1962)

Bartleson, C. J., & W. W. Woodbury, *Psychophysical methods for evaluating the quality of color transparencies: III. Effect of the number of categories, anchors and types of instructions on quality ratings*, Photo. Sci. & Eng. 9:323(1965)

Bartleson, C. J. & E. J. Breneman, *Brightness perception in complex fields*, Jour. Opt. Soc. Amer. 57:953(1967)

Bartleson, C. J., *Changes in color appearance with variations in chromatic adaptation*, Color Research and Application 4:119(1979)

Bartleson, C. J., *The combined influence of sharpness and graininess on the quality of colour prints*, Jour. Photo. Sci., 30:33(1982)

Bartleson, C. J., in ***Optical Radiation Measurements, Vol. 5 Visual Measurements***, C. J Bartleson & F. Grum Eds., Chapter 8, Academic Press, Orlando, FL 32887, 1984, ISBN 0-12-304905-9

Berglund, M. B., *Quality assurance in environmental psychophysics*, In Bolanowski, S. J, & G. W. Gescheider, Eds., ***Ratio Scaling of Psychological Magnitude***, Lawrence Erlbaum Associates, Hillsdale, NJ, 1991, ISBN 0-8058-0710-1

Berkson, J., *Maximum likelihood and minimum Chi-Square estimates of the logistic function*, Amer. Stat. Assn. Jour. 50:130(1955)

Bock, R. D., *Note on the least squares solution for the method of successive categories*, Psychometrika 22:231(1957)

Bock, R. D., *Remarks on the test of significance for the method of paired comparisons,* Psychometrika 23:323(1958)

Bock, R. D., & L. V. Jones, ***The measurement and prediction of judgment and choice***, Holden-Day Inc., San Francisco, CA, 1968

Bolanowski, S. J, & G. W. Gescheider, Eds., ***Ratio Scaling of Psychological Magnitude***, Lawrence Erlbaum Associates, Hillsdale, NJ, 1991, ISBN 0-8058-0710-1

Borg, Ingwer & Patrick Groenen, ***Modern Multidimensional Scaling***, Springer-Verlag, New York, 1997. ISBN 0-387-94845-7

Bradley, R. A. & Milton E. Terry, *Rank analysis of incomplete block designs: I. The method of paired comparisons,* Biometrika 39:324(1952)

Burningham, Norman & Yee Ng, *Image quality study of printers with various resolution and gray levels,* IS&T Proceedings of 8th International Congress on Advances in Non-Impact Printing Technologies, 1992, pp 500-505.

Burningham, Norman & Theodore Bouk, *Threshold visibility and objectionability of banding in reflection prints*, IS&T's Tenth International Congress on Advances in Non-Impact Printing Technologies pg 548 (1994), ISBN 0-89208-179-1

Carlson, C. R., *Thresholds for perceived image sharpness*, Phot. Sci. & Eng., 22:69(1978)

Carmines, E. G., & Richard A. Zeller. 1979. *Reliability and Validity Assessment.* Sage University Paper Series on Quantitative Applications in the Social Sciences, 07-17. Newbury Park, CA: Sage Publications. ISBN 0-8039-1371-0

Chambers, Edgar IV, & Mona Baker Wolf, Eds, ***Sensory Testing Methods, 2nd Ed***. ASTM Manual Series: MNL 26, ASTM W. Conshohocken PA 19428-2959, 1996 ISBN 0-8031-2068

Coe, Brian, ***The Birth of Photography***, Ash & Grant, London, 1976, ISBN 0-904069-079

Cornsweet, T. N, *The staircase-method in psychophysics*, Amer. Jour. of Psychology, 75:485(1962)

Cory, G. P., M. J. Clayton, & K. N. Cupery, *Scene dependence of image quality*, Photo. Sci. & Eng. 27:9(1983)

Culler, E., *Studies in psychometric theory*, Psychol. Monog. 35:56-137(1926)

Dainty, J. Christopher. & Rodney Shaw, ***Image Science***, Academic Press, London, 1974, ISBN 0-12-200850-2

David, H. A., ***The method of paired comparisons, 2nd Ed***., Oxford University Press, New York, NY, 1988, ISBN 0-19-520616-9

de Ridder, H., *Minkowski-metrics as a combination rule for digital-image-coding impairments*, ***SPIE Volume 1666 Human Vision, Visual Processing, and Digital Display III*** (1992), pg. 16

de Ridder, H., *Naturalness and image quality: Saturation and lightness variation in color images of natural scenes,* Jour. Imag. Sci. & Tech, 40:487(1996)

Diederich, G. W., S. J. Messick & L. R. Tucker, *A general least squares solution for successive intervals,* Psychometrika 22:159-173(1957)

Dixon, W. J., & A. M. Mood, *A method for obtaining and analyzing sensitivity data*, Journal of the American Statistical Association, 43:109-126(1948)

Dooley, R. P. & Rodney Shaw, *Noise Perception in Electrophotography*, Jour. Appl. Photo. Eng. 5:190(1979)

Dvorak, C., & J. Hamerly, *Just noticeable differences for text quality components* , Jour. Appl. Photo. Eng. 9:97(1983)

Emerson, P. L., *Observations on maximum-likelihood and Bayesian methods of forced-choice sequential threshold estimation*, Perception and Psychophysics, 39:151(1986)

Engeldrum, P., Glenn McNeill, *Some experiments on the perception of graininess in black and white prints*, Jour. Imag. Sci., 29:18(1985), errata Jour. Imag. Sci., 29:207(1985)

Engeldrum, P., *A new approach to image quality*, Presented at the IS&T 42nd Annual Meeting, May 14-1989, Paper Summaries, pg 461

Engeldrum, P., *Measuring Key Customer Print Quality Attributes*, 1989 TAPPI Symposium Process and Product Quality Division pg 101. Reprinted in TAPPI Journal 73:161(1990) as *Measuring customer perception of print quality.*

Engeldrum, P., *Print-Quality Requirements*, Proc. SID 32:141(1991)

Engeldrum, P., *A framework for image quality models*, Jour. Imag. Sci. & Tech. 39:312(1995)

Engeldrum, P., *Absolute graininess threshold and linear probability models*, Program and Proceedings Image Processing Image Quality Image Capture Systems (PICS) Conference, IS&T, pg 231 (1998), ISBN 0-89208-211-9

Engeldrum, P., *Image Quality Models: Where are We?*, Final Program and Proceedings Image Processing Image Quality Image Capture Systems (PICS) Conference, IS&T, pg 251 (1999), ISBN 0-89208-215-1

Fairchild, M. D., ***Color Appearance Models***, Addison Wesley Longman, Inc., Reading, MA. 1997. ISBN 0-201-63464-3

Freiser, H. & Biederman, *Experiments on image quality in relation to the modulation transfer function and graininess of photographs*, Photo. Sci. & Eng. 7:28(1963)

Frieden, B. Roy, ***Probability, Statistical Optics, and Data Testing***, Springer-Verlag, New York. 1983. ISBN 3-540-11769-5

Galanter, E., *Multiple moduli and payoff functions in psychophysical scaling*, Bolanowski, S. J, & G. W. Gescheider, Eds., ***Ratio Scaling of Psychological Magnitude***, pg 129, Lawrence Erlbaum Associates, Hillsdale, NJ, 1991, ISBN 0-8058-0710-1

Gescheider, George A., ***Psychophysics: Method, Theory, and Application, 2nd Ed.***, Lawrence Erlbaum Associates, Inc., 101 Industrial Avenue, Mahwah, NJ 07430, 1985. ISBN 0-89859-375-1

Gescheider, George A., ***Psychophysics: The Fundamentals, 3nd Ed.***, Lawrence Erlbaum Associates, Inc., 101 Industrial Avenue, Mahwah, NJ 07430, 1997. ISBN 0-80582281-X

Gibson, W. A., *A least squares solution for Case IV of the law of comparative judgment*, Psychometrika 18:15(1953)

Green, David & R. Duncan Luce, *Variability of magnitude estimates: A timing theory analysis*, Perception and Psychophysics, 15:291(1974)

Guilford, J. P., ***Psychometric Methods***, McGraw-Hill, New York, 1954

Gulliksen, Harold, *A least squares solution for successive intervals assuming unequal standard deviations*, Psychometrika 19:117(1954)

Gulliksen, Harold, *A least squares solution for paired comparisons with incomplete data*, Psychometrika 21:125(1956)

Hamerly, J., & Dvorak, C., *Detection and discrimination of blur in edges and lines*, Jour. Opt. Soc. Amer. 71:448(1981)

Hamerly, J., *Just noticeable differences for solid area*, Jour. Appl. Photo. Eng. 9:14(1983)

Hamerly, J., & Robert Springer, *Raggedness of edges*, Jour. Opt. Soc. Amer., 71:285(1985)

Hecht, Eugene & Alfred Zajac, ***Optics***, Addison-Wesley Publishing Co., Reading, MA 1974, ISBN 0-201-02835-2

Helm, Carl E., Samuel Messick & Ledyard R. Tucker, *Psychological models for relating discrimination and magnitude estimation scales*, Psychological Review 68:167(1961)

Hoehn, L. & Niven, I., *Averages on the move,* Mathematics Magazine, 58:151(1985)

Hohle, Raymond H., *An empirical evaluation and comparison of two models for discriminability scales*, Jour. Math. Psychology 3:174(1966)

Hunt, R. W. G, ***The Reproduction of Colour***, Fountain Press, Tolworth, England, 1987, ISBN 0-85242-356

Indow, T. & S. S. Stevens, *Scaling of saturation and hue*, Perception & Psychophysics 1:253(1966)

ISO 3664, ***Viewing conditions—prints, transparencies, and substrates for graphic technology and photography***, 1996

ITU-R BT.500-7, ***Methodology for the subjective assessment of the quality of television pictures***, (1995), http://www.itu.int

Jackson, J. E., & Mary Fleckenstein, *An evaluation of some statistical techniques used in the analysis of paired comparison data,* Biometrics 51:13(1957)

Jones, Bronwen L. & Pamela R. McManus, *Graphic scaling of qualitative terms*, SMPTE Journal 95:1166(1986)

Jones, L. V., *Some invariant findings under the method of successive intervals, in. H. Gulliksen & S. Messick (Eds),* ***Psychological Scaling: Theory and Applications,*** John Wiley & Sons, NY 1960.

Jones, L. V., *Invariance of zero-point scaling over changes in stimulus context*, Psychological Bulletin 67:153-164(1967)

Kendall, M. & Jean Dickinson Gibbons, ***Rank Correlation Methods***, Oxford University Press, NY, 1990

Klockars, Alan J. & Gilbert Sax (1986) ***Multiple Comparisons***, Sage University Paper series on Quantitative Applications in the Social Sciences, 07-061, Beverly Hills and London: Sage Publications Inc.

Kruskal, Joseph B, & Myron Wish (1978) ***Multidimensional Scaling***, Sage University Paper series on Quantitative Applications in the Social Sciences, 07-011, Beverly Hills and London: Sage Publications Inc.

Landy, M. S. & J. Anthony Movshon (Eds.) ***Computational models of visual processing***, MIT Press, Cambridge, MA, 1994, ISBN 0-262-12155-7

Lane, H. L., A. C. Catania, & Stevens, S. S., *Voice level: autophonic scale, perceived loudness, and effects of sidetone*, Jour. Acoust. Soc. Amer. 33:160(1961)

Liao, T. F. (1994) ***Interpreting probability models: Logit, probit, and other generalized linear models***, Sage University Paper series on Quantitative Applications in the Social Sciences, 07-101. Thousand Oaks, CA: Sage Publications. ISBN 0-8039-4999-5

Lieberman, H. R. & Alex P. Pentland, *Microcomputer-based estimation of psychophysical thresholds: The Best PEST,* Behav. Res. Methods & Instrumentation, 14:21(1982)

Lodge, Milton, (1981), ***Magnitude Scaling: quantitative measurement of opinions,*** Sage University Paper series on Quantitative Applications in the Social Sciences, 07-025, Beverly Hills and London: Sage Publications Inc.

Luce, R. Duncan & S. S. Mo, *Magnitude estimation of heaviness and loudness by individual subjects: A test of a probabilistic response theory*, British Jour. Of Math. & Stat. Psych. 18:159(1965)

Luce, R. D., *Thurstone and Sensory Scaling: Then and Now*, Psychological Review 101:271(1994)

Luo, M. R., A. A. Clarke, P. A. Rhodes, A. Schappo, S. A. R. Scrivener, C. J. Tait, *Quantifying colour appearance. Part 1. LUTCHI colour appearance data.* Color Res. & Appl. 16:166(1991)

Macmillan, Neil A., and C. Douglas Creelman, ***Detection theory: a user's guide,*** Cambridge University Press, New York, NY, 1991, ISBN 0-521-36359-4

Marks, Lawrence, ***Sensory Processes***, Academic Press Inc, New York, 1974, ISBN 0-12-472950-9

Massaro, D. W., & D. Friedman, *Models of integration given multiple sources of information,* Psychological Review, 97:225(1990)

Mees, C. E. K., a) ***The theory of the photographic process***, Revised Ed., Macmillan Co., New York, 1954, b)Mees, C. E. K. & T. H. James, ***The theory of the photographic proces***s, Third Ed., Macmillan Co., New York, 1966

Meilgaard, M., Gail Civille, B. Carr, ***Sensory Evaluation Techniques, 2nd Edition***, CRC Press, Inc. Boca Raton, FL, 1991 ISBN 0-8493-4280-5

Mellers, B. J. & A. D. J. Cook, *The role of task and context in preference measurement*, Psychol. Sci. 7:76(1996)

Menard, S. (1995) ***Applied Logistic Regression Analysis***, Sage University Paper series on Quantitative Applications in the Social Sciences, 07-106. Thousand Oaks, CA: Sage Publications. ISBN 0-8039-5757-2

Miller, George, *The magical number seven, plus or minus two: Some limits on our capacity for processing information*, Psychological Review 63:81(1956)

Morrissey, J. H., *New method for the assignment of psychometric scale values from incomplete paired comparisons*, Jour. Opt. Soc. Amer. 45:373(1955)

Mosteller, F., *Remarks on the method of paired comparisons: I. The least squares solution assuming equal standard deviations and equal correlations*, Psychometrika 16:3(1951a)

Mosteller, F., *Remarks on the method of paired comparisons: II. The effect of an aberrant standard deviation when equal standard deviations and equal correlations are assumed*, Psychometrika 16:203(1951b)

Mosteller, F., *Remarks on the method of paired comparisons: III. A test of significance for paired comparisons when equal standard deviations and equal correlations are assumed*, Psychometrika 16:207(1951c)

Newhall, Sidney M, *The ratio method in the review of the Munsell colors*, Amer. Jour. of Psychology, 52:394(1939)

Newhall, Sidney M., Dorothy Nickerson, and Dean B. Judd, *Final report of the O.S.A. subcommittee on the Spacing of the Munsell Colors,* Jour. Opt. Soc. Amer. 33:385(1943)

Noether, G. E., *Remarks about a paired comparison model*, Psychometrika 25:357(1960)

Norwich, Kenneth H., *The magical number seven: Making a "bit" of "sense,"* Perception & Psychophysics 29:409(1981)

Nunnally, J. C. & I. R. Bernstein, ***Psychometric Theory, Third Edition***, McGraw-Hill, New York, 1994, ISBN 0-07-047849-X

Paned, D. W., & S. S. Stevens, *Saturation of red: a prothetic continuum*, Perception & Psychophysics 1:59(1966)

Parducci, A., D. H. Wedell, *The category effect with rating scales: number of categories, number of stimuli, and method of presentation*, Jour. Exp. Psychology: Human Perception and Performance 12:196(1986)

Poulton, E. C., *Models for Biases in Judging Sensory Magnitude,* Psychological Bulletin 86:777(1979)

Poulton, E. C., ***Biases in Quantifying Judgments,*** Lawrence Erlbaum Associates, Inc., 101 Industrial Avenue, Mahwah, NJ 07430, 1989. ISBN 0-86377105X

Press, W. H, B. P. Flannery, S. A. Teukolsky, & W. T. Vetterling, ***Numerical Recipes***, Cambridge University Press, New York, 1986, ISBN 0-521-30811-9

Person, Annie H., ***Is there Annie Weight Out?***, http://www.ahp.net/annie.person/annieweigh.htm

Richardson, L. F., *Quantitative mental estimates of light and color*, Brit. Jour. of Psychology, 20:27(1929)

Rockwell, Christina & John I. Yellot, *A note on Equivalent Thurstone Models*, Jour. Of Math. Psychology, 65:19(1979)

Sachs, L., ***Applied Statistics, Second Edition***, Springer-Verlag, New York, NY, 1984, ISBN 0-387-90976-1

Sawyer, J. F., *Effect of graininess and sharpness on perceived print quality*, Proc. of Photographic Image Quality Symposium, Sept. 1980, Royal Photographic Society, pp 222-231.

Scheffé, Henry, *An analysis of variance for paired comparisons*, Jour. Amer. Stat. Assoc. 47:381(1952)

Shepard, R. N., *Psychological relations and psychological scales: On the status of "direct" psychophysical measurements*, Jour. Math. Psychology 24:24(1981)

Starks, H. T. & H. A. David, *Significance test for paired comparison experiments*, Biometrika 48:95(1961)

Stultz, K. F & H. J. Zweig, *Roles of sharpness and graininess in photographic quality and definition*, Jour. Opt. Soc. Amer. 52:45(1962)

Stevens, Stanley Smith, *On the theory of scales of measurement*, Science, 103:677(1946)

Stevens, S. S., *On the psychophysical law*, The Psychological Review 64:153(1957)

Stevens, S. S., *Review of L. L. Thurstone: the measurement of values*, Contemporary Psychology, 4:388(1959)

Stevens. S. S., *Ratio scales, partition scales and confusion scales*. In. H. Gulliksen & S. Messick (Eds), ***Psychological scaling: Theory and applications.*** John Wiley & Sons, NY 1960.

Stevens. S. S., & Miguelina Guirao, *Subjective scaling of length and area and the matching of length to loudness and brightness*, Jour. Experimental Psychology 66:177-186(1963)

Stevens, S. S., *A metric for the social consensus*, Science 151:530(1966)

Stevens, S. S., ***Psychophysics: Introduction to its perceptual, neural and social prospects,*** John Wiley & Sons, Inc., New York, 1975. Reprinted by Transaction Inc., 1986, New Brunswick, NJ 08903, ISBN 0-88738-643-1

Stevens. S. S., & Volkman, J., *The relation of pitch to frequency: A revised scale*, American Jour. of Psychology 53:329-353(1940)

Stokes, M., M. D. Fairchild, M. D. and R. Berns, *Precision requirements for digital color reproduction*, ACM Trans. Graphics11:406(1992)

Stokes, M., M. D. Fairchild, & R. S. Berns, *Colorimetrically quantified visual tolerances for pictorial images*, Tech. Assn. Of the Graphic Arts Proc. #2, 757(1992)

Strang, Gilbert, ***Linear Algebra and its applications, 2nd Edition***, Academic Press, Inc., New York, NY, 1980. ISBN 0-12-673660-X

Swets, John A., ***Signal Detection Theory and ROC Analysis in Psychology and Diagnostics***, Lawrence Erlbaum Associates, Mahwah, NJ, 1996, ISBN 0-8058-1834-0

Taylor, M. M. & C. Douglas Creelman, *PEST: efficient estimates on probability functions*, Jour. Acoust. Soc. Amer. 41:782(1967)

Thurstone, Leon Lewis, *A law of comparative judgment*, Psychological Review, 34:273(1927)

Thurstone, L. L, *Rank order as a psychophysical method,* Journal of Experimental Psychology, 14:187-201(1931)

Thurstone, L. L., *Stimulus dispersion in the method of constant stimuli*, Journal of Experimental Psychology, 15:284(1932)

Torgerson, Warren S., ***Theory and methods of scaling***, Robert E. Krieger Publishing Co, Malabar, FL 32950, 1985, ISBN 0-89874-722-8 (This is a reprint of the book originally published by J. Wiley & Sons, 1958)

Toothaker, Larry E. (1993) ***Multiple Comparison Procedures***, Sage University Paper series on Quantitative Applications in the Social Sciences, 07-089, Beverly Hills and London: Sage Publications Inc.

Tyrell, M. P., R. E. Jacobson, & G. G. Attridge, *Interval and ratio scaling of photographic image quality attributes,* Jour. Photo. Sci. 38:225(1990)

Tyrell, M. P., R. E. Jacobson, M. R. Pointer, & G. G. Attridge, *A study of colour-film granularity and print-image graininess,* Jour. Photo. Sci. 41:48(1993)

Velleman, P. F., & Leland Wilkinson, *Nominal, Ordinal, Interval and Ratio typologies are misleading*, The American Statistician, 47:65(1993)

Wandell, Brian A, ***Foundations of vision science***, Sinauer Associates, 1995, Sunderland, MA 01375-0407, ISBN 087893-853-2

Watson, A. B. & D. G. Peli, *QUEST: A Bayesian adaptive psychometric method*, Perception and Psychophysics, 33:113(1983)

Watson, A. B., *Probability summation over time,* Vision Research 19:515(1979)

Watson, A. B., & A. Fitzhugh, *The method of constant stimuli is inefficient*, Perception and Psychophysics, 47:87(1990)

Watson, A. B., (ed.), ***Digital images and human vision***, MIT Press, Cambridge, MA 1993, ISBN 0-262-23171-9

Wegener, B. (ed.), ***Social attitudes and psychophysical measurement***, Erlbaum, Hillsdale, NJ, 1982

Weibull, W., *A statistical distribution function of wide applicability*, Jour. Appl. Mech. 18:292(1951)

Weller, Susan and A. Kimball Romney (1990). *Metric Scaling: Correspondence Analysis.* Sage University Paper Series on Quantitative Applications in the Social Sciences, 07-75. Newbury Park, CA: Sage Publications. ISBN 0-8039-3750-4

Westerlink, Joyce H. D. M, & Jacques A. J. Roufs, *Subjective image quality as a function of viewing distance, resolution and picture size*, SMPTE Jour., 98:113(1989)

Wetherhill, G. B. & H. Levitt, *Sequential estimation of points on a psychometric function*, Brit. Jour. Of Math. Stat. Psych., 18:1(1965)

Whaley, C. P. *Collecting paired-comparison data with a sorting algorithm*, Behavior Research Methods & Instrumentation, 11:147(1979)

Wilks, Samuel S, ***Mathematical Statistics***, John Wiley & Sons, New York, 1962, pg 274.

W. W. Woodbury & C. J. Bartleson, *Psychophysical methods for evaluating the quality of color transparencies: I Comparison of categorical and comparative-judgment data,* Phot. Sci. Eng. 6:10(1962)

Yellot, John I., *The Relationship between Luce's Choice Axiom, Thurstone's Theory of Comparative Judgment, and the Double Exponential distribution*, Jour. Of Math. Psychology, 109:15(1977)

Yellot, John I., *On a Functional Equation Related to Thurstone Models*, Jour. Of Math. Psychology, 266:17(1978)

Zwick, D., D. L. Brothers, *RMS granularity: determination of just-noticeable-differences*, Photo. Sci. & Eng., 19:235(1975)

Zwick, D., *Psychometric scaling of term used in category scales of image quality attributes*, Proc. Symposium on Photographic and Electronic Imaging, Cambridge, England, October 14, 1984

Zwislocki, J. J & D.A. Goodman, *Absolute scaling of sensory magnitudes: A validation*, Perception and Psychophysics, 28:28(1980)

Zwislocki, J. J, *Group and individual relationships between sensation magnitudes and their numerical estimates*, Perception and Psychophysics, 33:146(1983)

Symbols

A, B, C	Sample designations.
a_{xx}, b_{xx}	Coefficients; regression, function, etc.
d_i	Discriminal dispersions.
F( )	Function of ( ).
f_{xx}	Frequency, a number.
i, j, g	Indices.
H( )	A function. Usually a Cumulative Density Function or a psychometric model.
J	Number of observers
k	Elements of a category frequency matrix.
l	Logit
m	1) Number category boundaries. 2) Number of categories minus 1.
n	Number of samples, stimuli, etc.
N	1) Number of threshold estimates. 2) Number of observations.
p_{xx}, P_{xx}	Proportion, experimental probability, of event xx.
P`, p`	Estimated or modified probability or proportion.
p*	Parameter of a binomial distribution.
P( )	Probability of ( ).
R	(σ_2/σ_1) - 1, a parameter equal to the ratio of two discriminal dispersions minus 1.
r	1) Number of ranks. 2) Number of "yes" or correct responses.
s	Estimate of standard deviation.
S_A	Scale value of sample A, etc.
t_g	The gth category boundary.
x_j	1)The jth threshold estimate. 2) Physical value of a stimulus, say lumens.
$\bar{x}$	Mean value estimate.
z	z-value.
A	The adjusted matrix for graphical rating scale. The rows, observers, are scaled so the average value is zero and the standard deviation is one. The rows are the observers and the columns are the samples. Size is J by n.
b	Vector, solution for least squares-fit for "stitching" scale values.
B	Coefficient matrix for the Case IV solution of Law of Comparative Judgment (LCJ). Size is 2n+1 by 2n

C	Matrix with all ones on and above the diagonal. Used in category scaling data analysis.
D	1) General data matrix for graphical rating scale. 2) The singular values in Singular Value Decomposition (SVD) method of category scaling. 3) Data matrix for paried-comparison plus distance method.
D	1) Discriminal dispersion vector using SVD of category scaling. 2) Vector of distances in paired-comparison plus distance method.
E	1) Vector of scaled z-values used in the Case IV solution of Law of Comparitive Judgment. Size is 2n+1 by 1.
F	Frequency matrix from paired comparison. Rows and columns are samples and the entry is the number of times the column was chosen over the row. Size is n by n.
G	A column solution vector for Case IV. The first n rows are the scale values and the next n rows are the discriminal dispersions. Size is 2n in length.
H	Data matrix for ranking. Rows equal rank number and columns are samples. The columns are histograms of the ranking for each sample. Size is n by n.
K	Category data matrix. Columns are categories and rows are samples. Each element is the frequency that the sample was placed in the category.
P	Proportion matrix in paired comparison. Size is n by n.
R	Data matrix for ranking. Rows are observers and columns are samples and the entry is the rank given the sample by the observer. Size is J by n.
S	1) The scale value difference matrix from paired-comparison. Size n by n. 2) Scale value matrix.
t	Vector of category boundaries.
U	The u-vectors of SVD used in category scaling.
V	The v-vectors of SVD used in category scaling.
X	"Design" matrix for the LSF of the incomplete PC or category ***Z*** matrix.
x	Data vector
y	1) Solution vector of category boundaries and scale values, size is (n+m) by 1. 2) data vector
Z	Matrix of z-values for PC. Size is n by n.
Z'	Matrix of z-values in a category scaling that are row normalized; row mean subtracted and divided by row standard deviation.
z	Vector of z-values or distances.
z*	Vector of boundary minus scale values, z-values
α	1) Intercept parameter in psychometric models. 2) Alpha risk.
β_x	Slope parameter in psychometric models.

Δ	Small increment added to one of the discriminal dispersions in deriving Thurstone's Case IV.
ΔS	1) Just-noticeable difference, JND. 2) Scale difference.
ϵ	Error, error in estimating discriminal dispersions for Case III from Case IV model.
μ_x	Population mean.
σ_x	Population standard deviation.
ρ_x	Population correlation coefficient.
π	1) Population proportion. 2) Proportion confidence limit, when used with subscript.
θ_x	Angle in radians.
Φ	Cumulative frequency matrix for category scaling.
χ^2	Chi-square value.

Index

A

B

C

D

E

F

G

H

I

J

L

M

N

O

Q

R

S

T

U

V

W

Z

CD–ROM Instructions

License Agreement

The CD-ROM on the back cover includes software that illustrate the methods described in this book. General information on each MathCad® sheet is contained in the appropriate chapter in *Psychometric Scaling: A Toolkit for Imaging Systems Development.*

If you open the CD-ROM package, you are agreeing to be bound by the following terms and conditions. If you do not agree with the following, do not open the CD-ROM package and promptly return the book and CD-ROM to Imcotek Press, P.O. Box 17, Winchester, MA 01890.

All of the software on the CD-ROM is copyrighted material. The author and publisher retain all rights. You may use this software on one computer. One copy may be made for backup purposes. Making copies for any other purpose violates the United States copyright laws. THE SOFTWARE IS OFFERED AS IS, WITHOUT ANY WARRANTY OF ANY KIND, EITHER EXPRESSED OR IMPLIED, INCLUDING WITHOUT LIMITATION, IMPLIED WARRANTIES OF MERCHANTABILITY AND FITNESS FOR A PARTICULAR PURPOSE. NEITHER THE AUTHOR NOR PUBLISHER WARRANTS THAT FUNCTIONS CONTAINED IN THE SOFTWARE WILL MEET YOUR REQUIREMENTS OR THAT THE SOFTWARE WILL BE ERROR FREE. Neither the author or publisher assumes any liability whatsoever arising from the use of or inability to use the software. This product is not designed for use in or with life support devices and the author or publisher make no representations to the contrary. Life support devices are those devices which are used to measure, diagnose, or evaluate the tissue, systems or functions of the human body; or other devices employed to support or sustain life or good health.

Using the CD-ROM

The MathCad® sheets are in individual files. If you do not have a copy of MathCad®, you can obtain an evaluation copy from MathSoft.

1) Insert the CD-ROM in your computer's CD-ROM drive.

2) Click the CD-ROM drive to display the drive contents.

3) Click the file "readme.htm." This should start your browser and the "readme.htm" page will be displayed in the browser window. Follow the instructions on the page to obtain the MathCad® evaluation software and install the files.